# DARK WITNESS

# DARK WITNESS

## When Black People Should Be Sacrificed (Again)

### RALPH WILEY

**ONE WORLD**

**BALLANTINE BOOKS • NEW YORK**

For Colen Cypress Wiley
and his mother, Holly;
William Garrick Smith
and his mother, Jackie;
**&**
D.K.M.J.

# CONTENTS

# PREFACE

This is, for the most part, a personal narrative about life and death at the *fin de siècle*, and the end of the twentieth century too. No other claims whatsoever can be made for it. It has no miracle method for losing weight, making money, finding love, overcoming the base emotions or engendering false self-esteem; there is scant headway into gossip, too little blame-shifting, not enough gunplay, not nearly enough sex, and no innuendo worth noting. Yet the author dares ask you to come along compliantly, hoping there is a Word or two herein you will find laughable; hoping not to be brained by hard political planks, or backshot by a devious social science. The author says you probably won't be as disappointed as often as he's been lately. Driven by a question—why *are* "black" people so stupid?—he plows a furrow or two in the American nature, first offering one caveat: At the *fin de siècle*, and the end of the twentieth century too, "Black" and "White" were not strict racial or biological definitions. They were political and social camps, carefully maneuvered people dividers. In the most dependably absurd American sense, "White" means privileged, and "Black" means unprivileged. If you can agree to keep that thought in mind, the following pages may or may not turn easier.

"At a time like this, scorching irony, not convincing argument, is needed. Oh! had I the ability, and could I reach the nation's ear, I would today pour out a fiery stream of biting ridicule, blasting reproach, withering sarcasm, and stern rebuke. For it is not light that is needed, but fire; it is not the gentle shower, but thunder . . ."

—FREDERICK DOUGLASS
July 4, 1852

sat•ire (sat i r), n. L. *satira,* **satura** (full plate filled with fruits, mixture, medley, full of food, sated) 1. a: ancient Roman verse commentary on prevailing vice or folly. b: a usually topical literary composition holding up human or individual vices, folly, abuses, or shortcomings to censure by means of ridicule, derision, burlesque, irony or other method, sometimes with an intent to bring about improvement. 2. a branch of literature ridiculing vice or folly. 3. a: raillery used to convey rebuke or criticism. b: caustic comment.

—*Webster's Third New International Dictionary*

"You can find in a text whatever you bring, if you will stand between it and the mirror of your imagination . . .

"Yes, take it all around, there is quite a good deal of information in the book. I regret this very much, but really it could not be helped . . ."

—MARK TWAIN
*Roughing It*

# DARK WITNESS

# 1

## Why Black People
## Are So Stupid

**D**id you know there is a way to travel overland from a certain high bluff above the Mississippi River to within sight of the U.S. Capitol rotunda while crossing only one state line? It is a hard way to go. There is a way to do it nevertheless. There are five ways to go overland from that same commanding bluff to the bottom of the Atlantic Ocean or the Gulf of Mexico while crossing but one state line, but since we are not trying to go there, we will just let that one go.

Suddenly it was 1995. It took me a quarter-century to take the long road from Memphis to Alexandria from the time I first struck out from that bluff in '70. Took a while to find the short way. I traveled under and in spacious skies, past purple mountains majestically, through the plains and grains, camping out in the coastal cities, as near to rivers and bays as I could come, according to my means at the time, not being one to live beneath them. I tried to hack out a decent living in a variety of ways. Careers eluded me. Debt did not. It would add needed cachet if I confessed to a good many murders. Since I have not committed any, they might be hard to bring off believably. We will labor on without them.

I plied my hand at banking and finance but had no taste for robberies from either side of the window. Then I tried retailing and exhibited an instinctive touch for the five-finger discount. Since I displayed no similar talents at arson, the boss had little reason to keep me on. His decision led to a brief fling with the insurance industry, where I was told to curse the claimants and leak lies about them to the press, whose memberships I was to cultivate. Cursing and lying I was pretty good at, which led to much time spent among the press. This proximity led to my embrace of the press as vocation. No lifting or felonies were necessary to sign up; so I did, enthusiastically. I took it up as the last resort, and shake it still like a terrier on a rat. Even if I was disenchanted by this media careering and resulting spin-off avocations, and by the company and scant pay they engendered, I was satisfied by now that at least the *land* came as advertised—give or take prime spots the real estate people never showed me.

All the above is supposed to serve one point: In America, it is the people who usually constitute "the problem." That they also happen to constitute the solution to "the problem" is the most unutterable of small consolations. Especially in the press.

By now the buffalo were nearly all played out, and those descendants who remained of the buffalo soldiers seemed about to follow suit. The deer, antelope, NRA and tobacco plant had a more effective lobby in Congress. And so, while temporarily camped within eyeshot of the Potomac River and the U.S. Capitol, I was summoned to a new engagement, gruffly asked to confront an old conundrum: "Why *are* 'black' people so stupid?"

That was how both "white" and "black" people framed it up for me, usually in a display of more words, or an odd assortment of pictures. How many people framed this question? Too many to adequately address in this part of the drift. We shall arrive at most of them indirectly. I was beginning to ask the confounding question of myself, with my own embroidery attached:

"Say, old dude, can 'black' people be so stupid that they allow themselves to be defined, represented, shaped and directed by a grotesquerie of degraded deformities that would defy even your next-door neighbor's imagination? Are they so stupid they cannot see where such questioning might lead them?"

Thus I was impelled to seek out the soul of such questions; in doing so, as is common in soul-searching, to face my own.

I had to put my own house in order before setting out for souls. Turns out there is a traitor under my roof. The bone of my blood, my own son, who betrayed me by sauntering home from school with a perfect score on some state-wide mathematics achievement test. I considered reporting him to the authorities, but he is my son and I care for him in spite of his regrettable precocity. I decided to risk living with him occasionally and trying to keep him quiet. This was a dangerously sentimental thing to do. But he *seems* to be a decent sort of boy, in that he's yet to point out the inconsistencies between what behavior I will not tolerate in him and what all I will exhibit myself. He *appears* docile enough, his cousins *act* as though they revere him, his grandparents *feign* a desire for his presence, his male peers *grumble* as though they half-respect him beneath their nonsensical competitive bluster and envy and would like to emulate the ease of his manner. Some of them are "black" people, so what could they know of respect, kindness, child-rearing or a human sort of love? We know "blacks" are inhuman beings; the wise numbers have told us so—as long as we keep manipulating them until they say what we want to hear.

In spite of the statistics I decided to withhold judgment on my son, until he had a chance to mature—or at least until I came back from hunting up souls—as long as he would straighten up and fly right in the meantime. My son is no statistic. A voice in my head just said, "Not yet." And it is not *my* voice I hear, meaning there are, at minimum, two voices in my head, making me seem like a curiosity if not worse. This is not always a bad thing to be. And although my son is no statistic to me, he may be one to you. Yes, he blundered awfully on the test. Youth is the best time for blundering. There was a period when I nearly made a career out of it myself. If he were thirty and blundering, I might be inclined to think less of him. But he is not thirty and has some room for growth. I told him he must take this test again and again until he sank to levels more befitting his father's potential. He must try and try until he failed and quit. This might be said to be a correct thing to do. He smiled impudently at paternal suggestion, as if it were all some sort of joke, and a private joke at that, between us. Have no more doubt about it—this boy is out of line.

Here is that cold dagger, the letter, itself:

### Prince Georges County Public Schools
14201 School Lane
Upper Marlboro, Maryland 20772

To the PARENT/GUARDIAN OF: 13430   December 9, 1994
COLEN C. WILEY                00200713

Dear Parent/Guardian:

Students who graduate from a public school in the state of Maryland must demonstrate competency in functional reading, mathematics, writing, and citizenship skills in addition to other graduation requirements. The functional/skill requirement is met if a student scores 340 or higher on the prescribed Maryland functional test.

Listed below are your child's scores for the Fall, 1994 administration of the Maryland Functional Math Test. The total test performance is reported using a 3-digit scale score which is determined by the number of questions answered correctly and the difficulty of the test. The scores range from **182** to **419** for this test. Students whose total test score is **340** or above should be congratulated for successfully completing one of the requirements for high school graduation.

If the total test score is less than 340, the functional/skill graduation requirement for Math has not been satisfied. Students who fail to satisfy the requirement will be provided appropriate instructional activities which will be followed by another opportunity to take the test. The seven Domain Scores can be interpreted as the percent of the items answered correctly. This information will help your child to see his/her areas of strength and weakness. Please note that the total test score is not the sum or average of the Domain scores. If you would like to discuss any aspect of your child's test result, please call the school for an appointment.

Maryland Functional Math Test

Fall, 1994 Result: **419** PASS

100% Number Concepts          100% Measurement
100% Whole Numbers            100% Using Data
100% Mixed Numbers/Fractions  100% Problem Solving
100% Decimals

Sincerely,
Sylvia A. Markham
Principal

You can see how this might upset me. I blame his mother for the most part. My own mathematical and scientific leanings do not lean so well; they lie paralyzed and cannot get up at all. If something needs figuring out, a guess will do me, if it is a good guess. But the boy's mother can fix what's broken, is inspired by disassembled hardware and truly believes Humpty-Dumpty's plight says volumes more about the king's men than it does about broken eggshells. Nothing pleases her more than a box containing pieces of an appliance chopped up into parts no bigger than those of a jigsaw puzzle; nothing enhances her pleasure more than if the parts come accompanied by tiny plastic packages of microscopic screws, nuts, bolts, etc.; the rapture itself is a white slip of paper with what appears to be Latin printed on it. Give the boy's mother rigging of this sort and she is in heaven, while I think so much of it I could barely enjoy Christmas Eve when the boy was younger. Boxes with contents needing assembly in some mathematic way missed my line of vision. The boy's mother didn't mind, judging from her scarce commentary on it. She did present the fact that I seemed to think myself capable when it came to rigging checkbooks. I admitted the truth of it, then aimed her skillful eye back at Christmas boxes.

My son is at an age when he has to act as though nothing moves him—certainly no folly promulgated by his parents. But last Christmas he was like a small boy again. He wanted to put up a tree, decorate, warble carols, give gifts. I think it made him feel secure in the knowledge that while might makes right, right is already made and paying a strong dividend. He wanted to lose himself in the memory of parents smiling down at him after having exhausted themselves and their pocketbooks to gain his favor. And I think he wanted to forget the atmosphere of subtle foreboding around him. All of which was fine by me, except the foreboding part. It was for the boys and girls anyway. Christmas, that is.

He has a gift to give. I don't mean a gift in a box with a bow, or like gifts some children have to tell the square root of twenty-four-digit numbers off the tops of their heads or work with thirty-six-digit numbers the way other children work with nerve endings. My son has a penchant for nerve endings when it strikes him, as it seems to do more often these days. But he doesn't mind figuring out other things in his spare time as long as nobody is around to make a federal case out of it.

If he insists on it, I'd rather he know that the one quality Poe, Douglass, Lincoln, Whitman, West, Geronimo, Banneker, Bethune, Will Rogers, Percy Julian, Picasso, and Einstein had in common was no IQ rating or SAT test score—or any particular need of them.

The boy has this surpassing gift. I know because he has surprised me with it four times. The first time came when he was nine months old. His mother and I were chauffeuring him to New Jersey. We had left his pacifier behind—a glaring omission he vocally stressed to his fledgling parents by upsetting even the most distant livestock throughout the Garden State and parts of Pennsylvania. Once arrived we found a stopper and plugged it in, and prayed. He spat it out, looked at us and "said" in a laconic expression with his crystal-clear brown eyes, "I don't want *that*. I wanted to *talk* to you all and ask you to attend to me in some other way." He never allowed a pacifier to touch his lips again.

The second time he surprised me was around six months after the pacifier became extinct. We went to a restaurant in Pennsylvania near his mother's hometown. Hung imperiously across the entrance of the establishment was a banner announcing this coup: "Biggest Best Brunch." The boy craned his neck off my shoulder, gazed at the banner, then back up at me; then he said, "Bingest Best." He said it with a stentorian gravity that dared correction. His eyes then slid sideways, followed shortly by a dramatic swivel of his head in pursuit of them. It was a studied movement. He looked me off *twice*, as if to say, "Don't think I'm a fool, old man." What we ate, I don't know, but it was shortly after this when my in-laws began to note with deep sighs of resignation that the boy seemed doomed to resemble his father.

The third time was later—the last trip we made to the circus together. Just to pass the time, I asked him, "Why do you think those clowns are out there right now, making the people laugh?" Without looking at me, he said, "To keep their minds off what else is happening. The acts in the three rings are changing. We aren't supposed to notice."

The test score was the fourth time.

So he has the gift some might call a curse. Name it what you will. I want him to know test scores mean nothing in terms of knocking about in the states of the America. Curse or gift, it means *nothing* of itself. Risking ridicule, I'd say it's all in the application. If used to divide, wreck, exploit, humiliate, destroy or apologize for any of that, it's a curse. If used to uplift, create, encourage, amuse or teach, it's a gift. Either way, he will need help implementing. Some who can help will be as gifted, only in a different way; some will be less gifted; some few will be more so. He will need equanimity and humility to discern the value in each—if any extractable ore does exist. He must be able to equate and account for people if he is to prosper in ways that bank failures, insults and tragedies cannot threaten.

There are people gifted with numbers, sciences, pictures and words who are not so good when it comes to people. I want to tell him to be very good with figuring out people, and the rest will take care of itself. But his public behavior beats me to it. He never lets on to his true nature when I am around, never gives me an opening to lay him out about changing his ways.

So I want him to keep figuring it out. If he goes into a jewelry store to pick out some small diamond earrings for his mother's birthday, and if the jeweler takes them away to polish them, then brings them back and they seem less bright, that's an unbalanced equation; his value is greater than the sum of the transaction, and he should walk out at an appropriate velocity no lighter in mass, purse-wise, than when he walked in.

I want him to know, if he is shown an apartment to let with one window, that one overlooking the panorama of the garbage dump—if he is shown any apartment at all—that is buzzard luckonometry. He should fire off a flat trajectory out of there. I want him to know whenever any salesman says a thing, he should say much less than, otherwise he will pay greater than the normal usury—and he can surely count on this. I want him to learn the greatest of the unwritten theorems: Life is a tradition of people attempting to separate him from the fruits of his labors. Until he learns this, he will need more seasoning and schooling, no matter how ripe his test scores are.

Mind you, I do not make so much of this measuring and scrutinizing that I frown upon an offer of free tickets. As apt punishment for blatant excellence, I proposed to my son his banishment to a National Basketball Association regular season game.

"You will atone by going to the game with me tonight. I have to go to New York tomorrow," I said.

He choked back all the gnawing resentments of youth and admitted he deserved the discipline. You agree that it would seem a basketball game would be a good place to hide from numbers? I thought so, once, before a man explained—but I am outpacing myself. A snowstorm was forecast for midnight. Being the kind of boy who loves the snow in part because of its prospects for the cancellation of the school day, he smiled. Being the kind of man who would father such a boy, so did I. Under a pinkish night sky we went to see the Washington Bullets vs. the Miami Heat, hoping to beat the storm back home afterward. We arrived and watched the players warm up. My son watched intently. He doesn't warm up to talking much to me in public anymore, so I found myself carrying the conversation.

"C. Web's back from that dislocated shoulder. There's Juwan, working on his low-post game. Remember being down in Memphis last Thanksgiving and going to Garrick's high school game, then going over to the Pyramid? The wind was blowing *that* day. Remember? Tornadoes were touching down all over. And Arkansas blew out Georgetown. We can say we saw the Iverson boy's first game."

"Iverson's just quick," he replied. "Garrick's better."

"True, in a way. But he's got something else. I can't say exactly what, but it catches hold of the eye, and he's got it."

"Not many do, huh, Dad?"

"Nope. There's Rex. Rex can get his shot off, but he can't stay in one piece. Good athlete, though. Glen Rice. Glen can see. Look how the ball comes off his hand. See that rotation? Hitting bottom—that's why the nets pop like that. Not catching the rim or the high part of the net. If the rotation's bad, might not go. If the D is tight, probably won't. It's one thing to be able to shoot. You can shoot some now. The question is, can you get your shot?"

*"There is something fascinating about science. One gets such wholesale returns of conjecture out of such a trifling investment of fact."*

— MARK TWAIN
*Life on the Mississippi*

It took neither imagination nor talent to reheat such classic leftovers as those left festering in *The Bell Curve, Intelligence and Class Structure in American Life,* co-authored by Richard Herrnstein and Charles Murray. It was published in 1994 to fanfare posing as handwringing. It was purportedly a book; and as if that were not bad enough, it was said to be an *exciting* book, a book of import, of revelations, of which this was the main one: Some "whites" have tests showing they are smarter than "blacks"! Such findings would be unprecedented, a novel state of awareness! Other projections were strewn about it, but this was the punch line, the moral, a popular one making it a bestseller among some of those to whom it gives the high end of the deal and an unsubtle declaration of war to those who made use of what little intelligence they had. This was no book. This was the gauntlet.

Yet I think I am not being forward in calling it a classic, if by classic we mean, as Mr. Mark Twain suggests, "a book people praise but don't read." Some similar estimations about the inner capacities of inscrutable brains have been cast upon the waters here for two hundred years, were used as moral buttress against the horrors of manumission and continue to surface, like a whale for air, every decade or so, as needed, up until the day after tomorrow. The steady dosing of this snake oil was gobbled down by a general public anxious to feel better about its biscuit-hoarding by declaring plague among its starving cousins. The same medicinal value is found in Thomas Dixon's "book" *The Clansman*, published in 1895. It too helped change the political landscape and led to a resurgence of the Klan that Dixon so warmly idealized. His book was turned by D. W. Griffith into the first Hollywood blockbuster, *The Birth of a Nation*, which also did not aid digestion in "black" people; the 1915 movie induced lynching bees instead, and those caused many "blacks" to listen less disdainfully to the back-to-Africa exhortations of Marcus Garvey. (Even more of them might have listened if they had not been suspicious that *had* they gone, Garvey's first act there would have been to declare the continent Garveyland.) Other "blacks" organized protests about the film and got a bargaining session, though not much of one, and forced copies of it to be edited. Other "blacks" began making their own movies as a counterweight. All this history-making effect must be noted for *The Clansman*.

Duly observant of the publication of *The Bell Curve* and its speculations about a social eventuality of national doom, and duly observant of inescapably ensuing conclusions that "black" people ought to go first, one notes how far the arts and sciences and literature have come in the last hundred years. No matter that the republic has postponed these eventualities and repeatedly escaped these conclusions for *220* years—a Houdini of a republic it must be in that way. The only inescapable conclusion about the United States is that it suffers from an overreliance on misinterpreted statistics. At this rate, the world will be turning flat again here, not far into the twenty-first century.

No more "books" about grandiose theories of the mental and "racial" royalty, thought up in England, interpreted by American neo-fascists (if fascist is not too kind a word), concerning man-made tests (they are invariably man-made, and quickly change in content whenever women outscore men) are necessary to make you seek out "black" stupidity. This effort did make the question a bit more complex: "So, are 'black' people so stupid they try to answer a book like *The Bell Curve* with logic? Do they not know once they accept the 'question' as legitimate, they are lost?" The premise here, in the realm of the Curve, is that they cannot think; so they cannot say, "An interesting presentation with ample data, but the *cause* of this sort of discrepancy is, I think . . ." You've been disqualified from thinking, relieved of its manifold burdens. As Mr. Ian Hacking wrote in the *London Review of Books* on January 26, 1995:

". . . at this point reasoning falters. This is because 'it does not follow' is a very imperfect reply to demagogues."

That Hacking's review was titled "Pull the Other One" shows all may not be lost. The speculations offered by *The Bell Curve* are not to be answered but ridiculed—in a manner so deft as to be not recognizable as ridicule for the *next* hundred years or so. Then the old ridicule, disguised as "art," can be brought up as alternative to the next dose of whatever combination of strychnine, arsenic, cyanide and cobra venom they will be calling medicine in those days. That dose is surely coming. But anytime you think of the bitter draft, you can think of the surest way out of swallowing it. Then you can smile. And then you can laugh at it. And then you get your own mind back. Such awful powers of ridicule are beyond our ability to execute; they are not quite past our notion to try.

As Mr. Twain observed, "There is no character, howsoever good and fine, but it can be destroyed by ridicule, howsoever poor and witless." I take that as the green light.

Who are these gods who can think up questions that presume to encompass the mind, who construct this papier-mâché anti-world where you and I cannot exist, then call all this naked ambition "writing a book" or "performing a patriotic duty" or "working in the interest of science"? There are questions we might ask that they too do not know the answers to. Or they might know and not want to admit they know. Secret questions of brown-skinned boys. Unspoken answers of golden-faced girls. Now suppose these little girls and boys *choose* not to answer certain questions, or even to face up to them? Would they not be emulating *all* of their fathers? If they, standing at the beginning of their lives, do not know the answers, how are they so different from any of us? Does this mean that if they are told the answer, or shown a way to find it, the information will not stick? Are "intellectuals" and politicians saying not only are the children's brains empty—we would not be rushing to disagree with them there—but also that they are spray-coated with Teflon?

Who are the conniving "gods," these "dukes" and "kings" who seek to invent a reality, and then stand back and act all innocent as though it is some other divine intervention they are merely pointing out to the ignorant, at the expense only of the wicked?

Odds are they are also rotten frauds; as despicable as the "duke" and the "king" in *Huckleberry Finn*, giving off the same strong waft that stinks like all the nation; pseudo-intellectuals wielding moldy tests, politicians spewing out sulfuric clouds of bad rhetoric. And who are we but puppets on the string? Odds are they'd *like* to be demigods; demagogues; it follows. Only they could be so enchanted by a child's refrain:

"*I'm* better than *you* are, *la*-la-la-la-*la*-la."

You remember children who chanted this. You may not recall what happened to them, because nothing of interest did, not until later, when they wreaked revenge on a world that *is* dumb but not so very as to unanimously agree with their hilariously inept self-assessments. They took revenge on us by infesting colleges and radio stations, running for Congress, and taking the onus off general failings and dropping them at the feet of my son. And gaining ratings and public office and lunch money for doing it, for bullies of all stripe, physical or mental, have always been able to intimidate us. Odds are, we—the royal we and the all-of-us we—will wind up skint unless we find a better way.

There is a better way, an infallible way to circumscribe minds without the subcontracting, double-billing, suspiciously high fuel allowances and other expenses involved in demagoguery. The infallible test exposing the ineradicable, inherent "black" mental inferiority is—let the trumpets herald—*the typographical error.*

The typo is the foolproof tester's foolproof test. It's fairly safe to say there isn't a "black" person living who can type twenty pages without making not one but multiple typos. No amount of nutrition or rubbing up against schools can change it. Your common "black," even after tutoring, can check over his or her work for any amount of time he or she deems appropriate and still not recognize all the typos. A good social scientist like Murray can type ten pages without typos as easily as pulling a hood over his head while whistling Dixie. (That may be harsh. If Murray has never witnessed a burning cross, I apologize.) Another test is spelling. The "blacks" constantly misspell words all over the lot, as you can see by taking representative samples from any former professional athlete up on double-homicide charges.

Conversely, "whites" do not misspell words, not even the felons. Oh, your average garden-variety computer hacker might, in theory, misspell a word here or there—but only because he's out of practice, having become so proficient with the computer mouse that there is no need for the tedium of typing. Point-and-click: The keyboard and the alphabet itself are passé—or no doubt will be, should "black" people study them harder. The smart "whites" in the think tanks, the ones who get entitlement grants to put new spin on the same old sad refrain—they're all descendants of Noah Webster! No misspellings! None! Not even a flutter! Oh, sometimes the pen may slip into a sort of *dementia notmyfaultia* because it was moved by stupid "blacks" as they cleaned up the laboratories and latrines at night.

If you asked the think-tankers to cite a witness to this "crime," they'd answer: "You are that witness. Say what the privileged want people to hear. If it comes from *you* it will give pause, and you will be rewarded. Fail and don't eat. Don't eat and die. That is what we call justice."

Well then, if you put it that way—I for one didn't need *The Bell Curve* to remind me of "nigger shit." Have you not heard of (and depended upon) "nigger shit"? Of course you have. You are American and you know it is important that "black" people are and remain so stupid. How else to stay busy making a profit? And if you haven't depended on "nigger shit" you'd best bone up because the test is being handed out real soon. "Nigger shit" is anything not up to speed— anything done badly, or done late, or done not at all. "Nigger shit" is when a person is envious and petty and jealous and stupid. I repeat, stupid. "Nigger shit" in a nutshell, stupid. When a thing is missing the mark and any persons owning a hint of discernible or even undiscernible African blood are available (or, in a pinch, even if they are not) you proclaim it "nigger shit"—unless it was your mistake and there is no other shoulder available. Then that was a horse of a different color. That was misfortune and you were a victim of circumstances. It could be rectified if you were given a chance/more time/a leg up. Yet when estimating your brother you never said, "My fault, mostly—my own bad choice in delegating." Or "Chalk it up to her youth." Or "So he failed. Failure can be overcome; only surrender to circumstances is unacceptable." Or "People *are* covetous—it is human." No, none of that escaped the crumpled aluminum can you call a heart or met your dry discerning eye; it was all "nigger shit." You call yourself human (superbly so, you think), and you can well imagine there are vacancy signs posted in the lesser minds. If you can't imagine what's in lesser minds, demagogues will do it for you, and you'll take their word, lest they turn their examinations more directly upon you. You are not here to protest leaps of logic, but to enshrine them.

Within the community that does (and does not) call itself African-American, there are those who are talented, industrious, some who went contrary and criminal, some who are envious back-stabbers and many who are profoundly, demonstrably, even proudly ignorant. The crooks and ignoramuses get most of the attention. They are seen on television, picked because they make the most sordid spectacles; they claim the central roles in books and movies; they are nominated for juries; they are given official awards for ordinary but myth-befitting work; they are handed out jobs that would not task a cadaver; they are allowed to make a place in all our minds even though they lack the moral center we portray so nobly in our writings and other celebrations of their ignorance. They do not see why they are there—as the vital justification for hating whatever spawned them. Do not send to know for whom the bell curve tolls. It tolls for me. But if you think it tolls for my son, then you've got one coming. I told one of my friends about my son's testing iniquities and said he'll have to go through life, because of lies like *The Bell Curve*, hearing people who are less talented say, "Who wrote that for you?"

He'll not only have to stay sane and steadfast in the face of such challenges, he'll need a good sense of humor about them. He'll have to suffer some genius's changing the landing coordinates he'd calculated, because the "genius" needs him to be inadequate to cinch his own spot. My son will have to walk from the wreckage home, making him late for dinner, which his wife will be quick to point out.

My friend said that I about had him in tears. I hoped they were tears of laughter, for I'd invented this tale not to describe some coming tragedy, but to offer up in a disarming way some statement of present-day fact.

After the game, we returned to Alexandria under a low cloud cover that both lightened the night sky and warned of the coming storm. The snow began to fall softly, quietly, ahead of forecast; fluffy, heavy flakes, clinging fast to whatever stayed still, blurring outlines and shapes we passed. Everything appeared as a grey nothingness as we schussed by the Department of Labor and Statistics building in Washington, D.C. There, the week before, I had offered up some material about my son to scant effect on an audience of government employees and high school students. Some of the employees were "black," which made sense, because if anyone should know about labor and statistics, it is them. Readers of *The Bell Curve* who also happened to be newly elected to Congress suspected there was no more need for the Departments of Education, Housing and Urban Development, Health and Welfare, Energy, and Commerce—much less the Bureau of Labor and Statistics. It should be eliminated first, just to get the feel for the ax.

One woman rose when I was done attempting to cut these issues down to size. She trembled with emotion, wavering on her feet. "How can you? How can you make us laugh about it so, when you don't even know if your son will get to grow up?" My heart went out to her, because what she said was from her own personal chronicle, from deep within her soul, and I could sense her loss—yet I could not imagine what she wanted me to imagine. Not by the light of day.

Shadows cast by the falling snow through the car windshield dappled and distorted my son's golden face. At length we arrived back at base camp in Alexandria, and read some before retiring. We needed to rest up, though he anticipated having the snow relieve him of any scholarly obligations the next day. I told him I would have to go to New York anyway, snow or no.

At the time my son was launched into *The Adventures of Tom Sawyer*. He was twelve, so this was a good book to begin to read. I told him I envied him in a way; that he was a changeling, embarking on a great adventure. He said I was the one leaving in the morning. Later he said he'd enjoyed the way Tom ducked out on Aunt Polly and was of an independent, imaginative mind. He liked how Tom spooned the Pain-Killer Aunt Polly had prescribed for him—"it was fire in a liquid form"—into a crack in the sitting room floor instead of his own gullet, then one day spooned it into a yellow tomcat only because the cat, oblivious to the dangers of medicine, meowed for it. My son rolled on the floor like Tom Sawyer, laughing as that cat sprang up, snarled, overturned furniture, arched its back and toe-danced in that eerie way cats have, shot for the ceiling, made it, turned a double-somersault and streaked through the window, followed by a tablecloth and flower pots, lighting out for open spots where there were no bad boys and worse medicine.

My son said the book made him want to read *The Adventures of Huckleberry Finn*. I said that was what it was bound to do.

"But, Dad," he said, "one thing, in *Tom Sawyer*. In that fence-painting part . . ."

"Yep . . ."

"It says, 'He . . .' "—he's talking about Tom right here—" 'He had discovered a great law of human action, without knowing it—namely, that in order to make a man or a boy covet a thing, it is only necessary to make the thing difficult to attain. If he had been a great and wise philosopher, like the writer of this book, he would now have comprehended that Work consists of whatever a body is *obliged* to do, and that Play consists of whatever a body is not obliged to do.' " He looked at me with clear, brown, wondering eyes. "Dad ... 'like the writer of this book'!?"

"I know ..."

"But that's ..."

"I know. It doesn't *seem* like the thing to say ..."

"I know!"

"... but then ..."

"I know!"

"... why are we laughing?"

"It's *funny*!"

It was at that moment, as my son and I were dying laughing, that I decided I would go forth the next day impelled (it is such a charming and archaic verb, but I have overworked it enough and promise to disabuse it henceforth and forever, until the next time I think I need it) by my own hypothesis for his survival into the twenty-first century in America: *If you know a little math, can understand Mark Twain's writings and, most difficult of all, can avoid being a victim of ever-ominous Circumstance, you have a fighting chance; if you show some "heart" (a word we use when we want to convey a certain state of mental acuity, an ability to act decisively in spite of fear and fearful odds), then you pretty much have living in America licked.* This is a rather hopeful hypothesis, I know. I blame my son for the overly rosy optimism. He is not a good model for me. I hope he overcomes the staggered start his mother provided. I watched over him as he slept. It dawned on me: I'd been watched over when I was his age.

"*Mama, I like that* Tom Sawyer *book. Gooood book.*"

"*Better than* The White Deer? *Better than* Charlotte's Web?"

*"Way better. Ain't never read none like that . . ."*

*"Haven't* read *any* like that . . . *fooling around out there in the street, learning how to talk crazy . . ."*

*"That's how people* do *talk . . ."*

*"I know. And I know you know the right way to say it. I know you know how . . . that's what Mark Twain did."*

*"I know it!"*

*"He could hide it many ways."*

*"I know—hide what?"*

*". . . Well . . . let's just say Mark Twain's one of those who took over where God left off."*

*". . . Not many of them, huh, Mama?"*

*"Only a few."*

*". . . zzz."*

*"Damned few."*

*"Ooo, you said dammmmmn . . ."*

*"Boy, you better gon'on to sleep before I—"*

*"ZZZzzz . . ."*

I retrieved *The Adventures of Huckleberry Finn* and began to read at a choice spot in the book as my son slept. I read in the spot where Pap Finn is holding his son Huck as a hostage, keeping him locked up, whipping him at his whim, putting the fear of God and a few other hair-raising subjects into the boy, and along the way revealing his original conspiracy theory about "their" plight:

"Oh, yes, this is a wonderful govment, wonderful. Why, looky here. There was a free nigger there from Ohio—a mulatter, most as white as a white man. He had the whitest shirt on you ever see, too, and the shiniest hat; there ain't a man in that town that's got as fine clothes as what he had; and he had a gold watch and chain, and a silver-headed cane—the awfulest old gray-headed nabob in the state. And what do you think? They said he was a p'fessor in a college, and could talk all kinds of languages, and knowed everything. And that ain't the wust. They said he could *vote* when he was at home. Well, that let me out. Thinks I, what is the country a'coming to? It was 'lection day, and I was just about to go and vote myself if I warn't too drunk to get there; but when they told me there was a state in this country where they'd let that nigger vote, I drawed out. I says I'll never vote ag'in. Them's the very words I said, they all heard me; and the country may rot for all me—I'll never vote ag'in as long as I live. And to see the cool way of that nigger—why, he wouldn't 'a' give me the road if I hadn't shoved him out o' the way. I says to the people, why ain't this nigger put up at auction and sold?—that's what I want to know. And what do you reckon they said? Why, they said he couldn't be sold till he'd been in the state six months, and he hadn't been there that long yet. There, now—that's a specimen. They call that a govment that can't sell a free nigger till he's been in the state six months. Here's a govment that calls itself a govment, and lets on to be a govment, and thinks it is a govment, and yet's got to set stock-still for six whole months before it can take a-hold of a prowling, thieving, infernal, white-shirted free nigger and—"

My gaze rose from the page. The snow descended so thick and uniformly until the world behind it disappeared. Looking at the falling snow as a background made the building I was in appear to rise. This was an illusion. I thought of my dear mother, English professor of the awfulest sort, and the nicest, too. I thought of what she said to me once about Mark Twain. I looked down again to the page, where Huck had made the moral break from Pap, and from all weak-minded men who were like him:

Pap was a-going on so, he never noticed where his old limber legs was taking him to, so he went head over heels over the tub of salt pork and barked both shins, and the rest of his speech was all the hottest kind of language—mostly hove at the nigger and the govment, though he give the tub some, too . . .

Huck had seen that his father was just a petty little man so busy blaming his troubles on other people that he could not even see where he was going. My eyelids disobeyed, and I dreamed . . .

. . . *Hucky, you tells 'em if dey feel like dey gots to take somebody, take me. Not mah son. He kin hep us, Hucky. Or dey kin take him an' me. We jes' piss po' mutts. Mutts, I say—mutts if it ain't no "white" folks to it a'tall. Our blood come up out Oklahoma an' we didn't have to be here in'a fust place from dere. One woman who married her cousin aft'a dey parents was manumitted in Texas was surrounded by dem of a Cherokee kine as she hung wash out twix Chandler and Boley, when Oklahoma was de Territory. Dem Injuns said no words but melted on 'way. We dem delta ones too, "black," "white," tannish, yella, brown pumpin' red under sandskin and showin' in dey face—what, you ig'nant?—den swung low in Memphis. His blood gots freemens of Philadelphia swappin' 'round. Count no "white" boys to it a'tall and we'se mutts. B'fo dat, who knew? Yoruba, Ibo, it all sound good. Who knew befo' dat? How'd dey get where dey was at? What dey go thoo gettin' dere? Some calls on Af'ica like Af'ica a county, and a dry one at dat! You know how many kines come up out'a Yourup? Is a Swedish man Spanish? Know what an Af'ican's answer to dat is? Yes an' no. You know you kin put two'a Yourups in half a Af'ica? Ain't nobody in dis worl' kin be from all over no Af'ica—an' cain't nobody not be, 'specially dem ol "white" boys, 'specially dem ol mad-assted ones. Truth's real close to whatever makes you mad, or laugh, eyether one. We'se mutts 'fo you get to dem. "White" folks's somethin' else, but somethin' dere, if not by sight—dough I wants for you to show me one'a dese hairy-assted Amer'can niggers where it ain't in sight—den in a'doin'. Somethin' vaguely— er'body? Aw, best take us both an' hell 'long wit it. One set'a monkeys won't stop no show, and strong mens keeps on keepin' on, and all dat'll wash, 'cause it's been washed 'an hung befo', an' by better. Wouldn' a'vize dey takes him and leaves me, Huck. Dat I'd reconsider as unnatch'el, and not quite smart as dey claims, by an' by . . .*

# 2

## What's Up with the Mad Mark Twain?

Let us first consider the lay of the land: a bloody, divisive war in the '60s; a social battle undertaken in the name of humanity; an assassinated president that same decade; the end of the divisive war; a period of reconstructive, affirmative action in the '70s; economic and political backlash against these actions in the '80s and '90s. Then a long-festering disease rent the air and thickened until it took shape and hung from the trees like insect pupa. At closer glance you could gather these were not pupa at all. Suffice it to say George Santayana's nineteenth-century dictum "Those who cannot remember the past are condemned to repeat it" might itself bear repeating into the twenty-first century, if not beyond.

One hundred years ago, in 1895, at the end of the nineteenth century (which we continue sketching, the better to observe the demise of the twentieth), a former student of Santayana's at Harvard, W. E. B. Du Bois, took a Ph.D. from that university and soon began to write the essays that would form his 1903 magnum opus, *The Souls of Black Folk*. In it he stated his dictum: "The problem of the twentieth century is the problem of the color line." We could now say, The problem is the *translation* of the color line. Or we could leave well enough alone and backtrack.

Frederick Douglass died in 1895. That year, José Martí, a cultural observer, author of *Our America*, was killed in Dos Rios, Cuba. In 1895, Booker T. Washington spoke out at the Atlanta Exposition, stoutheartedly countenancing a separate-but-equal doctrine that has taken some hundred years since not to completely overcome. The separateness was accomplished well enough to satisfy most; but the "equality" is a thirst only lately slaked and as yet unquenched, with no more water in the well. Booker Washington's conciliatory remarks were made in deference to a case wending to the 1896 Supreme Court—much as *Paxman v. Piscataway* wends its way to the 1996 Court. In 1895, the notable case was *Plessy v. Ferguson*. It was the curious case of Homer Plessy, of New Orleans, Louisiana, who had wanted to ride on a public streetcar. He had the nickel for the fare but not the dime lineage. One of Plessy's great-grandmothers had been "black," though this was not something you would notice right off if you looked at Homer Plessy. You would have to look hard at him to think about calling him "black." But that is beside the point.

The year 1895 was not all bad. Yes, at least two premium examples of manhood died, *The Clansman* dreck was unleashed and Harriet Beecher Stowe, author of *Uncle Tom's Cabin*, fell ill. She died on July 1, 1896. She was Mark Twain's next-door neighbor in Hartford, Connecticut. In the space of a year, Twain lost three friends of the spirit—Stowe, Douglass and Martí. If you consider the collected literary and oratorical efforts of only those four people—the woman, the "black," the "Hispanic" and the "white"—you'd have to admit today's authors, intellectuals and other good talkers do not keep up our end of the bargain by any pull of the imagination. And if you further realize that the collective works of those four, tinged by relevance though they be, were not enough to stop *Plessy, The Clansman* or all the hell, lynching, wars and death that broke loose afterward, in the long, murderous twentieth century, that does tend to give you pause when you consider the upcoming millennium.

Where were we? In July of 1895, when *The North American Review* published Twain's "Fenimore Cooper's Literary Offenses"—one of the most instructive criticisms posing as a satirical essay ever to meet these hungry eyes. In it, Twain levels famed Ivy League academics who had showered James Fenimore Cooper's *The Pathfinder* and *The Deerslayer* with their most delusional praise:

> It seems to me that it was far from right for [academics] to deliver opinions on Cooper's literature without having read some of it . . . In one place in *Deerslayer,* and in the restricted space of two-thirds of a page, Cooper has scored 114 offenses against literary art out of a possible 115. It breaks the record.

He next impales the whole notion of literary criticism as it is most often practiced:

> There are nineteen rules governing literary art in the domain of romantic fiction—some say twenty-two.

Then he gives a lesson on writing that anyone considering the suicidal act should be made to read, and I will not be the one to spoil it for you. It is enough warning to suggest that Twain's essay has an embarrassingly high profundity content and makes one begin to wonder how one was occupied all this time when one *thought* one was doing some reading. It is of more potential utility than *The Clansman*, though much more actual utility has been made of the latter. If Twain wrote that up today, and was equally incisive about some equally deserving novel, the essay might not be published; or if it was, critics would accuse Twain of first-degree "multiculturalism" and then broil him on a spit.

But let us not exalt those good old days: When *Huckleberry Finn* was published, it was banned in Concord, Massachusetts and Louisa May Alcott was among the many who all but accused Twain of pedophilia. Twain would be savaged today, and not for being right or wrong in his perceptions, but for cleaning up another "white" man's slipshod work. He would be laid out and gutted like a catfish by critics for attacking unquestionably classic virtues of a "dead white male," no matter how deserving, redemptive or even necessary his attacks might be—all because he takes *The Deerslayer* and exposes it as not being all it's cracked up to be, saying with a few well-chosen words:

"Shakespeare, this ain't."

> There have been daring people in the world who claimed that Cooper could write English, but they are all dead now . . . A work of art? It has no invention; it has no order, system, sequence, or result; it has no lifelikeness, no thrill, no stir, no seeming of reality; its characters are confusedly drawn, and by their acts and words they prove that they are not the sort of people the author claims that they are; its humor is pathetic; its pathos is funny; its conversations are—oh! indescribable; its love-scenes odious; its English a crime against the language.
>
> Counting these out, what is left is Art. I think we must all admit that.

As you can plainly see, 1895 was not *all* bad.

You may ask why there are references to Mark Twain in this book—indeed in every book I have inflicted upon an unsuspecting public thus far. I offer you several reasons. The first is the best: fair play. Twain saw clearly, thought clearly and wrote abominably well. He took the language that Americans I know speak and made a beautiful quilt of it, threw it over the whole country and warmed us up—made us a little *too* warm at times. If it's deeply, *really* American, Mark Twain has already written about it—and in such a manner that even today the writing does not cry out for much revision.

And that would be true of the worst of what he wrote. The best, like *Huckleberry Finn*, is so ethereal, knowing, sublime, all-encompassing of American nature as we know it, you sense neither "black" nor "white" was responsible for writing this. Something Else wrote this.

To wit: In *Huck Finn*, Twain-as-Huck, describing his decision to help Jim after the latter has been re-enslaved:

> "I went right along, not fixing up any particular plan, but just trusting to Providence to put the right words in my mouth when the time come: for I'd noticed that Providence always did put the right words in my mouth if I left it alone."

I have been snidely asked if I aspire to be "the 'black' Mark Twain." That aspiration has already been aspired. I could never be the "black" Mark Twain: Mark Twain is the "black" Mark Twain—and the "white" one, too. I aspire only to be some of the Ralph Wileys, and all any one of us can do in relation to Mark Twain is to point out where the best of him is camped out so that if this book does not move you, you can go off and read Twain, and that is *sure* to work or else the lights are too dim in those rooms where you do your reading. I also am running a deficit owed Twain. He has shown me the beauty in absurdities. Contrast that subversive wit with a Nobel Prize–winning American author of the twentieth century who could draw himself up and haughtily ask, "Who is the Tolstoy of the Zulus?" As if there were no reply. *Tolstoy* is the Tolstoy of the Zulus—unless you find a profit in fencing off universal properties of mankind into exclusive tribal ownership. Apparently, this Nobel Prize-winning author does find profit, and has passed the trait on. His son was editor and advocate of *The Bell Curve*.

Twain put it this way: *"If you pick up a starving dog and make him prosperous, he will not bite you. This is the principal difference between a dog and a man"* (Puddn'head Wilson's Calendar). The Nobel Prize is exclusively for humans, then.

Twain demonstrated how well he knew the demarcation between *right and wrong*, knew the boundaries are consistent, the same for all: There is no separate-but-equal category, no territory of right-and-wrong-for-"black"-people. No one, "black" or "white," is exempt because they think they ought to be—otherwise we should all soon be suffering the same exemption. Twain illustrated that the American "white" male cannot only be angry; he can be supremely privileged, yet treacherously just; outrageously talented, but terribly insight-ridden—and not three out of five at best; a *decent* "white" man who drew upon the true complexity of America without infantile denial—denial that would be funny were it not so pathetic. We should all get down on our knees and thank Providence for Twain, for he paid the deficit owed by giving something money cannot buy. And so if I am going to borrow concepts, pass them off as my property without permission, then they might as well be the very best concepts, taken off a dead man who can't put up much of a wrangle over them and probably wouldn't even if he wasn't dead. I have thought up two or three "original" concepts on my own, but those were heisted, and the better my concept the quicker the bite, it goes without saying without a favorable mention for me. I am not quite dead, as yet. I plan to save on the aggravation of scratching my head bald in search of more original concepts that people are going to palm off as their own without my permission, when some perfectly good Twain is sitting there all available and everything.

Now, if you want to go and call this stealing, or even sacrilege, well, what can I do about that? Hungry eyes are no different from empty stomachs and parched throats. They all are going to eat or drink. At least I am open, fair and fool enough to say that Mark Twain is the only man I would call master, and *mean* it. I say this as a reader and a would-be writer and an African-American. I've read articles, short stories, essays, sketches and novels and scripts for screenplays by writers far and wide, and a precious few of them have moved me to low whistles of awestruck amazement and recognition. I have read great writing and been moved by it, and after all the moving was done the worst effect it ever had was to sentence me to a lifetime of trying to write something good myself. But only after reading much of Samuel L. Clemens, a.k.a Mark Twain, did I think I had possibly gone into the wrong line of work. For within his writing, the recognition was complete, the mastery of the form was total, the lesson finished. He had refined, mastered and retired the form I'd put in thirty years attempting to identify: satire.

Only Shakespeare could be Shakespeare—although Twain did say Shakespeare could be Francis Bacon, maybe to keep up his end of his running feud with the Victorian novelists. Running feuds themselves are irrational: Shakespeare and Twain pointed that out in both life and art. Yet they could not help but be swept up in them, though their circumstances were completely different.

Humanity was what they had in common.

What Americans say when relaxed is based on the tongue Shakespeare wrote in, though it's not the same—not nearly the same, sometimes. The standard is different, and riffs on the standard, the vernacular, idioms and dialects, make it more so. Twain is the Shakespeare of the American standard language—where methods of expressing standards are different.

Shakespeare wrote, "This blessed plot, this earth, this realm, this England—" Can't do any better by it, as far as England is concerned. But we've got a sight more than a plot here in America. We are bigger situated land-wise and have a condition we carry over it wherever we go. This may be one reason why Sam Clemens the reporter was not overly concerned with plot, even of the bookish sort, or so he most deviously claimed. For why seem concerned with plot, a bloody thing requiring many pages, when you can ring the bell at one swoop:

*"I'm told [Richard] Wagner's music is better than it sounds."*

And that wasn't even Twain; that is a line from a fellow who looked *up* to Twain, a fellow named Nye who followed along in Twain's way of approaching and saying things; it is the American way.

So Twain took the universal human nature Shakespeare plumbed in a different mode of expression, in language the same but different and threw it in a pot where Americans could get at it. "Our prose standard," he wrote, "was ornate and diffuse; some authority or other changed it in the direction of compactness and simplicity."

It didn't matter if you were "Indians" meeting Marquette and Jolliet, or "white" "black" "nigger" "Chinaman" "Filipino"; it was the manner in which you were called these things that stood for something. It didn't matter who you were when it came to right, wrong and the human proclivity to ignore the difference. That was how he wrote it up, in a voice as subtle, simple, absurd, compact and complex as people he met. He was in a constant state of complaint about these people (remember, Twain went to Europe "on $500 the plumber didn't know I had"), as they so richly deserved, but he loved the land he'd occupied, from the banks of the Mississippi, Missouri and Ohio rivers to the Sierra Nevada to San Francisco Bay to New York City to the meadows of Connecticut. Everywhere the land seemed indescribably beautiful. It was people who made it so incredibly daft. Of course, even the land was up for review every once in a while. Like some land his family owned: *"This Tennessee land had been in the possession of the family many years, and promised to confer high fortune upon us someday; it still promises it, but in a less violent way"* (Roughing It).

Many have called me on my annoying admiration for the appropriateness of Twain's intentionally rustic, robust, laconic style; have told me my liking stems not from Twain's execution but from his being "liberal," seeming to tolerate "black" people occasionally. Then again, I have been questioned about my admiration because Twain knew how people had used the word "nigger," and what they meant by it, and when, and who it most reflected on. To me this was subtle craftsmanship of the sweetest, tenderest sort, but it still upset some of the selfsame "black" people Twain supposedly had tolerated a little too well. Mainly, I have been questioned.

I have no answer. If they have read Twain and don't get it, then how am I going to help the situation any? I can only speak of my own shortcomings: *If I could have said it that way first, I would have.* Mark Twain is not master of the school in which I am enrolled—he *built* the school, forced its accreditation, made it known and honored worldwide and kept the admissions policies liberal so that even a wretch like me could get a berth. Not a soft berth, mind you, but in this school who ever has time to rest?

I suppose you could say he was a "divine amateur," as Mr. Arnold Bennett put it back in the roaring '20s. Mr. Bennett himself was a pro's pro writer. He wrote at least twenty-four novels, a clutch of plays, countless essays—the titles of which escape all but the most diligent historians of today. Twain was a self-described "hack journalist"—a hack who happened to be the demiurge of his age; a registrar of humanity more than events; a keeper of times and perpetual human dilemmas and the manner in which they are expressed; a human motion-picture camera already whirring away in a time when no one in his neighborhood knew that technology was just aborning. Twain was more those things than a promoter of "ideology." You know the titles of a few of his books even if you've spent your life heeling it from historians.

Twain wrote *The Innocents Abroad* (1869), with his own frank style struggling to appear from the impenetrable techniques popular in that day; it was Victorian on top but itching underneath, an incorrigible boy in Sunday clothes; this fit the subject of *The Innocents Abroad* like a glove, even if it did not fit Twain. In his next book, *Roughing It* (1872), this definitely Twainlike sentence emerges: *"It was on this wise (which is a favorite expression of great authors, and a very neat one, too, but I never hear anybody say on this wise when they are talking)."*

From then on, though he "wrote off in a thousand different directions," as a friend of mine says, Twain's style changed. He wrote what people *said*, and about the differences between that and what they *did*. He also wrote with descriptive beauty such as that displayed at the beginning of Chapter 19 of *Huckleberry Finn*, or with the utter thoroughness of the first 214 pages of *Life on the Mississippi*. He wrote with rectitude, as in Chapters 49 through 51 in *Roughing It*, or in the recollection "A True Story Repeated Word for Word as I Heard It, or My First Lie, and How I Got Out of It."[1] And he wrote with a brilliance of controlled and telling imagery, never better displayed than in Chapter

12, "Jim Standing Siege," from the never-mentioned story *Tom Sawyer Abroad*. In this sequel to *Huck Finn*, Twain finds a plausible way—plausible, within the absurd burlesque he weaves to hide it—to have Jim, the mild ex-slave, holding a small American flag while striking poses, then standing on his head while *perched on the head of the Sphinx!* as Tom and Huck sail by in a hot-air balloon, getting "effects and perspectives and proportions." No need to go on about it. I've included it in the Notes section.[2] You may go there now and sample some. I'll wait.

. . . Well, *shit*. That is the only word I have available for what I (and others) have been writing in comparison to *that*. *Shit* is a common word, a crude word, but crude is not quite it. What I have written needs a slingshot to get up to crude in comparison to what Twain wrote. His writing reduces mine to precisely that—*shit*. What have I been writing by comparison? Say it all together now. *Shit*. There. It takes a good bit of the sting out of having been bad when you own up and accept it. Yet there is also an American way of saying "shit" that implies excellence. If you say of a book or song or painting or movie or some other attempt at art, "That's the shit!" then that is a high compliment—the highest, really—among certain young American people who can and do talk that way and, even more miraculously, understand each other when they do.

I've spent two books, an aggregate 559 pages, trying to capture an image Mark Twain spends all of *four* pages capturing better—not counting his fifty-page setup. All I can do now is keep trying to live up to Twain's long shadow, to the tradition of that voice. But, just between you and me, I think he has set the bar *too fucking high* for me to do anything but jump under it. I can't touch that bar. I can barely *see* that bar, but that is some consolation, because most people can't see it at all. Twain took a common American expression such as "He'd sell his own mother down the river," a phrase often said admiringly in market-driven America, and get to the root of it, put the pliers to the root, worry it out, and then reconstruct it as the novel *Pudd'nhead Wilson*; or what about when Twain—

Well, no need; the citings could be ceaseless and you haven't got all day. Most authors would like to write one book they might hang their hat on; two qualifies the author for one pantheon or another; three sets you up for retirement. Three great books seems to be the limit for even the most gifted American writers. Consider—Twain wrote *ten* such books.[3] Some are good books you might not get around to because you're busy being knocked cross-eyed by the top five, amazed to find how easily great literature can be swallowed. For not *just me,* Twain's writing is a fine point of art, the literary equivalent of the best blues and jazz, and would be had it no qualities other than a summation of a hidden history, a re-creation of life by the tongue of spoken rhythm, and beauty. Twain raised the "mongrel child of philology": *readability.* He can be read at the end of this century without need of a machete.

My admiration further swells for his repeated reminders of this cardinal truth: That a person, place or thing is dead, praised or said to be regal, doesn't make it classic, royal or better than average. Its actual nature does that. "Real Americans" are the ones who sniff out the difference. Finally, Twain *could get that down aright on paper.* There are wits who can talk, can get a joke when one is loaded up on them, but can't preserve or retell it. Twain wrote—*spoke*—for them because he wrote/spoke in a way they can appreciate—or should be *made* to appreciate.

That here and there in life I traced a path similar to his does not hurt my sense of intimacy with his writings. A slave woman shoos away a dog with "Begone, sah!" circa 1844 in

*Huck Finn,* and an electric shock courses through me as I sit book in hand; my own grandmother chased away curs with the similar " 'Gone, sah!" in 1964 (a mere coincidence, maybe; to me, some precious links strengthened). In his mid-twenties, Twain went west off the river into northern California and soon was engaged by the press. Then he came east to New York and was soon further engaged by the press. He slung lectures in his spare time. I did some of all that. Before-hand, at the age of twenty-one, Twain struck out from his temporary camp along the Ohio, in Cincinnati, to New Orleans, grubstaked by a fifty-dollar bill he found on a Keokuk, Iowa, street, tantalized by a book he had read that inspired him to plan to sail to South America and bivouac on the Amazon, then bring the wonders of the powder of the coca plant to a waiting world, his way of becoming a captain of commerce. Even you must admit it sounds sort of like me—what you may think you know of me, anyway.

Today, Twain could have watched the movie *Scarface,* and been similarly moved to get rich quick. I've met young men who were. No need to seek verification from them; they are now permanent residents of the quietest neighborhood of all. Fortunes made from cocaine are an unbelievably stupid goal. Young men don't see it because unbelievable stupidity is a young man's primary employment. Twain never made it to the Amazon; the trip was beyond his reach and his means; for our sons, it ain't necessarily so. Circumstance, leveler or booster of youthful ambition, will be accounted for.

Twain took an apprenticeship in steamboat piloting on the Mississippi. He's got me beat there. I went to college. Twain turned into a humanitarian. Oh yes, a shaggy, wounded, mis-anthropic humanitarian in the end—but a humanitarian still. One cannot be greatly disappointed unless one has enter-tained some reasonably high expectations to begin with. If Twain's being a humanitarian is a problem today, who does that problem reflect? Him, or us? And even humanitarianism has *function* in art. Why, it is the *height* of the artistic act. Was Shakespeare a humanitarian? What *truly* "classic" artist is not? What else but humanitarianism—Emerson's "universal heart"—sitting in judgment gives a story timelessness? In "The Turning Point of My Life," from the book *What Is Man? And Other Essays*, Twain writes:

> Such vast events—each a link in the *human race's* life-chain
> . . . link by link took its appointed place at its appointed
> time . . . If the stranger, with his trumpet blast, had stayed
> away (which he *couldn't*, for he was an appointed link) Cae-
> sar would not have crossed [the Rubicon]. What would have
> happened, in that case, we can never guess. We only know
> that the things that did happen would not have happened.
> They might have been replaced by equally prodigious things,
> of course, but their nature and results are beyond our guess-
> ing. But the matter that interests me personally is that I
> would not be *here* now, but somewhere else; and probably
> black—there is no telling. Very well, I am glad he crossed.
> And very really and thankfully glad, too, though I never
> cared anything about it before . . .
> *A nation is only an individual multiplied* . . . (Italics mine.)

A friend of mine, upon whom I have forced a familiarity with Twain's work, raised her eyebrows after reading that, and *The Tragedy of Puddn'head Wilson*, and "My First Lie, and How I Got Out of It," and Chapter 12 of *Tom Sawyer Abroad*, and then she said, "Well, this is pure D genius, of course. But, you know, I think this man was 'black'—you know, Homer Plessy style."

She was speaking of Twain's sympathetic and empathic responses, which were not limited to "black" people, though he concentrated so much of them there because that was where much concentration was needed. Writers are known for that—well, the better ones are.

*"I knew how an emancipated slave feels, for I was an emancipated slave myself."*

Twain wrote that in *Life on the Mississippi,* ostensibly about his liberation from a miserable period of apprenticeship under a resentful and tyrannical pilot, but with the best writers there is always something between the lines. Also, Twain thought he was responsible for the death of his brother Henry, horribly burned in a steamboat disaster on the Mississippi. Henry was laid up in Memphis awhile before dying from his injuries. Twain had given him morphine to ease his pain and felt he had given too much. Likewise, during his brief fortnight as a member of a Missouri militia (I told you, the man had done it all, or come close), an innocent passerby was shot and killed by untrained militiamen who were nearly petrified by their fear of the unknown future. Twain had fired his weapon at the man, as had six compatriots. Twain felt it was his bullet that found the mark, though no bullet he had ever loosed had found any sort of mark before.

It was more likely his empathic response that made the hit.

My friend interested me greatly when she said, "Not that it matters if he was or wasn't 'black.' He could *see* 'black' folk. He saw the situation—the way we're compromised. So I understand him. Even if he *was* passing, he is the only one I ever heard of that I *can* understand. Because of what he did. When we weren't supposed to be reading, here he was *writing,* and like *this*—making up a new way to write. He really couldn't have been himself, he wouldn't have been allowed, if he had been 'black.' I understand. He probably thought, 'Only here can I get to be me—and tell everybody about themselves at the same time.' "

For me, it is a matter of the commonality of the naturally satiric voice. Not that I'm a humanitarian (quite otherwise, it appears), but I do recognize the voices and the situations Twain uses—and so, I believe, can you, for he is the one nineteenth-century American writer whose writing is not faux-Elizabethan or Victorian, but a thing forever *fresh*.

Ever laugh at a joke, roll on the floor wrestling with it, thinking of it, day and night, laughing some more at inappropriate times just thinking about it, and not being able to wait to collar a group of your friends so you can flatten them with it, and when you finally do sit them down and try to regale them with the magic of this humorous story—they seem to resemble Mount Rushmore? They don't laugh much. But they do wonder how long you've had the fever.

So maybe you don't get this. But if you dare open Twain, you will get that, guaranteed.

For first one reason then another, Mark Twain's name appeared on the news pages and the letters-to-the-editor section of *The Washington Post* nearly as much as those of the President and House Speaker combined during the years between 1994 and 1996—and in that respect those years were no different than any other year in America in the last century. In 1995 and 1996, people were still arguing over the suitability of *Huck Finn* for high-schoolers to read. I agree. I say flog 'em with it in middle school first. They won't really begin to get it until much later anyway. Come to think of it, there's a Mark Twain Middle School not three miles from my base camp in Alexandria! An administrative aide there, a Mr. John Wallace, a "black" man, had wanted to delete any references to that archaic/contemporary word "nigger" from Twain's book. John couldn't delete it anywhere else *but* this book so that was where he wanted to start, in the one place where such copious use of the word in society was first best put in perspective—where it was used to describe a *condition*, not people; where it reflected on the *speaker*, not the subject. There is not one usage of "nigger" in *Huck Finn* that

I consider inauthentic, and I am hard to please that way. Twain was writing about 1844, remember. Now, if you were writing about today, say, you'd be able to use "black" (with or without quotation marks; it's your choice), "African-American," "colored," "Negro" and most certainly "nigger"; back in Jim and Huck's day, you were pretty much shut up with "nigger." Twain did not invent the situation; he reflected it. I think Twain would be prejudiced against John Wallace. Not because he is "black," but because Wallace was prejudiced against Twain's work, or, worse, he was not as sharp as the fifteen-year-old Twain's "black" friend Jerry, who told Twain about "Corn-Pone Opinions."

In that essay Twain says Jerry was a *"gay and impudent and satirical and delightful young black man—a slave—who daily preached sermons from the top of his master's wood-pile, with me for sole audience . . . To me he was a wonder. I believed he was the greatest orator in the United States and would someday be heard from. But it did not happen; in the distribution of rewards he was overlooked. It is the way, in this world."*

Twain wrote that in 1900—fifty years after he'd hung out with Jerry, who once told Twain this: "You tell me whar a man gits his corn pone, en I'll tell you what his 'pinions is."

Fifty years later, Twain wrote:

I think Jerry was right, in the main, but I think he did not go far enough.

1. It was his idea that a man conforms to the majority view of his locality by calculation and intention.
This happens, but I think it is not the rule.

2. It was his idea that there is such a thing as a first-hand opinion; an original opinion; an opinion which is coldly reasoned out in a man's head, by a searching analysis of the facts involved, with the heart unconsulted, and the jury room closed against outside influences. It may be that such an opin-

ion has been born somewhere, at some time or other, but I suppose it got away before they could catch it and stuff it and put it in the museum.

I am persuaded that a coldly-thought-out and independent verdict upon a fashion in clothes, or manners, or literature, or politics, or religion, or any other matter that is projected into the field of our notice and interest, is a most rare thing—if it has indeed ever existed . . .

It scatters the breath to consider how many scholarly and literary essays have been written about *Huck Finn* over the years. Some beg for revision, but I will limit myself to this one;[4] it, to me, best relates to Jerry and John Wallace. Ralph Ellison once wrote a typically brilliant short essay—"Change the Joke and Slip the Yoke"—that summed up how those he called "Negro" were "reduced to a negative sign" in the "Anglo-Saxon branch of American folklore and in the entertainment industry." The first two paragraphs are as good as essays get. Then, in discussing *Huck Finn*, Ellison says:

> . . . It is not at all odd that this black-faced figure of white fun is for Negroes a symbol of everything they rejected in the white man's thinking about race . . . When he appears, for example, in the guise of Nigger Jim, *the Negro is made uncomfortable* . . . Writing at a time when the blackfaced minstrel was still popular, and shortly after a war which left even the abolitionists weary of those problems associated with the Negro, Twain fitted Jim into the outlines of the minstrel tradition, and it is from behind this stereotype mask that we see Jim's dignity and human capacity—and Twain's complexity—emerge. Yet it is his source in this same tradition which creates that ambivalence between his identification as an adult and parent and his "boyish" naivete, and which by contrast makes Huck . . . seem more adult. *Certainly it upsets a Negro reader* . . . A glance at a more recent fictional encounter between a Negro adult and a white boy, that of Lucas

Beauchamp and Chick Mallison in Faulkner's *Intruder in the Dust*, will reinforce my point . . . Lucas holds the ascendancy in his mature dignity over the youthful Mallison and refuses to lower himself . . . Faulkner was free to reject the confusion between manhood and the Negro's caste status . . . but Twain, standing closer to the Reconstruction and to the oral tradition, was not so free of the white dictum that Negro males must be treated either as boys or "uncles"—never as men. Jim's friendship comes across as that of a boy for another boy rather than as friendship of an adult for a junior . . . It is ironic that what to a Negro appears to be a *lost fall* in Twain's otherwise successful wrestle with the ambiguous figure in blackface is viewed by a critic (L. Fiedler) as a symbolic loss of sexual identity. Surely for literature there is some rare richness here . . .

It is as Jerry said. Ellison was of the "classic" school, of Faulkner; of James Baldwin, and Baldwin's hero and literary father, Henry James, who once said Twain was "an appeal to rudimentary minds." (Twain replied, of James's *The Bostonians*: "I would rather be damned to John Bunyan's heaven than read *that*." Didn't pay to anger either of them, apparently.) It is also as T. S. Eliot said: "*Huckleberry Finn*, like other great works of imagination, can give to every reader whatever he is capable of taking from it."

Mr. Ellison left us twin monuments, *Invisible Man* and *Shadow and Act*. One monument he did not leave was a son. He was working off partial speculation when Jim made him uncomfortable by how he spoke and acted and carried himself with Huck. Ellison was not alone in this discomfort among "black" people who tried to get familiar with the book. Jim can make us all uncomfortable because we do not fully appreciate his double-barreled dilemma—though we should. Jim was not in a stingy-brimmed hat and Stacy-Adams shoes, knowing his Faulkner pat, proving the value of his college degree, assuming and demonstrating his own equality, or even his superiority. Jim had no such luxury. He was a *slave*, a slave in slavery, denied education, denied right over himself or his family, denied the dignity Ellison wished he'd shown not for the sake of the authenticity of the book, or even for Jim's sake, but for the sake of the image of the Negro; for *Ellison's* sake. Jim was denied, but dignified. As the two go down the river, Huck notices Jim's not waking him for a turn at watch. He knows Jim is all torn up over the loss of his wife and children, the deaf Elizabeth and little Johnny; they are his drive to freedom. Though Huck is thirteen, an ignorant waif, Jim needs him, for Huck can travel the landscape with near-impunity. When Huckleberry comes back to the raft after they've been separated in a dense fog and Jim has spent all night banging into the towheads looking for him, Huck says the misadventure was all a dream. What was Jim to do then? Scowl? Scold Huck for lying? Be aloof? Huck provides the answer later, talking about his father:

*"If I never learnt nothing else out of Pap, I learnt the best way to get along with his kind of people is to let them have their own way."*

So Twain has Jim *fall quiet for five minutes.* What must Jim be doing then? He is *thinking.* Thinking of what? Thinking that he doesn't fully know this "white" boy—not down below the quick—and mustn't cross him, or it will be up, because he could get Jim caught at his whim. And Jim must not get caught; he would be sold down the river and never see his family again. So he does what Huck said was the thing to do with people like him. Jim lets Huck have his way. Jim says this "dream" must have been a sign, then, and tells what signs stand for, and on and on. When Huck tires of Jim's facility with the lie Huck had started, Huck points to the detritus on the raft, the leaves and broken branches fallen there when Jim had been running blind into towheads while looking for him, because Jim was worried about the boy (and worried about what the boy might be doing); Huck points out what Jim already knew, that it was *not* a dream, by asking, "Oh, well, that's all interpreted well enough as far as it goes, Jim . . . but what does *these* things stand for?" And here, Jim takes the chance and delivers the lesson:

"*. . . Dat truck dah is* **trash**; *en trash is what people is dat puts dirt on de head er dey fren's en makes 'em ashamed.*"

Jim enters the wigwam, wondering what Huck will do. It is not idle wondering. Huck does this: "*It was fifteen minutes before I could work myself up to go and humble myself to a nigger; but I done it, and I warn't ever sorry for it afterward, neither . . .*" It is *then* Huck becomes the son Jim had lost. At that point Jim knows him beneath the quick and becomes Huck's surrogate father.

Take away any master/slave/skin coloring connotations. I can tell you, being with a thirteen-year-old boy of any stripe, trying to raise him halfway right for either selfish or altruistic motives, is not a matter of preserving your own dignity; it is a manner of ongoing negotiations with the boy. It is a manner of compromise. Therein lies the universal heart of it. Because any thirteen-year-old boy is nothing but a budding man; as such, he wants to be right at least sometimes, and amusing in all others, in rehearsal for when he will become a man and want to be right *all* the time. The man teaching him has to respect this sobering fact, like it or not, or else lose the boy, just as Pap lost Huck, and have to bear up under the outcome. You cannot clutch onto or hang your foot off in the tail of such a creature, at least not as a habit. You have to let him go and then try to be there when you see him falling.

From the first moment Jim talks to Huck, we begin to see the dilemma of the father/stepfather begin. For Jim gives him a prophecy and wants to get paid for his services. Huck has "an old slick counterfeit quarter that warn't no good because the brass showed through the silver a little," and the coin was thick with grease. Jim tells him one night spent inside a freshly cut white potato will clear all that up. Huck says to himself, "Well I knew a potato would do that before, but I had forgot it." This is no different from Bart Simpson saying, after someone informs him of facts he didn't have at hand: "I knew that." The reason you smile is you know the ways of thirteen-year-old boys. Circumstances will allow room for the man to respect the thirteen-year-old's whims, if he lets "blame well alone," because there are times when a thirteen-year-old *is* going to be right.

Several other 1995 public brushfires were blazing away due to *Huckleberry Finn,* causing a spouting of columns on editorial pages in Washington, New York and elsewhere, also much published letter-writing back and forth. The magazine *Civilization* ran a cover story by Lance Morrow titled *In Praise of Huckleberry Finn: Instead of banning Twain's novel, we should teach youngsters how to appreciate it.* A book receiving much 1995 mail was titled *Was Huck Black?* A title sure to garner response in America. The response would have been bigger if the title was *Was **Twain** Black?* Twain was definitely the one who showed me it didn't matter if he was or not.

As for Huck, Twain made it clear: Huck was backwoods "white," drawn from a childhood friend named Tom Blankenship; Huck is also Twain at times, and also Twain's speaking idol, Jerry. Draw conclusions as you may. Huck's occasionally coming off like Jerry does not make Huck "black"; it makes Huck *American,* and in some clear yet inexplicable way indebted to Jerry. Huck/Twain pays off the debt, to Jim. Jim was based on several men Twain knew, and so on through the other characters meant to exemplify imperishable Americans. Twain took pains to perceive and to point up differences in vernacular and dialects.

*The New Yorker*'s June 26–July 3, 1995, double issue, devoted entirely to fiction, was anchored by a recently discovered "lost chapter" of *Huckleberry Finn*, called "Jim and the Dead Man." *The New Yorker* published this "lost chapter" and five essays by five noted authors on different aspects of Twain's magnetic effects.

I read it suspiciously; I am suspicious every time a "lost chapter" of a great author is found and published. I always suspect some wag is looking to put one over on all of us. "Jim and the Dead Man" was supposedly found in some hotel in Hollywood in 1990. Twain died in 1910, in Redding, Connecticut; I don't know why, his being an old Northern Californian and predating the movie business, he would have left any papers in Hollywood. What's more, maybe there was a reason he "lost" this chapter. After reading it, I could see why Twain would want to leave it in the closet of posterity. It's not quite there, not Twain's best. The dialect is fair, not near-perfect, and Twain's ear for dialect was near-perfect. Also, it doesn't seem to advance the novel, unless Twain's intent, through Jim, is to take Huck's mind off the identity of the dead man Jim had actually found (Huck's father). If *The New Yorker* had wanted to print what's missing from *Huck Finn*, it should have printed the "Raftsmen's Episode," which Twain first published as a revealing aside in Chapter 3 of *Life on the Mississippi*; it is one of the most humorous stories I've come across, and intends to advance the narrative of *Huck Finn*, and would have accomplished it, too, if some smart editor, a relative of Twain's, had not decided to leave it out because it would make the book "look too long"— bigger than *The Adventures of Tom Sawyer*. So *The New Yorker* gave us "Jim and the Dead Man," which I'm not sure was Twain. But if *The New Yorker* says it was Twain, then it probably was Twain, because they are known to worry a fact to death over there at *The New Yorker*, or so I've heard said.

Of more interest were the five essays about *Huck Finn* that followed the excerpt. Bobbie Ann Mason wrote about the similarity between the language Twain wrote in and the one her grandparents spoke while they were raising her in Kentucky, and I understood and recognized this. Roger Angell then wrote of the resonance he felt, having been raised near a big river (the Hudson) himself. Angell does something else interesting. He says the book invites re-reading, "but I find less sunshine in it each time around. Its cruel and oafish backwater crowds, and the itinerant grotesques who prey upon them, don't feel all that funny or far away, and the bitter pains of Jim's condition, on which Twain poured out his irony, are dated more in details than in substance . . ."

Here (and maybe without knowing it) Angell breaks one of the codes of literary critiques of *Huckleberry Finn*—that the great book "ends poorly." E. L. Doctorow follows Angell, but apparently has not learned as much in re-readings. That author opined Twain had no "plan," he was guided by "whim."

Twain had no plan in *Huckleberry Finn*? Such a statement, written by the author of *Ragtime, The Book of Daniel, Waterworks* and *Billy Bathgate*, boggles the mind—or reveals one of the seven deadly sins and Doctorow's inescapable human susceptibility to at least one of them. This might be envy. Twain is the wrong writer to envy. No comfort can be gained there at any future point. Only Doctorow knows the agonies he endured in ordering his books. And they are very good books, extravagantly great books for all I know, and possibly even one of them could crack into the top ten of Mark Twain's great books. But no more than one, no higher than Twain's top five. Consider then the agonies of ordering

Twain must have suffered. So to say he had no plan is denigrating. In a literary sense, denigrating Twain (in order to replace him) is devilishly difficult. Doctorow makes himself comfortable in this bear trap, though; he says the usual about the ending of *Huck Finn*:

> And then something terrible happens—terrible for Huck, terrible for American literature. [Actually, what happens next was pretty terrible for Jim, too, but Doctorow seems not to have noticed.] Jim is captured [Actually, Jim is sold by the "king" for forty pieces of silver, which prove elusive; Doctorow might have skipped over that part.] Though the moral mind of the book is Huck's . . . it is given to Tom Sawyer to stage Jim's ultimate escape . . . the book wallows in foolishness, playing out, long past credibility, Tom's nonsensical, overcomplicated, boy's-book fantasy escape plan.

Doctorow ends his feverish treatise with a bang, following up Ellison's verdict on poor old "gullible" Jim. Just as Ellison was not speaking of Ellison's feelings about Jim, but about Ellison's feelings about Ellison, Doctorow has not felt the rapier. He's bleeding and doesn't notice. The end of *Huckleberry Finn* is near-perfect.

Doctorow claims that Twain worked on Huckleberry Finn sporadically for eight years out of several kinds of laxity. I contend that Twain put the manuscript away for stretches because he had to see what was going to happen in American history—the river represents life, and history. The raft itself is both America and the only way to safely traverse America in that point in its history. When Twain's resolve was steeled, it was the 1880s, when backlash against reconstruction and "blacks" intensified—just as in the 1980s, when "liberals" gave way to the "dukes" and the "kings" and other hustlers. Twain knew Jim had been resold into slavery for a paltry pittance of silver. And I think the reason "liberal" reviewers hate Tom's reappearance is that it's *their* reappearance as well—and the adult Twain's reappearance too, for *he* is as much Tom as he is Huck. It is the reappearance of the adult American consciousness. For it knows the slaves are free, in the legal sense, as in Miss Watson's will, or the Emancipation Proclamation, or the Thirteenth and Fourteenth Amendments to the Constitution; as in the eyes of God itself, without all the "legal" rigmarole.

Yet we, like Tom, instead of giving Jim what was owed and moving on out of there together, construct a bizarre game of programs and schemes and plans and organizations and all whatnot just to give ourselves something to do and feel good about; so we can approve of ourselves by feeling it was our knowing hand that freed Jim. Not for nothing does Twain have Tom take his escape plans from the swashbuckling novels of Dumas, like *The Man in the Iron Mask.* Nor for nothing does Twain evoke the game of Evasion. Meanwhile, people who are not necessarily "liberal" but just good-hearted and honest folk, like Huck, stand idly by, going along with these ridiculous and outlandish measures when we wish they would do the right thing. It frustrates us. Imagine then what it must have done to Jim—made to sleep with snakes and spiders, close to the grindstone; forced to write his history in his own blood because Tom thinks it a novel and romantic way to get a man freedom. Jim's already free, but what fun is there for Tom and the adult American consciousness in admitting that and getting on with it? No adventure or romance or even much exercise in that.

Mark Twain had no plan in *Huckleberry Finn?* Well, it may be that he didn't. But Providence obviously did. Twain is asking, Who is the real nigger here? And who is the one being violated by the nigger's presence? Speaking of the unspeakable, Bill Styron and David Bradley then wrote in *The New Yorker* about the use of "nigger" in *Huckleberry Finn,* and Bradley, who is "black," seemed to understand the usage in the great book better than Styron, who is "white." Bradley is the author of the novel *The Chaneysville Incident.* It and Toni Morrison's *Beloved* are two of the better novels of the past twenty-five years, or not, according to those who would know such things. Both books use a haunting question of infanticide and suicide by slaves to keep their children from enduring slavery. This is a subject Twain plumbed one hundred years ago in the first twenty-five pages of *The Tragedy of Pudd'nhead Wilson*—coming to the unspoken conclusion that suicide *was* likely a better outcome than being in slavery—on either side of the "equation." *Pudd'nhead Wilson* is the only one of Twain's great novels never to be adapted to film. Once you read it, you will see why. It's beside the point. Right beside it, in fact.

Also in 1995, two movies based on *Huck Finn* were advertised and reviewed in the papers. (Cinematic dubs of the great American novel are yearly events now, though few of them convey the finer points of the book or are even true to its form and dialogue—as though either one could be improved; one 1995 release was called *Huck and the King of Hearts*—apparently Jim came to a bad turn.)

Back in 1895 Twain traveled to England, Germany and Austria to lecture for pay and to get out of a deficit. He owed $100,000, which in the '90s—any '90s—is too much money. You thought we invented deficits? Seems as if deficits are part of the American way of life.

Twain considered the journals and the language in Germany, wrote rivetingly and without much diplomacy about both in "The Awful German Language," from *A Tramp Abroad.* Riveting isn't diplomatic work. Twain thought the German language awful, I think, because he loved his American language; it and only it reminded him of his best beloved—a river that was liquid land as much as water, with a floodplain a hundred miles wide in some places, a living, quiet riot of river that levees and pegs and the best-laid plans of the Army Corps of Engineers and all other man-made forms of grammar-as-landscaping could not hope to contain when that river chose not to be contained. A mention of Twain's harsh appraisals of the German tongue appeared in the 1995 newspapers and *that* began a thirty-day exchange of artillery fire in the editorial pages of *The Washington Post*—a blitzkrieg in black-and-white rivaling coverage and glamorization of "inner-city crime" during the same period. For this flurry alone, Twain, no less lively for having died eighty-five years earlier, should be combed, reproduced and honored. The man still has no peer.

*Also* in the 1995 newspapers, excerpts were published from letters Twain wrote while he was working in Washington, in the office of Senator William Stewart from Nevada. After six months on the job of answering letters from the senator's constituents with replies that left them speechless and dissatisfied, and laughing when they didn't particularly want to, Twain left Washington—but until this very day, it appears Washington hasn't left him, nor his assessments of the brawling nation that founded it. Even a sportswriter, John Feinstein, drew from Mark Twain in titling his 1995 book about the Professional Golfers' Association *A Good Walk Spoiled*— Twain's evaluation of a day on the links. A prerequisite of satire is topicality, at least as Webster's defines it. Twain "qualifies." Topically, Twain is all over the place. He might just do.

Take *High Noon*, the 1951 movie with Gary Cooper and Grace Kelly, a masterstroke of storytelling playing on cable and in video rental stores in 1995. In case you don't know the story of *High Noon*: Three bad guys are waiting to shoot up the saloon and gun down the law (Gary Cooper's character, the town marshal/constabulary) and raise all kinds of sand in town just as soon as their leader and blood brother exits the noon train. His eminence had been sent down the river for murder by Cooper's character (dressed, interestingly, in black) and had promised to look the lawman up if he ever got out. Cooper's character was willing to face the trouble to the point of delaying retirement and his honeymoon with the beautiful and beautifully lit Kelly character, a moon-eyed Quaker girl. Nobody in the law-abiding and peaceful town was willing to take a stand with Cooper—especially not his friends, who suggested he hightail it because they would if it were them. The townsfolk were pious, moral and brave about being them, as long as they went untested on their convictions. When faced with lawlessness they deferred to higher authorities. If lawlessness defeated law, lawlessness would become the new law and the townsfolk would have to do a different deal. Most people believed doing right was somebody else's job, when you came down to the nub. Eternally, people do what is convenient for them at the time.

*High Noon* was drawn from Twain's story *The Man That Corrupted Hadleyburg*. It takes no deep insight or schooling to ascertain this; that fictional town in *High Noon* is "Hadleyville." As long as there's an appreciation for absurdities in human beings and their brief, collective history in America, Mark Twain will never go out of style.

I once had a dream. I am in a room with "white" men. No other "black" people. No other anybodys. Everyone is dressed to travel, but judging from the room's mood no one is much looking forward to any adventures that begin with running the river on a night such as this. For it is as if Twain's "firmament of black cats" hangs outside. By this tip-off and certain others, I figure we are in the pilothouse of a mighty stern-wheeler, where else but on the Mississippi, when else but on a starless void of a night. The men in a group speak loudly, some others quietly fill up a corner, alone, as do I. A few pace. Most are ashen.

We await someone, and I am figuring the someone better be the pilot of the boat. I know the others are accused of being pilots and give good spoken account of themselves in this regard and are here to "look at the river." The ones in the group scan me in a manner that does not ring out welcome, which is fine by me; piloting is not a group activity. The solitary ones nod at me when we make eye contact, but I do not maintain the contact long because I don't want them mistaking me for some wastrel they know and bear grudge against. I can hear a woman tittering, as if in the walls, and tickled by the situation. But I am not leaving the pilothouse because somehow I know the pilot we await is Mark Twain, or maybe his steersman. Why else would I be there?

Finally, he makes his entrance, looking about as you'd think—in a rumpled serge suit, with an untamed mane and mustache gone grey, impenitently reeking of tobacco, made comfortably at home by the Stygian darkness and the dangers beneath that treacherous river's surface. He smiles contentedly, a man with a full stomach, a spotless conscience and a firm grip on the best way to proceed. He nods at the motley assemblage of pretenders, who have all shrunk some since he came in. We return frozen poses that would resemble smiles if they did not resemble the clench of rigor mortis so much more. The man I think is Twain walks over to *me*, mustache raised at the corners like wings off an albino bat. This does not thaw out the room. But I am delighted. I smile—not too broadly. My mouth lists to starboard—as if there's an insidious joke and I get it. The man I think is Twain shaves at my elbow, steers us off to one side, has a word for me, then moves on to the next now-delighted man.

A "white" man comes out of a corner and asks me what the man I think is Twain said. It is when I say it that I remember hearing it. I answered him as I awoke from the dream:

"He only said one word."

"Relax."


Plot, T. S. Eliot said, was "the meat a burglar brings to distract the watchdog."

In *How to Tell a Story*, Mark Twain wrote:

> *There are several kinds of stories, but only one difficult kind—the humorous . . . [It] depends for its effect upon the manner of the telling, the comic story and the witty story on the matter . . . [T]he humorous story may be spun out to great length, and may wander around as much as it pleases, and arrive nowhere in particular . . . the humorous story is strictly a work of art—high and delicate art—and only an artist can tell it; but no art is necessary in telling the comic and the witty story: anybody can do it. The art of telling a humorous story—understand, I mean by word of mouth, not print—was created in America, and has remained at home. The humorous story is told gravely; the teller does his best to conceal the fact that he even dimly suspects that there is anything funny about it . . .*
>
> *[T]o string incongruities and absurdities together in a wandering and sometimes purposeless way, and seem innocently unaware that they are absurdities, is the basis of American art, if my position is correct. Another feature is the slurring of the point. A third is the dropping of a studied remark apparently without knowing it, as if one were thinking aloud. The fourth and last is the pause.*

So. It is the manner of the journey that matters; not so much what people say along the way as how they say it, how they act accompanied by and compared to what they say, and how they are situated. In the stories of the people you meet, manner and method add up to something as rich as the plot itself—maybe richer. Stories get told in brief tall tales, for the most part, because it is a big country and there are many stories to be told; a big country needs a like lore to describe it. That is what fits. Here the thing is *how* people say it is. America is a place steeped in irony. What other way to write it?

# 3

## One Day, When I Was
## on Exhibit

*This building holds in trust the records of our national life
and symbolizes our faith in the permanency of our national
institutions ...*

—NATIONAL ARCHIVES BUILDING

The coldest inconvenience accumulated outside Union Station as I arrived to board the train. Why go to New York
City in the middle of a snowstorm? Habit, most likely. I
once worked there, and lived. But also applying some spur
was *The New York Times Magazine*, which had recently
published a cover story entitled:

"The Black Man Is in Terrible Trouble: Whose Problem Is
That?"

No need to wonder long, eh? And no need to shirk in
vain when responsibilities are so obviously delineated, so
clearly headlined, so bickered over—then so cavalierly
tossed aside.

First, two New York art exhibits would incur my vigil.
Thus fortified by perspective, I would then cast out and

about for those whose job it was to give more exquisite rebuttals (or Amens) to such bold inquiries as the *Times's*—if
I could find such parties.

They were rumored to be on their way out of town under
cover of night, for this "black intelligentsia" was also standing siege. Months after the publication of *The Bell Curve*,
the "color-blind" *Village Voice*, bowing to a hurricane of
convention, prepared its article, "The Current Crisis of the
Black Intellectual," keeping it abreast of *The New Republic*'s
article "The Decline of the Black Intellectual."

These and like articles in *The New Yorker*, Washington's
*City Paper* and others were good enough reasons to try on
the art exhibits for size first. Their locations were fixed and
would be simpler to find than the nebulous whereabouts of
harried "black" minds.

One of the exhibits, at the Michael Rosenfeld Gallery,
above 57th Street, was named *Exultations: African American
Art: 20th-Century Masterworks II*. The other, at the re-
nowned Whitney Museum up on Madison Avenue, was
called *Black Male: Representations of Masculinity in Contemporary Amerian Art*. Surely these two might serve to
amuse, especially in February, a period of bitter deprivation
often slandered as "Black History Month." Being thought to
be so shallow that a mere month, headline, "book," politi-
cian's lying pronouncements or intellectual's babbling self-
service is enough to contain you, and accepting these blind
stabs as immutable facts of *your* life, requires a shortage of
confidence, or a lack of a good sense of humor. Just as soon
as the latter deficiency is corrected here—*if* it ever is—we will
be a lot better off.

It was a fine time to be shed of Washington, D.C., even
had I *no* agenda for leaving. The District had been found to
be some $750 million "in deficit." Layoffs and wage cuts
were in the offing. School lunches, libraries, fire and police

would be cut. People had "draconian" added to their speech if not their vocabularies. Fiscal control of the city was on the verge of being taken by Congress from less capable hands. There! That is absurd, to imply (or infer) there are hands less capable than those that pander in Congress. This absurdity was made mostly of passions. Passions had been whipped up into a froth in a variety of ways by popular radio and TV and newspaper "personalities" (names do not matter, since anyone can entertain the role) and their whiny and repeated entreaties about certain hinted-at epiphanies (little things like wealth, control, common sense, occasional debauchery, intelligence, morality on the day after the orgies, and the divine right to judge and then shoot any antagonist between the eyes) that ought to go hand-in-hand with the fine stock implied in lacking pigmentation.

My own stock was good, or so my family cared to insist, but I found I could not swallow that stock and have it nourish me; oh it nourished my pride, but my stomach grumbled for bread and water to be included on the menu. Blood passions bore sweeter fruit for others, as in the election to the 104th Congress of politicians (proper names don't matter; fill as needed) and consultants, lobbyists and blowhards the prior fall of '94 under a banner of "Whatever's Most Convenient" and on a promise to "End Big Government!" They all said big government consisted mostly of doling out "welfare," and "affirmative action," abetting "crime" while denying "real Americans" their constitutional rights. In reality, the promise to end big government was the hollowest of threats, considering that those who made the promise now made up the big government.

In some quarters this quantum absurdity was known as the uprising of "angry 'white' males." No need to wonder about the focus and direction of the anger. Not according to Pap Finn.

*. . . The nigger and the govment.*

Since Pap had been elected to Congress and had assumed the mantle of big government and had the "duke" and the "king" doing the Royal Nonesuch for the amusement and titillation of radio and TV audiences, that left you-know-who holding the bags. I wonder if "black" people shoulder this baggage because they are naive, or feel trapped, or because they are so accustomed to being defined by tragedy that they do not take much offense to it anymore. I don't know why this acceptance is so uniform—but others might. I decided to seek out, in addition to the art, the elusive Cornel West, Henry L. Gates, Shelby Steele, Derrick Bell, Bell Hooks, Michael Eric Dyson, Glenn Loury, Stanley Crouch, Gerald Early, Robin Kelley, Patricia J. Williams, Thomas Sowell, Stephen L. Carter, Manning Marable and a host of others who will be upset to go unmentioned by name—much more upset than those who *are* mentioned by name—and ask them. They'd all either written for or been quoted by *The New York Times* or *The New Yorker,* or had been in the employ of Harvard or Yale or Princeton or Stanford or come close to it at one time or another and would know what to say and how to say it soothingly, if not always in a refreshing way. Some of them said things that were not particularly dulcet but true, and some of them sometimes came near the truth refreshingly. It's up to me (and you) to figure out who does which. In a nutshell, this is why I took the train to New York during a snowstorm. I was hoping against the odds and what was put before me that a search for "black" intelligence was not some wild-goose chase.

## Commerce and Deficits Inside and
## Outside Union Station

Union Station is a honeycomb of reinvested Roman architecture whose chambers buzz with commuters and commerce all the livelong day. In addition to train lines and their personnel ranks, there are 130 gift shops offering everything from chocolate to shoes to books to sunglasses to jewelry to socks to brass fixtures to more and more until it makes a body's head and credit cards swim; also there are upwards of fifty restaurants and bars, four newsstands, and a movie theater with nine screens. And all that accounts for about half of the commerce occurring daily there. The station teems with people and is washed by the hum of life before 9 A.M., around the noon hour, and after 5 P.M., when government workers, bureaucrats, consultants and their lobbyists come to trough and bar, and take up air. Some even take the trains. The only tax they pay for a life of a relatively high leisure is one of quite open disparagement about "these people" who have their hands out, and utter amazement that amid all this wild commerce the District of Columbia's "black" custodians would be so incompetent as to run up a big deficit in an era of such obvious plenty.

Many of these autocrats live in Montgomery County, Maryland; or Fairfax County, Virginia; or Prince Georges County, Maryland; or Anne Arundel County, Maryland, east of Prince Georges, bordering Chesapeake Bay. None of these commuters pay a toll to enter the District of Columbia if they drive; their wages are not taxed by D.C. The federal government itself owns much of the choicest land in D.C. What it does not own belongs to the churches, church-sponsored universities and others with a tax-exempt status. A mortgage company, "Fannie Mae"—Federal National

Mortgage Association—sits astride *one hundred acres* in northwest Washington. It is a privately held company. The "Federal National" part of the title intends to throw you off on that count—and accomplishes it, apparently, at least as far as the tax assessors are concerned; though Fannie Mae is privately held, it pays no property tax to the District of Columbia. If it would move its offices over near the Pentagon in Virginia, and see what *Virginia* would say about tax exemptions, and meantime cut up all that prime D.C. real estate into one-acre parcels and give out mortgages on it, like it says in the title, then *I* would take this as good-faith collateral and agree to run a deficit in order to shepherd a double-lot toward tax profitability. Such actions are unlikely soon.

Meanwhile, the good citizens of the District of Columbia, 575,000 strong, pay the per capita third-highest federal income tax each year—some $1.6 billion annually—for the right to *not* have a voting member in the Congress but only to listen to the voting members castigate *them* as fiscal insurrectionists. You would think the Congress would say, "Washington has a deficit, and it is us." But Congress has never said anything resembling that before, and we marvel at its consistency in this regard.

By comparison, New York City does tax and toll the people who work there. If you are driving a car, you have to pay four dollars just to get in line to enter New York, with no promises given that you will actually make it alive, whether you are entering from out-of-state to work or just attempting to visit art exhibits. You must pay three dollars just to drive into the borough of Manhattan from some other boroughs of New York. Having worked in Manhattan, I can say unequivocally that New York State and New York City tax the wages earned there. It may be better put that the taxes are slightly waged.

And yet New York City was also running a deficit—as

were Philadelphia, Cleveland, California's Orange County, etc. And those were just the most publicized deficit-holders. At the same time, Mexico said it was a little overdrawn itself, so it was loaned $40 billion by the U.S. government to "strengthen the peso." The U.S. government itself was running a deficit many times that of the District of Columbia— over four trillion dollars' worth. But the government has the distinct advantage of being able to print its own money.

In keeping with these traditions, I too am running a little hot, deficit-wise. I have a loan for a house and one from when I had to bail myself out by groveling at the feet of a banker. I could not pay off these loans if asked to do it by tomorrow evening, but the bankers know they will get their money or their pound of flesh sooner or later: I have worked hard to rise up and pay my bills and become what any decent banker would call "high-risk."

I am not alone in my predicament. There are "white" people out there who are running deficits. They go into banks for loans, say, for the upkeep of a farm, or a business. If they are denied the loan, they are told that if they had been "black" they would gave gotten a loan posthaste, and a parade announcing it. This is a gurgling stream of verbal diarrhea serving to wash the banker's manicured hands of the matter and earning him a pat on the back from the one whom he has denied patronage; this is also marvelous hypnosis, although it usually seems to leave the now-mesmerized "white" person more bitterly disposed toward the next "black" person he bumps into, once he tears himself away from collegial times at the bank. For he has not taken the time to ask himself whether this was a lie. Bankers wouldn't lie. But a nigger would, and with a straight face. In the face of this particular financial tradition Washington's deficit was benign—unless it too wore The Mask.

## The Shoeshine Man Waxes Eloquent

Life was so situated as I came into Union Station. I saw a "black" man standing there. He had his hand out rather naturally.

"Spare a quarter?" he asked.

I frowned. "Don't you know what's going on out here?" I said, speeding off at a rate that discouraged a thoughtful reply.

I stopped off at the shoeshine stand. It was a lost art, shoe-shining, though it threatened a comeback judging from the four-seat stand that appeared to be the busiest enterprise in Union Station. I waited for my turn, rose to the appointment, opened the newspaper to another unholy reference to Mayor Whatshisname.

"Oh, why don't they write something about Eleanor Holmes Norton?" I asked. "There's a woman with something on the ball. She should be senator. Mayor'll do, come to think of it. The Senate's too low for her. She doesn't get to vote in Congress, but she's always running a town meeting or seminar about contract procurement for small businesses, or something else people can use. I never see *that*. All that's in the paper is Mayor Whatshisname, drugs, crime and obits."

The shoeshine man looked up.

"Me, I live in Myrrh-lun," he said. "What about Albert Wynn, the congressman? Smart as a whip. Don't hear 'bout him much in the papers neither. Be glad of it."

"Glad?"

"You know why, don'tcha?"

"Do *I* know why?"

"You *do* know what's goin' on out here, don'tcha?"

Not wanting to appear as slacking before the shoeshine man as the beggar had been before me, I said, "I got a good idea," and snapped the paper, waiting for the shoeshine man to give me a notion of what idea might be suitable. He kept on polishing. The stand was the most centrally located business in the station, in front of the gates to the trains. The foot traffic by it was unabating. "Must see a lot in this spot," I said in a moment of discernment. "Mister, I see er'body," he said. Once he unlocked, the torrents rushed forth. "Seen Lani Guinier, Mike Espy, Hazel O'Leary, Henry Cisneros, Ron Brown and Joycelyn Elders riding out of town on this here rail. Some of 'em hadda go, 'cause of what the papers said once't they got 'pointed to the Cabinet. Maybe you see why I say if you want to get somethin' done, best keep it out the paper. The day Eleanor starts being in the paper a little too much is the day she gone, far as me and you's concerned."

"I see what you mean . . ."

"Just this morning, Michael Jordan's business managers come through here. Judgin' from what they said and the bounce in they step, he's comin' back to the NBA." The shoeshine man said this sadly. I couldn't imagine why. At the mention of Jordan playing ball my heart leapt. I dared not hope so wonderful a thing could happen. It would be a relief from what else was in the papers.

"Jordan's retired," I said, hoping the shoeshine man would remain consistent in contradicting me. He fell into my trap, but his mood remained inexplicably somber. "Not for long," he said.

"Don't get my hopes up unless you know."

"I'm tellin' you what I *do* know," said the shoeshine man, "and doin' it nice, 'cause in three and a half minutes, you're gonna give me three dollars—five if you like the job I do on 'nese shoes. When was the last time they got shined? Ain't no way to treat a good pair of shoes like that. I want you to come back and see me sometime. So I wouldn't lie on you."

"Three bucks for a shine? It's . . . highway robbery!"

"Naw. It's Febearry 1995, and I gots to make payroll."

"Well . . . five dollars isn't so much to find out Jordan's coming. We need his classic artistry. If he comes back—that'll be great!"

"Yeah? For who?" said the shoeshine man.

"*Whom,*" I wedged in, though I was not sure of this correction. He appeared to ignore the advice anyway.

"He should come back, but with his own team."

"His own team? What are you talking about, man? Michael Jordan is a player. He doesn't have a team."

The shoeshine man snapped his rag and kept his head bowed. Presently he said, very quietly, "Oh, he's a player, all right. He just don't know it. Don't you know what's goin' on out here?"

I admitted something was going on and suspected I knew a great deal about it. I knew how he was hinting, but whatever was going on, it was not a conspiracy. I am not some kind of lunatic conspiracy theorist; instead, and in very fine stead, I am a good American. "Well, I'm rational about it," I said. "I'm against the welfare state. I am against it *as it is constructed.* It seems to me giving welfare to a family whose father is nowhere to be found only perpetuates the misery. I've seen what this kind of welfare can do to a woman's drive and to her spandex. I've heard of living off the fat of the land, but exploding off the fat of the land is stretching it. I'd say the only way to get the three hundred dollars a month is if the father is *in* the house, not the other way around. That would be a kind of welfare that forces families together, keeps a woman on her toes and out of the refrigerator, and might foster up productive adults from the children that those families would raise. I'm against 'affirmative action' too, because if all 'affirmative action' is giving me is a group of pathological or at best mediocre folks like Clarence

Thomas on the Supreme Court, Quinn Buckner—you follow ball, don't you?—as an NBA coach or analyst, and O.J. Simpson as a celebrity, then that's some action you can hold on to, right there. That's not no 'affirmative action.' That's some con action is what that is."

"Don't be talkin' 'bout Clarence," said the shine man. "He ain't done nothin' to y'all—yet. Jordan's the one let me down."

"I'm not talking about basketball."

"I ain't talkin' 'bout basketball neither. I'm talkin' 'bout what people need, and that's a job. Some bid'ness."

"What little birdie told you?"

"You mean, me being a shoeshine man? That ain't nothin'. I been worse. I was an editor at a magazine up in New Yawk. Before that I was a reporter for a few newspapers. This line promised more upward mobility. I just fell off to talkin' like this since the stand opened up. Makes everybody mo' comf'tible."

"How'd you come to this?" I asked, with my arm sweeping at his four fellows whose heads were bowed as they shined shoes.

"This? Oh, I own the stand," he said.

The four heads bobbed like corks in a sea of affirmation. "Owns it." "Yep." "Lock, stock 'n ba'el." "Straight up his'n."

"*You* own it?"

"Yep. And Jordan's got better leverage than me," he said. "When I started out I went to a barbershop owned by a 'black' man. You might know his son. Goes over to George-town. Plays ball over there. I came in one day and said I was an ex-journalist. He let me put a chair in the corner and shine shoes. Soon I had two chairs. Then I got the permit to set up here. Then the woman who approved it got laid off. I still had the permit. Got two more years to go. These men here? They need the work. They can make three hundid cash a week if they work hard. Here Michael is, best basketball player to ever live, or he was when he stopped. If he come back to the Bulls—just another dude with a bull's-eye on his chest. No leverage. You remember that commercial where he said, 'What if I was just another ballplayer?' He's 'bout to find out! Time don't wait, man. Might as well try and hold back water.

"I bet when he do come back, companies he does commercials for, they stock goes up two and three and four and five p'ints, first day. Money in a back pocket right there. If he do come back, ratin's on TV go through the roof. Money in a back pocket right there. Why not do a deal with the league? With the network? Own the majority of a *new* franchise? There's people who invested in me, so I know some are gonna wanna invest in Michael Jordan. So what he worth, twenty million dollars a year for three years—until he stops playin'? League can pay that outta petty cash from what he gonna generate. That's half a team right there . . .

"Now, judgin' off that look on your face, you might not like it, but there's bankers who'll sit down and listen to that. Might not sound like much unless you figure when Jordan came to the Bulls they was worth maybe twenty-five mil, playing in a decrepit gym, drawing flies, never won nothin'. Now they worth one-hundid-fifty mil—two hundid if *he's* there—in a new buildin', won three championships, in a state of sellout, on TV more'n a little bit. You mean to tell me Jordan cain't get a piece? I'm all for loyalty, but it cut both ways."

The shoeshine man paused for breath, and I am not one to let such opportunities go by. I said, "He's not a businessman."

The shoeshine man went unfazed by my assessment. "Long past whuther he's a bid'nessman. Hell, *hire* a bid'nessman," he said. " 'Cause we've got us a gang of angry men shootin' up this here Congress, talkin' 'bout ain't no more free ride, got to stand on our own two feet, no more entitlements. Well, who made the Chicago Bulls entitled to Michael Jordan? Plus they 'bout to kill the boy up there! Last two titles they won was on the cheap. Took three years off the boy's life for him to win that last one! He *ain't* gettin' no younger. His people talked about him comin' back with a new number, Number Forty-five instead of Twenty-three. Sell some more jerseys. Jobs for people in Taiwan. Money in some back pockets right'chere. One of 'em said if things went bad Jordan'd wanna go back to Number Twenty-three 'cause old ballplayers is real superstitious. I thought, 'He can't change one number. Thirty-one.' That's how old he is. And soon he'll be wearin' Thirty-two, and then so on. That's one number you can't change.

"So, seein' as how he ain't gettin' no younger, who'd he rather have pickin' the players he's going to play with now? A general manager tryin' to save somebody else some money? Or one who got to run who he get by Jordan first? It make Jordan's job easy if he get other great players 'round him and don't have to do all the work. Could play four more years easy as rockin' in a rowboat with the right kind of players. 'Cause he ain't gonna be able to stand to lose. Mark you that. Won't be able to stand it. Don't you think they's youngsters would love to play for Jordan's team? Don't you see opportunity up in there? Once they cut out affirmative action, where else a brother gonna get a job? If Michael comes back and plays for the Bulls for a weak salary, he's runnin' an entitlement, corp'it welfare for the NBA, shoe stows, Nike, NBC, companies he do them commercials for. Gonna be skinnin' 'n' grinnin' in them places, a level of Tommin' ain't got nothin' to do wit color. If I was him, I'd tell them Bulls and the NBA, 'If I can't get a chunk, then I gave you opportunity, gotta stand on your own two feet. On your own. Sink or swim.' "

He interrupted himself to put his hand out. I could not be irritated at him because he *was* owed. I told the shoeshine man if nothing else he had confused me. I gave him a five, put my shoes in a bag, and shod myself in boots and went out to board the train.

## Small, Irritating Talk on the Amtrak Metroliner

I took a seat in the third car, on the right side, facing forward. Soon the conductor came to request my ticket and punch it. He was a cheery young man who wore his conductor's garrison cap tilted back on his head and whistled while he worked. I was not feeling bad myself. The train was on time, all it took to make this an acceptable morning, although Amtrak was suffering layoffs, budget cuts and other symptoms of obsolescence. Critics called for its elimination, reasoning that most people drove or flew or walked or rode the bus or should stay home. The dead issue of the jobs in the railroads provided in the past was not greatly mourned.

I gestured out toward the snow and the conductor said, "Yeah, it's bad, and they say it's even worse up the line."

"Think you can get me to Penn Station by noon?" I asked. "Think so," he said, "but you're on your own after that."

A "black" man with a beard sat next to me, preoccupied with his work. He said he was a radio producer and TV newswriter, and presented a résumé as long as your arm to prove it. Then he asked me if I was hiring. I told him I was scrounging around myself. Then he seemed to start mumbling to himself. "Seems like some of them want to start some kind of race war," he mumbled. "I wish they'd get it over with, because the suspense is killing me."

"War will kill you quicker than suspense, for sure."

I rose away and he seemed to take no offense. As the train sped along I went into the food service car. Who was this "them" the man spoke of? Surely he did not mean a "white" man like that nice conductor or the one who stood behind the counter, outfitted in a vest often seen on "black" backs, having set up his routine and now bent over the figures of inventory, multiplying mightily with his pencil, pausing occasionally to doodle on his tongue, seeming not at all predisposed to any of these duties except for what appeared to be an unconscious taste for lead. It was a job—one now seeming to require an ill temper to do it justice.

"What?" he said, the weight of inventory heavy on his brow. Though put off, I ordered. As I waited for the order to take, I could not help but hear the conversation of a table of three: a "white" man, his pretty "black" wife and an old "black" woman.

"Your friends say, 'Toni, you aren't really 'black,' " she said. "Well, your friends say, 'Hey, Dan, you ain't 'white,' " he replied. The young woman sighed and said, "I wish they'd stop showing all this terrible stuff on TV—these daytime talk shows, crime on the news, these sitcoms. I guess that's what they're supposed to do—makes decent people believe that's all we are."

"Nobody thinks that," said her husband.

The old woman said, "It doesn't matter, dear. It just makes it easier. Even if all the 'black' people were doctors, or chefs, that would not change it. The Jews in Germany were educated, had jobs, money. That didn't change it. You are decent, child. But remember, it's not *your* decency that you have to worry about."

I hummed the tune the conductor whistled so I would not hear more as the counterman slammed down questionable comestibles. His attitude was unacceptable. In protest, after paying for a puddle of grease and lukewarm coffee, I dropped $1 on his plate. "Thank you, sir!" he said. I returned to my seat as the train rambled through one of many places in America that I consider home. The first stop was New Carrollton, Prince Georges County. On the way, the train passed through a small town that we shall call Certain.

## An Overview of the Curious Maryland Landscape

Maryland is not only the most curiously shaped state in the Union, it is quite possibly the most curiously shaped anything anywhere. On the map, it looks as though somebody took a razor to the top half of an amoeba and the bottom half has severe feelings about it. Maryland's southern and eastern borders are cilia-like tendrils of land surrounding hundreds of inlets of the Chesapeake Bay like the legs of a fat, twitchy caterpillar. Some of the legs are broken off into islands. The western border of the Free State follows the slow wind of the Potomac through the Appalachian and Allegheny mountains, downhill at the southeasterly zigzag all the way toward Washington, where it widens and slows some on the surface. But up the river there are many fast rapids. People drown in them every year because they don't grasp how quickly an underestimated river running fast can make a rock slippery, then break your arm, knock the wind out of you, then pull you under.

It is said if you had a big-enough hammer and the free time you could pound Maryland's borders into a flat line that could span Texas. Baltimore, largest city in the state, is one hundred miles inland and west by northwest of Ocean City on the Atlantic Coast. Yet Baltimore, and not Ocean City, has a good harbor. You can suffocate from heat and humidity down in the St. Mary's County lowlands and hours later risk hypothermia over in Frostburg or go ice-fishing on Deep Creek Lake in Garrett County, in the high green tips of Appalachia. Maryland's most southerly latitudes, on the Delmarva peninsula, lie south of Richmond, Virginia. Its northern border, the Mason-Dixon line, runs on the parallel with Atlantic City, New Jersey. No wonder there was a First Maryland Cavalry in both Union and Confederate armies in the Civil War.

And yet Maryland is one of the smallest of states in land mass, smaller than all but seven in the contiguous "lower 48." Though it is small it has more people in it than half the other states. They are interesting people with their own set of ways. The state motto in Latin is *Fatti Maschii, Parole Femine,* which, if Latin throws you, means "Manly deeds, Womanly words." It is a wonderful motto, if only because it should make you pause and think before you act or speak up again.

Speaking of speaking, if you pronounce "Maryland" as it is most commonly spelled, like "Dairyland," or "Merry-land," the natives will seek your immediate deportation. It's "myrrhlun" if you live there. Best not forget it, pilgrim. If we are to be frank in describing the human landscape, there are some proud and ignorant people inside Maryland who put the *k* in "cracker," and some of the same description who put the *ig* in "nigger." They only appear to be a majority. There are exceptions. Where these exceptions are located is another problem entirely.

Take, for example, the governor, a "Democrat" elected in November of 1994, the year of the angry "white" male, during a landslide "Republican" victory and resulting hoopla. Before he landed on his feet in Annapolis, he was from Prince Georges County, a former county chief executive, and he was named Parris Glendening. He'd had the intemperance to say he didn't mind admitting the complex identities among the proud and ignorant Marylanders, and didn't seem to be in the mood for hacking up their carcasses or their reputations or their schools or their futures, even the "black" ones; this was common sense, since the citizenry of Prince Georges County, including many of the "white" ones, are by some measure "black." It is a mixed-up place.

Glendening was elected governor though he carried only three of twenty-one counties. They happened to be the most populous counties: Baltimore; Montgomery, a rather ritzy-in-spots northwest suburb of Washington; and Prince Georges, northeastern, eastern and southeastern suburb of Washington. Prince Georges has less ritz—if by ritz you mean pricey sitdown restaurants, fancy hotels, and overpriced department stores. People take all that for ritz, but there are less expensive ways of showing royalty.

By train you cross water three times to get out of Maryland through Delaware and on to New York—or New Jersey, should you admit going there. One crossing is near Havre de Grace, where Douglass taught some of his fellows to read; where that graceful baseball immortal Cal Ripken, Jr., was born; where a forking Susquehanna empties into the upper reaches of the teeming bay. Should the train go the way of the buffalo, there are hummingly good roads in Maryland—no shock, since Maryland is efficient and insistent about its tax collections. Maryland is not known for basketball. Knowing Maryland for basketball is like knowing Brooklyn for crab cakes. But even on the fine points of hoop, Maryland and some of those living within its absurd borders can surprise you.

## Apt Lessons of Sport for Growing Boys and Men

Within Prince Georges County stands USAir Arena. Eighteen thousand people can be herded into it at one pop, and often are. This saddle-shaped edifice is where home games of the Georgetown Hoyas and Washington Bullets are played—up until a new arena is built, in Washington, D.C. Blueprints for this edifice are being drawn up and overcharged for even as we speak. Don't ask me how. Some bank must smell money in it. Also within Prince Georges is a bucolic neighborhood, incorporated as a town. It is well inside walking distance of the District itself, a green-and-gold epaulet on the eastern shoulder of the capital city. It is not far from USAir Arena.

It's the kind of place you hear about less often than you'd like to these days. Along the meandering and tree-lined streets are homes of differing shapes, sizes, types, colors, description—so different it is hard to find any two alike. Most have yards big enough and sloping enough and ter-raced enough to discourage mowing, although they usually do get mowed, to the accompaniment of some potent profan-ity. Within the houses and yards there are people—families. Certain boasts "white" and "black" families, or vice versa, however you tend to look at it, perhaps in the percentage of Maryland itself—say, 65 percent "white," 30 percent "black," "others" fitting in, or vice versa; all finding them-selves (to their occasional disbelief) getting by in some trying times. Certain has a police force, its own maintenance crews and parks, including the one with the flagpole, where Cer-tain Day is celebrated once a year with a colorful shower of fireworks. Certain has its own Town Center and Boys and Girls Clubs. And on one of those tree-lined streets is a gingerbread-colored house where my son and aspirations reside.

The best way to have people relate and get along is through the common efforts and travails of their children. Children will attempt baseball; it is usually the first game they try to play, especially the boys. It is unintimidating at first blush, quite accessible. The spot where most of the action takes place and where the scoring is done is called "home plate," two familiar enough places to children, and it is right underfoot. Children can step on home immediately, and that is the goal of the game, so they feel they have accomplished something just by showing up.

The baseball itself can be held and thrown and lost by any child. In basketball, for counter-instance, the goal is ten feet off the ground, well out of reach of even the child's parents—the child is not a fool, though even a fool would notice this right off; a regulation basketball is of a considerably larger circumference than a baseball and cannot be easily held in one hand or hoisted upwards of ten feet by a young child. This discourages the child some more. Baseball also includes bats. Give a boy a stick and he is going to want to hit something with it, so you'd best make it a ball.

Baseball tryout at Town Center in Certain, Maryland, was where my son and I first met Cameron and Darius, two of the five "black" boys who initially made the twelve-man Certain 10-and-under baseball team of the county Boys and Girls Clubs. My son had not played a sport competitively before this and he desired to wet his feet. I wanted him to try it on for size too because of the lessons lurking inside the games, and the good, clean fun of it, the exercise in fresh air, the honest sweat, the busying of idle hands, the beginning a process of learning how to get along with other boys even when that is completely impossible.

I thought Cole was good-sized until I saw Matt and Warren at age nine. Matt was bigger—big and thick. Warren was taller, and fluid, and he loped along at a fast gait. One made

Cole look small, the other made him look slow. "This is the way of things," I told myself, acutely aware of the shortage of endowments I had passed along. Cameron and Darius were more Cole's size, but even then, as nine-year-olds, Cameron and Darius already stood out if you're talking about ballplaying. Didn't matter what game. They could play it. In this the earliest case it turned out the game was baseball.

Cameron's parents pronounced his name "Cam-Ron," so that is what we did. Cam-Ron was a catcher, a good one from the get-go. He had an older brother and was serious about playing as familial necessity. He was squat; piano legs, barrel chest, hands as big as a man's, a smile he fired indiscriminately. Once Cam-Ron threw out four would-be base-stealers in two innings of a game, then threw in a pickoff of a runner on first base for good measure.

(In another game, years later, he got bored and threw a peg away, putting Certain down 7–5 to Bowie; it's not that I minded being down so much—it was being down to Bowie at Bowie that grated. After the half-inning, I told Cam-Ron, "Son, you're too good to make a play like that, even if you are bored. You owe me one." In the last inning, with a man on, Cam-Ron hit it nine miles, tied the game 7–7 with a two-run home run. The game ended tied. I congratulated him upon his return to the dugout. He made sure no one else could hear and said, "Will that do?")

After watching him play I told his father, "Cam-Ron's like Campanella." No parent likes to hear what his or her child is like when that child is playing ball—or at any other time I can think of offhand. Cam-Ron's father was no exception to this rule, but, to his credit, he spied the compliment in there anyway:

"But . . . but . . . aw, you're right. He *is* like Campanella."

Darius was a starting pitcher and the best we had. He was

shorter, had a good arm, good body control, and he could hit. But the other boys said Darius's *real* game was basketball. Matt was bigger than Darius or Cam-Ron, Warren was taller, rangy, faster, but if they wanted to play baseball they'd have to put in their good sweet time. They made the team. Cole did too. He had a good arm, a "live" arm, which surprised me, and he'd have to take it from there. He pitched, played third and outfield. Another good player was Mike, whose father coached. Mike was small, even for nine, almost tiny. He could pick it up at short like you wouldn't believe. Then there were Bobby, Paul, Josh, Johnny, Greg, a few others—far fewer after the first game of the year Certain played in the 10-and-under league (and in Cole's case, in life), against Bowie.

Bowie is home to the Class AA Bowie Baysox, part of the Baltimore Orioles' farm system. Bowie is in the western reaches of Prince Georges County, where there are more wide open spaces, more parks and more budget. They take their baseball seriously in Bowie: They came to Town Park and made that too abundantly clear. Cole was stationed in center field that first game and he got in some mighty good exercise chasing after all those balls the Bowie players struck into the far gaps off Darius or whoever else was throwing to them. His first time at the plate Cole looked lost, just as most boys do the first time, and he struck out. The ten-run mercy rule was instituted in the fourth inning. Later on, I watched him peel off his uniform, mired in gloom. I thought, It is the way of it. Now comes the lesson, if he sticks with it.

As I say, Mike was a good shortstop, Cam-Ron was Cam-Ron, we had some decent filler, the other "white" kids, especially the second baseman, Paul, who also would end up on the 10-and-under basketball team. Darius pitched. Cole pitched too. Pitched well. The boys caught on. They struggled the first year, in Triple-A. There are two classifications of teams in Prince Georges County, AA and AAA, reflective of the populations of the townships they represent. In any particular age group, Certain might have half a hundred boys to choose from, where a larger township like Bowie or Clinton would have upwards of a thousand boys to choose from. Numbers do matter some in baseball. Almost as much as people.

The Certain boys were put in the AA classification for the 11-and-under league the next year. Cole started and won the first game as a pitcher and, later in the year, began to hit. Coach F. said he didn't understand it, that Cole popped the ball hard in practice, but during the games it was all that man could do to restrain himself when Cole took strike three. I understood. It wasn't his son. This went on for a while. Then Cole came to me one day and said, "I'm going to hit a home run soon, Dad." Over the next three games, he hit two. That was against AA pitching. I don't think Certain lost a single game that year.

The next year they were put back up into the AAA for the 12-and-under league. Bowie and Clinton were still in business. Same boys, only older. Certain's boys had learned how to play. Certain won the county championship, beating out Bowie and Clinton. It was a tremendous feat, akin to David felling twin Goliaths. Though Cole had won his two or three games as starting pitcher, he didn't hit as well that year. And he was not so young he couldn't see he was passed over to pitch the middle game in the best-of-three finals. Cam-Ron was installed to pitch, which ruined the whole defense by the process of declension, and Certain lost the middle game, 10–1, with Cole scoring the only run. The loss would have been just the same even if Cole had pitched and lost. Cole was not so young that he didn't see the lack of confidence within this decision, and not so old that he might not question himself on whether such concern about his reliability might be legitimate. Darius won the final game with tight defense behind him, Cam-Ron behind the plate.

When the boys celebrated after the final, Cole did too, less triumphantly—in it, alongside it, party to it, but not *of* it. There is a difference. He'd interrupted baseball season by going to Big John Thompson's Georgetown camp for basketball, as he does each summer with his cousin Garrick, whom he reveres as an older brother, tortures and all. Cole awaited the start of the 13-and-under basketball league with a vengeful anticipation. My son had seen Michael Jordan play enough by then, and others, too, though only one Jordan. Slowly he had begun to gravitate to basketball, but with his live arm and good eye, I wondered if baseball might not be a better bet, as far as any ballplaying and lesson-giving went. But with basketball there was no negotiation: He must try.

A year can make a big difference to a boy at this age. By the time a boy becomes nearly thirteen, some parameters are set, and possibilities are becoming inevitabilities in his mind. The 13-and-under basketball team now had no "white" players. Paul, who played infield for the baseball team and had always been on the basketball team, decided to give up basketball, not because he wanted to but because he felt it was for the best. He said it was because the coach had "decided on his five" starters. The 13-and-under AAA league was tough. Paul, an outstanding kid, wasn't tall. I wonder if things are so simple. As ten- and eleven-year-olds, the boys, including Paul, played AA hoop and did well, led in scoring by Darius, the point guard. They were coached by Darius's father, Coach C. Coach C. is a cop in Certain, a military vet, doing some security jobs on the side to help ends meet in this particular tree-lined neighborhood—the kind of guy likely to give you a speeding ticket if you broke the 25 mph limit in

Certain but unlikely to passionately pump fifteen slugs into you if you found yourself handcuffed in the backseat of his patrol car only because you nearly fit into some amorphous profile.

So there was this core group of boys: Cam-Ron, Darius, Warren, Matt, Cole. Matt was a fun-loving kid, handsome, hazel-eyed, with skin the color of banana pulp; Warren was brooding, pensive, mahogany. Matt and Warren had played on the baseball team, but then they'd given it up, as Paul had given up basketball. Warren and Matt, like Cole, felt they *had* to play basketball.

Why, I can't say, other than to observe that baseball coaches seem to feel a "black" boy must be in the image of Willie Mays by age eleven or he has no future in the game (Cole was born on the same date as Willie Mays and there the similarity between them seems to end, the occasional mood swings and triple to right-center field notwithstanding); other than to point out that all the basketball games are on television; other than to cite a b-ball's loud promises of a college education for those so inclined; other than to bemoan that academic scholarship set-asides have gone the way of the buffalo; other than to deplore the promise of riches beyond belief that is made to all the rest. Such promise is an empty boat without stevedores of work filling it up. That part of promise is rarely stressed in any meaningful, unintimidating way. I can't say why so many young "black" boys entertain the *promise* of basketball; I can only say that all boys entertain this *notion* of playing basketball, until the day they see it contains as much hard work as other vocations and maybe much more than most. If these boys do not at least entertain a notion of "playing" as if their livelihoods would depend on it one day, other people around them, in particular the family members and those till-recently despised girls, want to know, "Why not?" And basketball, taken all around, is a good game to play in the first place without all the sociology.

Other than all that, I don't know why a boy would take up with such foolishness when all it is is *everything* when you are growing up around peers, girls and a warm television set.


The core group of the team—Matt; Warren; Cole; Cam-Ron; Darius, point guard and leading scorer. Darius and Cam-Ron had better hand-eye skills than the other boys, but both Warren and Matt had traits recommending them. Warren was a good athlete. You could see him running 400 meters on an Olympic track one day. He could run, jump and block shots. Matt was nearly as wide as he was tall, and he ate up space; he shot better than Warren, though he couldn't move or jump as well in getting his shot off. Cam-Ron could shoot, had the good catcher's hands and a head for the game—a "good idea," as coaches say—but wasn't tall. Darius had the handle, he could dribble and shoot, wasn't tall either, but was very quick. Darius could just flat-out play. He let the other fellows know it too, which is the fashion now—maybe always has been, in some cases; I think so. Darius busted their chops, I'm sure, except for Cam-Ron, who didn't care. I told Cole if he was going to play, he would need to be able to dribble the ball reasonably well—that was the way to be sure to be able to get his shot off. I told him such knowledgeable dexterity takes time to accumulate.

Though Cole was not short for twelve, he was not very unusually tall, but his feet were size eleven, thus bigger than mine. The rest of him hadn't caught up. I'm afraid my bestowal to him in the area of height is as meager as my bestowal of wealth. I had always threatened to leave him a fortune. I still threaten it, but in a less eloquent way. Cole didn't yet move as fast as Darius or Cam-Ron. His jump shot had not yet become picture-perfect—indeed, it had yet to rouse itself in any but the most modest of manifestations. He mostly used a set shot. But among the kids we had, he had height, and fair hands. He was destined for big forward. At the 13-and-under AAA level—any level, for that matter—playing "4," strong forward, is tough sledding.

There were four boys joining this nucleus on the thirteen-year-old AAA Certain basketball team for the 1995 season. McDerrin was a sullen, surly kid from a nearby, less promising neighborhood; technically, it was in Certain, but it was a good distance away, up off the main drag, Landover Road, Route 202, which leads right to the USAir Arena in Landover, where the Georgetown Hoyas play. Bad things have been known to happen up on that drag. McDerrin lived in an apartment complex over there, one where the property management seemed to be particularly uninspired. There were no such complexes in Certain proper, only different homes under all kinds of trees, with a 25 mph speed limit, and police cars and people like Coach C. in them to back up the law, within reason.

Then there was Steve, a slight, dark-skinned chatterbox who looked like someone Leni Riefenstahl would not take a picture of, if she'd ever gotten the chance to reject him. Steve followed McDerrin around for protection. McDerrin heckled the other boys and seemed to itch for some confrontation. He seemed desperate for a starting position; such was unlikely, but that didn't quell his desperation for it. Warren had always been the one most likely to disagree, but now here was McDerrin, who had the potential to be the worst kind of bully. He was the type to pick out the designated bully before him, or the most ominous guy in the crowd, and take him on, settling all hash at once. McDerrin decided he should be on the starting team instead of Warren; he was wrong, but that did not stop McDerrin's deciding. He and Warren came close a few times and may have exchanged the manly pleasantries when nobody was looking—nobody except maybe Steve, who threw in his lot with McDerrin; wisely, since they both sat on the bench and went to middle school in Greenbelt together.

Tyrone was a skinny beige boy with pipestem legs and knobby knees and greenish eyes and a full hairline some student at the barber college cut back into a rectangular box. The hair would begin to grow back in, giving Tyrone the effect of a five o'clock shadow, only above his temples. He was wiry, had a handle, but not much physical strength. Darius didn't get along with him from the start because it had always been Darius's team and he figured it would need to be more so now that the boys were going to Triple-A for the 13-and-under league. Instead of being happy to get some help, Darius at first seemed to resent Tyrone's ability to play, while Tyrone may have suspected Coach C. of nepotism for not recognizing his singular talent and presenting him the reins of the team and a new Lexus automobile.

The fourth newcomer was Johnny, son of a Jehovah's Witness family. Johnny was as skinny as Steve, and there are shoots of bamboo not as skinny as Steve. Johnny didn't have deep wells of stamina, but he was taller—that helps—and determined, and he had a quick first step.

So this was the final roster. They were all good kids, deep down somewhere, and no two were alike. Yet I knew if you waited six years and lined them up and ruffled them so everyone's hair was unkempt, then took black-and-white photos of them from front and side with numbers hung from their necks, somehow they would all look alike. I know they are *not* alike, if only in looks and temperament and potential. This was the roster:

1995 Certain, Md., Wolverines
Prince Georges County
13-and-Under Boys Basketball AAA League

| | |
|---|---|
| Darius C. | g |
| Cam-Ron J. | g/f |
| Tyrone B. | g |
| Matt M. | c |
| Colen W. | f/c |
| Warren R. | f/c |
| Johnny R. | f |
| McDerrin J. | f |
| Steve W. | g/f |

Right from the very start, things fell apart. The boys had done fairly well in AA ball, but this was Triple-A, the highest level for their age group. Some boys grow up quicker than others. When you are a boy, logic has nothing to do with anything. You don't realize that if your community has five hundred boys, and the other community has ten thousand boys, they are likely to find better ballplayers. You don't realize some boys develop much earlier, some boys are as big at thirteen as they are going to get; that as the formative years go on, things even out.

I told Cole, "It's who can play at eighteen that matters, mostly, and even then it doesn't matter a lot." This is no consolation when you are twelve going on fourteen, playing power forward, matching up with somebody who is four inches taller, feels thirty pounds heavier when he lays into you, looks five years older, on a team beginning the season 0-and-9. I attended as many games as I could. Coach C. did a good job, the record to the contrary; I saw the boys getting better, just as they had in baseball; *they* could not see it; getting better is a long, featureless haul when you are the one doing it. But I knew Cole, Cam-Ron and Darius had learned the lesson from baseball: The determined could and would turn. It was hard, though. Darius distanced himself from a collection of mediocrity with which he was saddled. There was not one win for them to use as a hat-rack. They began to miss practices, reasoning, I suppose, that not much practice was required to lose.

The starting team listed Matt at center, or "5" position, Cole at power forward, or "4," Warren at small forward, or "3," Cam-Ron at off-guard, or "2," and, of course, Darius at point guard, or "1." That was the group Coach C. decided should start and, more importantly, finish games, until he had to get Tyrone in at off-guard. This put Cam-Ron out of the starting lineup, which he didn't enjoy but understood better than he let on. Cam-Ron was still in the end-game lineup. As John Thompson says, it's who finishes the games, not who starts them. McDerrin brooded on the bench, lashing out at Warren and the others, even at Coach C., who did his best to tolerate the boy's petulant outbursts.

Steve often echoed McDerrin's sentiments where they were safe and appropriate: "Yeah, go'n, McDerrin!" These are recurring roles in the long history of boys, and you know two such yourself.

Warren, becoming thirteen, losing boyhood, had begun to do not as well as before at school. I don't know the reason for the slippage; the most well-meaning teachers in this era of bell curve balls might say, "Well, it's not *my* kid." The boys said Warren's parents—he had both to choose from—were making him eschew practice in favor of a more obvious scholarship of homework.

Matt, bigger at the AA level, and still wide as thirteen-year-old boys go, found himself surrounded by taller, meaner opposition. The chore for rebounding at this level fell squarely to Cole.

As the losses mounted, we began to lose players. Warren

had to hit his books. Johnny, who could score but didn't have a lot of stamina, began to miss the practices and games because of his family's religious beliefs and scheduling conflicts. McDerrin was threatening to pull the team apart, and Steve would do whatever McDerrin was doing. Cam-Ron, not to mention Cam-Ron's father, seemed quietly dissatisfied that he wasn't starting.

Finally, it came down to the final three games of the year, two of them at home at Certain Town Center. It was beginning to dawn on the boys that they couldn't hope to out-physical the other Triple-A teams. But they could win if they passed the ball well and shot it smartly and played team defense and blocked out on the boards and did what Coach C. said, and got it to Darius for the clutch shot. The final three games were against teams that had beaten them in the regular season, but I felt while watching those games that these were teams the boys could beat as they played better.

There were some teams on the schedule, like Largo-Kettering, and especially mighty Greenbelt, that I felt the boys could not beat, not yet. Greenbelt in particular was rough duty. The boys played on the road there and were blown out by twenty-five. In the handshake line after the game, Steve was the last player. Last for Greenbelt was their star, designated tormentor, George, a thirteen-year-old who looked seventeen, his muscles defined, his voice an adolescent yodel. He was a good player, but in the main he'd just developed early. I don't know if Steve said something to George, but I don't think McDerrin had, so it wasn't likely Steve had, since he was a follower, but then again it's possible because Steve could be sneaky that way. In that sneaky way, he was a normal and very human boy. George had a bad word for Steve.

I said, "Hey! None of that. You'all aren't enemies."

At first George was startled that he had been heard, and

made himself scarce by reflex. Later I saw him looking at me from a distance, whispering to his buddies. I thought nothing of it because I'm not thirteen. But I looked at George in a manner that said:

"I've been there, and I don't want to go back."

At least three of the boys on our team went to school with George and his cronies at Greenbelt Middle: Cam-Ron, McDerrin and Steve. How the latter two must have felt after the losses, when at school, I can only speculate. I knew Cam-Ron couldn't have cared less. Cam-Ron was good and he knew it. A bully would know better than to go there without a lunch. McDerrin and Steve were the ones derided; "joned on," as the boys said. Greenbelt's boys saved their laughter expressly for McDerrin when he got in for a few minutes during the game. I'd gone over after the last of nine losses, at home to Greenbelt, and said to our squad, "Don't quit. No matter what, as long as you don't quit, I'm with you."

Actually I said, "I'm wit y'all," a presumptuous statement to make, even to twelve- and thirteen-year-old boys, but they all seemed to understand me. All of them, that is, but McDerrin, who had not gotten enough playing time to suit. He wheeled away in disgust.

The Certain boys won the tenth game, the nucleus playing well. They were very cool, but I could feel that weight lifting from them. I went over and congratulated Coach C. To McDerrin I said, "See?" McDerrin was cross. So I said, "Cheer up. You won."

"I didn't win! They won!" he said, pointing to the other boys on his team wearing the same colors as his.

"Well, if you feel that way," I said, and spun around to congratulate Cam-Ron and Cole, who had settled into the job of being a good passer and rebounding and scoring if and when the opportunity presented itself. As we left the Center, McDerrin was outside, stomping on his game jersey.

I smiled to myself and kept walking with Cole and his mother to the car. It is *so* much nicer to be forty than thirteen. I knew what McDerrin needed, and I wasn't giving it to him yet. I went to my car, and there stood McDerrin, Steve on his shoulder like a parrot on the shoulder of a pirate or some scavenger fish safely riding the flank of a shark.

"What are you boys going to do?" I asked.

"Beat you up," said a laughing Steve. He said this not because he meant it, but because he was short anything better.

I said, "You better grow some first."

Later, I was not surprised when I heard that Coach C. had suspended McDerrin for conduct unbecoming a Certain Wolverine.

The boys won the last two games, though I missed the away game, when Coach C. said he'd had to get in Cole's face and tell him he was standing around, and if he didn't play hard—Warren was still on punishment—the team wouldn't rebound, and if we couldn't rebound, we couldn't get the ball to Darius, Tyrone and Cam-Ron, and we couldn't win. So Cole had three straight ten-or-more rebound games and they won all three. In the final game, he'd also put in fifteen points. The Certain Wolverines' season would have ended at 3-and-9 were it not for the Greenbelt Tournament.

It was said Greenbelt only invited teams that it figured it could beat. I don't blame the citizenry of Greenbelt one iota—if parents go to the trouble and expense of buying trophies, they want them to be handed out to their own children. The Certain Wolverines were "invited" to enter this tournament as the bottom seed, No. 8. It was an invitation that the boys and Coach C. most cheerfully accepted. I didn't have to find a gentle way to tell them that Greenbelt invited them because Greenbelt figured it could beat them. I didn't have to find a way to tell them and neither did Coach C. In fact, they told us. That's the best way.

I went to the quarterfinal game of the tournament held at Greenbelt's Spring Hill Lake Recreation Center. It was a sparsely attended game. The boys all did their jobs, and Darius and Tyrone took care of the scoring well enough, and they beat the team from Landover Hills, advancing to the semifinals—against Greenbelt.

The Greenbelt team had sat behind the Certain bench during the quarterfinal game, mocking both teams, but saving their best slings for Certain. However, there was an unmistakable current running beneath their harsh banter; they seemed to be pulling for Landover Hills. After what I felt was a particularly offensive call against our group, I wondered aloud about the amount of money the referees were expecting from the civic coffers of Landover Hills. One of the refs wanted to know if I was in the mood to double it. Landover Hills shortly mounted a comeback. Coach C. seemed to discourage any more efforts to engage the refs in rudimentary philosophy. When another play was disputed and the rule explained, I turned to George, bully captain of Greenbelt:

"George, is that right?"

George, surprised that I would include him in a rational conversation while he was plotting the collective extinction of the community and very memory of Certain, nodded in disbelief. The other boys from Greenbelt had rolled up sheaves of paper and were pounding them on the metal grandstand seats, attempting—begging, actually—to gain the attention of someone in authority to tell them to knock it off, or keep it up, depending on that authority's good sense. I sat with Cole's mother, quite calmly. A weary man going grey who was from Greenbelt came out and said the boys should stop that, but he did it rather reluctantly, so they desisted in the same manner. But they let our boys know they planned no mercy in the semifinals that following Saturday.

I did not attend the semifinal, but beforehand I spoke to Cole about being a Stoic, doing his level best. I felt a lesson coming on. Later on, I heard about it. Certain dressed only six players—the nucleus of Matt, Cole, Cam-Ron, Warren, Darius, plus Tyrone. Six was plenty. These six, under Coach C., went into that hostile gymnasium, with a strange, capacity crowd screaming for their heads, against a team that had wiped them out twice in the regular season, a team headed by a bully who intimidated even our bully, McDerrin, before McDerrin was dropped. Certain went in outsized, against thirteen players. With everything going against them, with small chance of winning, much less of gaining beyond winning, they won. They held fast, played the way they'd learned to play, and won. In fact, they won going away, 41–29. They may have won because Greenbelt may not have been ready, what with George and his crew thinking they could come in and scowl and cock their fists and make noises and the boys from Certain would shrink if not faint dead away. However you choose to add it up, the Certain boys won going away. And from an 0-and-9 start, they would play in the championship game of the Greenbelt tournament.

Words cannot describe my pride—but there is a check to Springfield Trophy, drawn on the bank that owns me, that can verify it. I went to the Monday practice before the championship game, to be contested the following Sunday. The boys were all back by now, of course, all nine, including McDerrin. There is nothing like winning to guarantee the lure of players to practice. But only six of them had gone into Greenbelt and won a game that two months ago would have been impossible to consider winning, and that bit of it would always belong to those six, and Coach C.

I asked Coach C. if I could speak to the team before practice, and he allowed it, calling the boys over for me.

"Fellas, you found out something important. If you don't

quit, and you keep working hard, good things will happen. You can't know more than that, but it's all you need to know. And I want you to know this: I'm proud of you. Really proud of you. Not because you won—but because you didn't quit. You kept trying to get better. Even though you didn't notice it, you did. You learned a lesson. You went into a hostile environment, crowd was up against you, outnumbered two-to-one. You learned if you prepare you can will your way through. You learned that you can win, and that you will win, sometimes. You played like men. I'm proud of you."

It was standard issue as motivational speeches go. But some of them wore rip-roaring smiles, especially Warren, because his smile had become such a rarity, and Matt, because his was so big. Cam-Ron, Tyrone, Darius—they smiled coolly. Cole hung back.

"Now, who do you play in the finals?"

The boys explained that one of the teams was found to have a fourteen-year-old posing as twelve—not a rare occurrence in this league, if you ask me. The two losing teams from the semifinal would have to play again, to see who would play Certain in the final game.

"The other semifinalists?" I asked.

They explained that yes, Greenbelt was included.

". . . You'll be playing Greenbelt in the finals," I said.

How did I know, they asked.

"You'll be playing Greenbelt. Trust me."

It was then I went to have the trophies made up, figuring somebody from Greenbelt was doing the same. I went to get trophies I figured would be at least the equal of those Greenbelt would have. I went to a shop near Alexandria and ordered nine of the best trophies they could muster, with a gold-colored figurine atop it. Usually the pose of the figurine helps define the trophy, and this was a beatific, wavy-headed, tall guy going up for a one-hander off one foot. This figurine was put on a three-inch column. There was a choice between two columns—one had a red-white-and-blue striped piping, and one was midnight blue laced with silver stars and silver Spaulding basketballs. I chose the silver and blue columns, and a wide granite base, with a brass plate, on which was to be inscribed:

1995 CERTAIN WOLVERINES
TOURNAMENT FINALISTS

While whatever trophies Greenbelt was ordering would undoubtedly have "champions" in the inscription, mine had only "finalists." I did have the luxury of having each boy's name embossed on these trophies, as they'd already earned them, and if they also won those Greenbelt was making up, all the better. But they would not go without. My little operation is not much to speak of; I do have an account for "advertising/public relations and community service," and it could stand the hit that week. So if my little shop never accomplishes another goal, one was met. I also had a plaque made up for Coach C., and on it was inscribed *Coach C., 1995 Coach of the Year.* The players' names were to be etched on the trophies, save the last one. On that one, the words were printed larger, and there was no room for the player's name.

Upon returning home after placing this order, as if fate could hardly wait, I received a phone call from Coach C. He said he would not be able to be at the tournament final at Greenbelt next Sunday. His eldest daughter was graduating from military school out in Kansas City. I heard all this rather vaguely until he said he wondered, since I had been involved, and knew the kids, and tried not to miss too many games, would I mind coaching the team, in the finals? Rather absently I said, "Sure. Why not?"

As Coach C. spoke further to me, assuring me that the kids knew their assignments and plays and basic defenses, and how it wouldn't be much of a problem, it began to dawn on me, what I'd taken on—though not as fully as it would on the next Sunday.

We had one more practice, on the Friday before the game. Six boys showed up: Cole, Matt, Darius, Cam-Ron, Johnny and McDerrin. Cam-Ron said, "You're going to coach?" I said, "For the most part, you're going to coach yourselves." I wanted to know where Steve and particularly Warren and especially Tyrone were. I had taken to Tyrone because he seemed to listen to me. I often spoke to him from the stands during the games and encouraged him to keep playing through any mistakes and not bemoan them so at the time he committed them, to use his speed, to wait until afterward to dwell on mistakes. I also talked to him after games and could tell he was listening. Steve and McDerrin said Tyrone was probably at home, and that sounded reasonable, so we got on with practice.

I told Cole to shoot free throws, but he didn't move fast enough to suit my new position as the "black" John Wooden, the Wizard of Certain. "This weekend, I'm Coach, not Dad," I said. "I know," he said. I knew what caused a lack of enthusiasm. Earlier, in my role as the cheering lunatic in the stands, I had yelled, "That's you, Coley!" Or "C'mon, Coley!" The giveaway is "Coley" if we are talking names parents give babies who then proceed to grow into boys who will be teased mercilessly by other boys who didn't have parents to give them cute names when they were babies or who aren't there to call them by those names anymore. I can remember hearing McDerrin, parroted by Steve, teasing Cole later, calling him "Coley, Coley"; I recalled Cole's crimsoning face, and my feeling bad, because no one should have a father that is so stupid. Now he wouldn't leap to at my command even if I was calling myself Coach this week. I had to, and did, understand.

We worked on a couple of other things. We practiced the 2-1-2 zone defense with McDerrin and me and a young man in his twenties named Bill (who Coach C. had said would be available and of some help but not much) passing the ball around the zone and trying to penetrate it. I was surprised when I tried to get the ball by the boys and couldn't—surprised at what they could get their hands on. Thirteen-year-olds had changed some since I'd been one, particularly when down amongst them. We practiced extending the zone, and fronting the post, and helping out on the lob pass. I had Cam-Ron practice catching and shooting from beyond the three-point arc. Then I had them work on the only new play we'd have. I decided I owed it to the profession and the legacy of John Wooden of U.C.L.A. to put in at least one play. We would call it "Fist," with the signal for it being an up-raised one. I decided to keep things simple for an obvious reason: I could not be counted on to remember any more than that. "Fist" was simply the high screen-and-roll. Darius would bring it up. At first we had Cole setting the pick, Cam-Ron popping out on the wing. Darius was to drive off the pick and slice through the middle and score. If Cam-Ron's man came over from the wing to help, Darius would kick it to Cam-Ron for an open three-pointer. As the pick man, Cole would roll to the hoop if his man jumped out on Darius, and crash the boards if Darius shot. But Cole could not get the pick set to my liking. So we worked on Fist for a while with Cam-Ron setting the pick.

Cole and I gave McDerrin a ride home. That's how I found out he lives over by the drag where bad things have been known to happen. "You live with your mom and dad?" I asked as we let him out. "My uncle and godmother," he said. And they were probably good, decent people, trying to do the right thing, this uncle and godmother—trying to do whatever it was that needed doing for McDerrin, who for one reason or another was not with his parents. The uncle and godmother were to be commended for doing the best they could. They couldn't help some of it. He wasn't their child.

I didn't think much about the game until Sunday, unless you are counting the time I was awake. I had considered myself prime coaching material while watching games from the stands, or the press box, or in front of the television, ever since playing the game when younger. I once told John Thompson what most impressed me was the way he taught, how the young men seemed to get what he was trying to teach, how they were educated by an experience of schooling, playing *and* living, and not by the fact that he had won 70 percent of the games he coached. I told him I figured I could do the latter. Due to this absurdity, Mr. Thompson thinks I'm a good American lunatic and wisely maintains his distance. Once when I was watching a Georgetown game I became all apoplectic because it seemed as though the team was not playing well and that Thompson didn't mind. The Hoyas tightened their vise in the second half, came back and won. I felt foolish for being all apoplectic for no reason. How had he stayed very calm in the face of self-inflicted adversity? How had he known the tide would turn so inexorably? "Years of experience," he rumbled. I figured it must be so, and had also half-figured why Thompson insisted he'd learned better lessons from *losses* than wins—and taught better behind them.

On Sunday afternoon at 2:00 I picked up Cole and headed to Town Center. I'd told everybody at practice that if anyone needed a ride to Greenbelt, I'd be at Town Center between 2:00 and 2:10. The game was set for three. Darius (and Coach C.) assured me that he'd have a ride, Cam-Ron said his parents would be bringing him. Matt was never late. His mother saw to it. I'd asked about Tyrone, Warren and Steve. Everyone agreed they'd get there. When Cole and I gave McDerrin a ride home after practice, we asked him to be sure to tell Tyrone that if he couldn't get a ride, to be at Town Center at 2:00. If I was going to coach I wanted Tyrone to play because he would give us a better chance to win. And, as you know, I liked him. I figured that I'd somehow tell Tyrone and Darius they needed to stop the catfight already and that they needed to play together, and if they did that, nothing could stop their success. So on Sunday when Cole and I arrived at Town Center, I was not all that surprised when we saw two boys there. I was a little surprised about which two. McDerrin and Steve. No Tyrone. I asked about Tyrone, and they said they thought he'd be there. I told them to get in the car, and we went off to play Greenbelt.

Coaches hate to lose ball games. But you can lose a game and still feel good. I'm not talking about losing, period. I'm talking about losing where the other guy looks to find you to shake your hand, then grins like there's some joke between you as he does; grinning, but not broadly. I'm talking about losing in a way that the winner is not looking for you the next day. If you must lose (and you must, sooner or later), that's the way to go.

I was thinking of this while leaning against the concrete wall of the Spring Hill Lake Recreation Center as Greenbelt filed in, green-clad, thirteen strong. I had four players: one who was coming off suspension; one who had suspended himself in sympathy; my son, who has the uncanny sense for playing best in games I do not attend, much less coach; Matt, whose mother makes sure he never misses anything. I had no time to linger long on the slim roster because a woman began telling us to move out of the way; not to leave our coats in so unseemly a pile; not to warm up too near the exterior glass doors because they might break and she didn't know about me but she didn't have three hundred dollars for a new one. She was "white," seemed to be Jewish, had something Jewish about her, as Jewishness has been advertised to us—pushy and all, you know. When we'd entered, she was telling off a "black" man from another team. If anything, his outrage at her instructions pleased her. While we waited outside, the man came out fulminating: "If that woman says another word to me, I don't know what I'll do!" This reaction seemed to warm her heart. There were two ways I could read this: "Watch me make these grownup little boys come to heel, because they want it—they want to be told what to do." Or, "This is my turf and I will challenge you on proper use of it. I live here and you're just visiting."

Soon she brought her craft to me for close inspection.

"I said, don't let them play with the ball near these doors. I said, I don't know about you but I don't have three hundred dollars."

"Understood," I said, and bade the boys cease.

"Don't stand *there* with your team. It's too close to the court. There's a game going on. Your game is not the only one."

"Understood," I said, and encouraged the boys to get back.

I gave her nothing to feed off, so she left us alone. I was not about to challenge or resent her authority. I had enough to do on my own. Greenbelt was warming up. I noticed their coach had on a suit and two-toned shoes. I have a pair of two-toned shoes. I save them for notable occasions, occasions so very special they rarely arrive. This might be a special occasion to the Greenbelt coach—well it might, since the team from Certain had experienced such reversal of fortune in the semifinals against his team and won a twelve-point victory. Greenbelt would be stoked. They had even brought out the two-toned shoes.

It was then I recalled Coach C. saying a play might work once in the 13-and-under AAA league, but the guys coaching in this league were sharp and you couldn't do a thing twice to them without putting something in between to throw them off. Not only did I not have a strategy, I was minus the full complement of five players. We might forfeit. Some coaching that would be.

Warren came with his father and his grandfather; then Johnny came with his sisters. That made six. But we were without the starting backcourt of Darius and Tyrone; without Darius, the go-to guy. I had the boys shoot free throws to warm up, then the buzzer sounded and the game started. "Good luck, Coach," I said to the man in the dark suit and the two-toned shoes. He assumed a bucked-off look, as though it didn't happen very often, people wishing him luck. Or perhaps he was thinking, "Why is he wishing me luck when he's the one who needs it?"

Then Cam-Ron showed up, leading his parents, in uniform, wearing radio earphones. Rarely have I greeted someone with such animation in my life on earth.

Cam-Ron's father knit his brow and said, "Where's Darius?"

I told him I didn't know.

"Do you want me to find him?"

"His father told me that he was going to be here, that he had a ride," I said. "So it's his responsibility."

"Do you want me to help out?" said Cam-Ron's father.

"Well, you can sit here with me, if you want," I said, and he made a little "humpf" sound in his throat, but I hadn't answered him in any sort of backhanded way—all I'd planned on doing myself was sitting there; indeed, it was all I *could* do, with my mind in such a distracted swirl no distinct thought would rise above it.

Cam-Ron sucked his teeth when he saw Darius was missing. I gathered the boys into a huddle. "Look now, men," I said. "You don't need Darius or Tyrone to play. What you should do is have fun." Actually, Cole's mother had gone by the playground before the game and found Darius shooting on a goal. She'd offered him a ride, but he said he had a ride—Bill—and would be along. The day before he'd told Cam-Ron he might not play because he "might get a headache." It was his way of getting under Cam-Ron's skin. Why? Boys do it for no reason, other than they are boys.

No one had heard from Tyrone.

"Cam-Ron, you've gotta run point," I said.

"Aw, non*onaw*," Cam-Ron said. "Let Johnny run point."

This was not childish recalcitrance. Cam-Ron was being punishingly logical. He needed to be on the wing, available to shoot. Without Darius or Tyrone, where were the points going to come from? Running point guard might wear him down. I remembered Coach C. saying the boys knew the game by now, and that if you suggested a strategy they felt was improper, they would suggest right back to you, "That's stupid," and then there you'd be.

". . . You're right. Johnny, can you run point?"

Johnny nodded. It was unfair to put Johnny in a position he'd never practiced. But life was unfair. So be it. I pointed into McDerrin's face and said, "You watch the forwards," and then to Steve and said, "You watch the guards." Then we sat down and watched Certain, minus starting backcourt, go out for the tip.

The game began with the familiar theme: disaster. George and his fellows had vengeance on their brains and ran their plays and scored again and again. Johnny tried to bounce pass the ball inside from the top of the key twice, and twice he had the ball intercepted. Cam-Ron's father, mindful of decorum, yelled out, not at Johnny, who was not his son, but at Cam-Ron, who was. He yelled, "Cam-Ron, you can't make that pass from the top like that!" Cam-Ron yelled back, "Well, I didn't do it!" Which goes to show, you can't yell anything at a thirteen-year-old. Greenbelt raced to a 15–4 lead. Such a lead is like the death knell, for these games fly by. They play four six-minute quarters with a running clock unless there is a shooting foul or a time-out. But it seemed they had already played for hours as Greenbelt converted steal after steal into layups. Cam-Ron switched to point. He knew it, so when I said, "Cam-Ron, we need you up top!" he knew what that cryptic phrase meant. Another Greenbelt layup made it 17–4.

Then Cole stepped out on the wing and attempted three consecutive three-point jump shots. The first, launched from the left wing in front of the Greenbelt bench, nineteen feet from the hoop, was accompanied by derisive cries from the sitting Greenbelters:

"No shot! Off! Nothing! Rebound! Short!" Quietly, for the lack of anything better to do, I stood up and whispered, "Yes."

The ball split the net with a pure rip—a rip no less resounding than those conjured by Glen Rice, or Jordan himself. Cole's next shot, on the next possession, also catapulted from directly in front of the Greenbelt bench, was accompanied by silence all around. It too found nothing but net. On his third shot, renewed yells came from the Greenbelt bench. The content had changed some: "Get him! Get him! Get him! Get him!" Too late. Cole's shot left his hand, cleared George's desperate leap and, if anything, was even more perfect than the two preceding it.

*Swish.*

*Swish.*

*Swish.*

Then, with the defense drawn to him, Cole hit a cutting McDerrin with a bounce pass and the latter sank the shot and made a fist. Greenbelt called time. At this point the score was 17–15 in favor of Greenbelt, and I was not thinking nice things about the I.Q. test and bell curves. I was thinking about what you can do with them. If the bitter truth be told, putting the women and children away, what I was *really* thinking was: "M———k an I.Q. test and the horse it rode in on with a red-hot poker. That has *nothing* to do with *him*, that has to do with *your* own self-approval." I was thinking in such a disreputable way because it disturbed me that anyone hoped to off-hand the totality of a twelve-year-old son who had reasoned, and while on the fly, thusly:

"My team is in deep trouble here; not only that, my old man is in deep trouble down there. We need points. Darius and Tyrone are not here, Cam-Ron is busy running point. Somebody's got to do something. Somebody's got to stand up. I'm going to step out here and try my hand. If I make them, fine; if I miss, my miss is no different than anybody else's. But I'm going to try." If you want to measure something, measure this: Greenbelt assigned its best defender, George, to Cole for the rest of the game. That opened up the court for the others. Cole did not take another shot—or, if he did, it was not a bad shot, else I would remember it.

Later on I was proud Cole had taken those shots: I was glad for my reputation's sake that he made them—but I was proud for him that he tried. These are lessons schools do not teach.

Greenbelt recovered from the hail of threes to take a 21–16 halftime lead. It was at this point Mr. Darius showed up, with an apologetic and immaculately dressed Bill in tow. I had written Darius's name onto the official game roster and pointed him to the court rather impatiently. Some coaches might have benched him for the entire game. I'm not a coach, let alone one of those. Two lessons had already been learned. The boys had learned they could play without Darius, and Darius had learned no matter how good he could play, he still had the responsibility for showing up, because nothing was bigger than the team; the game would be played whether he was there or not. He just makes it a lot more interesting.

The second half was hotly contested and well-played, and I say it confidently after having watched many games at all levels. Certain matched Greenbelt basket for basket, play for play, and likewise; you could see the Greenbelt boys realize they were in a long battle. Late in the first half, Warren, taking a breather from rejecting many Greenbelt shots, had mentioned something:

"We should run some more plays."

Casually I mentioned back, "Second half. We'll hit 'em with something fresh in the second half."

Warren nodded. That made sense to him. I was grateful for his evaluation. I seemed calm but only because I didn't know what I was doing and was manfully trying not to show it off; but also, nothing unusual or untoward was happening that would allow me to exhibit proper coaching behavior. I was watching everything and seeing nothing. I longed to jump up and scream instructions at them and make them feel belittled, but there was no call for it. The offside defensive rebound was being accounted for, protected, and kicked to Darius in such a manner as did not call for loud protest on my part. I was vaguely aware that often this rebound being gathered to my stunned content was gleaned by my son. I was distantly aware that he was my son. If you had blown a whistle, stopped the game and asked me, "Is that your son?" I would have said, "Of course it is." If you had thrown a punch at him, my presence, if not my vengeance, would have been swift and immediate. But as far as being the guy responsible for the offside defensive rebound, my son had entered into the realm of Competition, and that is a landscape where blood doesn't count; the only blood that counts there is the red kind. All I could see was that my power forward was yanking and cranking, baby. I could be proud of him later. At the time he was just doing the job as called for.

At the beginning of the fourth quarter, Certain was down by seven points. Halfway into the last period, it was down to four. Darius brought up the ball, glanced over and held up a fist.

"Fist! Fist!" I yelled.

The Greenbelt coach stood up and made a megaphone of his hands. "Watch the three-point shooter!" Sharp guy, as Coach C. had said. I told Cam-Ron to set the high screen. Darius rubbed by, the wing defender dared not leave Cole, and Darius had a lane to the goal. *Swish.* Certain was down two. A time-out by Greenbelt. I said to the boys that I was glad they seemed to be having fun. As the huddle broke up, Cole said, in a loud and much deepened voice I did not recognize, "Two-one-two!" In coachly fashion, I repeated, "Two-one-two! Extend it!" Their hands were quick, and they made a steal. Cam-Ron had it, gave it to Darius, who walked it up. As Darius passed half-court I said, "Fist! Fist!" Warren gently said, "Uh, Coach. They switched to zone." "Oh." (I said.) I looked at the man in the dark suit and two-toned shoes who was coaching Greenbelt.

Our side managed to adjust without me. Darius, Matt and Cam-Ron punched passes in a triangle, on one side of the zone. They had known how to attack it on their own, which was a good thing, because my expertise in these matters had been completely exhausted and I was now a formerly loud, anonymous spectator, one silenced and becalmed by my new, more official position. With Matt in the post, Darius out high right and Cam-Ron in the corner right, they passed the ball rapidly in a triangle; three passes, six passes, nine passes, edging Cam-Ron closer into the baseline shot. I suggested, "That's the way to play!" Finally, Cam-Ron was shaped up for a shot; it rimmed out, but that result wasn't the point. They'd defeated the defense for the shot we wanted. That was the point. Greenbelt rebounded and brought it up with less than a minute to play. The Greenbelt crowd was on its feet. Greenbelt went into its zone offense. Cole fronted the post in the face of George; they tried to lob it in over him, and Johnny came from the backside and tipped it away from George over to Darius, who flipped it out to the streaking Cam-Ron, who was wisely fouled.

Cam-Ron stepped to the line with sixteen seconds left, with Certain down 32–30. "Take us to overtime, Cam-Ron!" said a loud voice from our bench. I looked over and saw it was McDerrin, who had said he didn't care. Cam-Ron nodded and hit two free throws like there was nothing at all to it, and the score was tied.

"Stay up! Stay up on them on D!" I beseeched.

Certain's extended 2-1-2 that fronts the post and helps from the backside is a puzzle Greenbelt has a year to figure out. Another steal, Darius streaking to the goal, and fouled. Darius at the line now in a 32–32 game with nine seconds left. Greenbelt called time-out. I told the boys I was proud of them, and to play until there was no time left. Play all the way to the end. Darius toed the line—and missed the front end of the one-and-one. But that happens. We fouled the rebounder, George, and the Spring Hill Lake Recreation Center's roof was lifted by the Greenbelt fans' joy and relief. We let them line up, then called time-out. Six seconds left. I told the boys no matter if George missed or made the free throws, to get it to Darius, and for Darius to take it all the way. I knew the sharp guy in the two-toned shoes would figure that out. I wanted to have Cam-Ron run to the three-point arc and have Darius get him the ball—but it might go better this way. George made both. Cole got it to Darius. Darius streaked to the goal with George running alongside. George reached in. Maybe it was a foul and maybe not—definitely not because there was no call. I should've told Darius to take it in stronger, or drive up then pull up behind the arc and take it, or pass to Cam. Having been left to his own devices, Darius dribbled off his foot.

And that was the ball game.

I walked onto the court to gently touch Darius on the top and back of his head. He had given it everything he had. Tyrone walked up to me, distressed, his eyes shining and wet, his gold uniform clean, unsullied by sweat. "My ride," he said sadly. "My ride was late. But it wasn't my fault." "That's all right," I said, "but I wanted to coach you, boy. You know I did."

Meanwhile, Darius was fuming, "The ref should've called that foul!" I told him it was all right, because that was the thing to say, but it turned out it was also the thing that was mostly true. The referee came over and said, "Great game, Coach, great game, shame somebody had to lose that game." He was saying it more to himself than me, much as the late Earl Strom would say it while running off the parquet floor of old Boston Garden after a heated NBA playoff game between the Celtics and the Lakers.

"You gave us a good call today," I said, knowing full well this is all a ref ever wants to hear out of a coach.

Then the Greenbelt coach came over and said, "I'm sorry. Either team could have won. Great game. *Great* game." The teams lined up and slapped hands. I looked at George and said, "That's the way to hit the free throws, son." He smiled and ducked his head. I saw the Greenbelt players slapping hands with the Certain players. And then I saw George slap McDerrin's hand, and then Steve's. Then our stuff was moved off by the lady so that other, older teams could play, and everything could stay on schedule.

We held our awards ceremony right there at Spring Hill

Lake Recreation Center in Greenbelt. I pulled the trophies out and the boys—well, you would be surprised how far a ten-dollar trophy will go when it comes to lifting the lowered spirits of the recently vanquished. I gave an honest thumbnail sketch with each award:

"Guys, you can't be getting mad at each other. You have to care about and support and help yourselves out, because nobody cares about you but you. So you have to care for yourselves.

"McDerrin, you quit. Your trophy has no name. If you want your name on it, put it there yourself." (McDerrin took the trophy anyway, so transfixed by it he may not have heard me.)

"A flexible player, our most determined shot-blocker, a good athlete who's got to not let his books slip. The books are the real game . . . Warren R." (Warren took his trophy to applause from the Certain players and parents and guardians—applause so strong and well-met that most of the Greenbelt people stopped to look. This strong applause continued for each ensuing player.)

"I call this guy Instant Offense, best hands on the team, best athlete in the neighborhood—Cam-Ron J." (Cam-Ron took his trophy and gave Darius a look; as noted, Darius had teased Cam-Ron by saying, "Aw, I might not play today, I got a headache," and that made Cam-Ron mad because he is a "gamer"—I would not be all that surprised to see him in the major leagues one day.)

"A young man who is our space-eater inside. He had some good looks at the basket today. They didn't drop for him, but if he keeps putting them up there soft they'll drop sooner or later. And he never misses a practice, a game, or anything. Matt M.

"A young man who can really score the basketball. We asked him to run point today, and it wasn't fair, but he held up. He missed practices and games because his religious beliefs caused scheduling conflicts. I like a man with principles—Johnny R.

"This young man, I'm particularly proud of—the leading rebounder for the season, hit three big treys to bail us out in the first half; the smartest passer on the team, and the kind of guy we want on the court at the end of the game—Colen W.

"A young man who can become quick, and who's only got to learn to think for himself out there—Steve W.

"The Most Valuable Player. We could've used him in the first half today, but he played his heart out in the second half, and gave it his best, which is all we can ask—Darius C.

"And this is a really gifted player, with quickness and instinct. He is as good a guard as we have. If he and Darius learn how to play together, I don't really think anybody could stop them. He had a little trouble with his ride today, but that's not his fault. I'm glad he came anyway—Tyrone B."

A lady from Greenbelt called us over and gave us a big runner-up trophy and ten medallions hung from ribbons. Standing alone they would not have made the most comforting sight. Taken with the boys' other trophies made them a welcome surplus. The boys had a big trophy for the Certain trophy case and individual trophies and individual medallions—quite a bounty. Greenbelt had won the biggest trophy and some individual trophies that were no better than Certain's. Greenbelt's boys deserved them because their parents bought them—and because they had played well. So it was one of those games where losing was the least of it.

I took Steve and McDerrin home. McDerrin carefully and lovingly pulled some tape off his trophy and said, "Don't know why, but it don't hurt today, like it did when we lost before."

"That's because you didn't lose," I said. "You won what you play for . . ."

He frowned, wondering what that could be.

"Old George? He won't be talking about that game at school tomorrow," I said. "He knows you—we—could've won as easy as lost. We didn't have our starting backcourt for the whole game, our MVP only half of it. You won't be hearing from George about *this* game. From now on, he'll say, 'They play a li'l bit over there.' If he says anything. And Greenbelt might not be so quick to invite you back to their tournament next year. In fact, you probably won't be invited, I'd say. That's why you play."

McDerrin frowned even more formidably. I don't know what he thought. I only know that he was thinking. I don't know which way he will go. He's not my child. But for a second there . . .

"Fist worked, you know," he said finally. "Darius scored off of Fist . . . it made a difference when you said have fun . . . I'm going right to the court . . . you gonna coach us next year?"

"It's a possibility, on an as-needed basis, but nothing's guaranteed. If you whine or throw fits because you don't get your way, it won't matter who's coaching the team—he'll bounce your bee-hind off the squad again. Assume my blessings on that.

"Now, go show your uncle and godmother."

He got out over near to where bad things have been known to happen, and got out heavier than when he'd gotten in.

Steve was quiet as I drove him to his parents' nice new home in Certain proper. As we turned the corner of his street, Steve raised up his hand, acknowledging some playmates standing astride their bikes. Steve raised the hand with the trophy in it.

"Well, go'on and show your mother and father," I said, and Steve was out of the car and gone before my mouth closed.

I went to the gingerbread-colored house and exchanged winks with Cole's mother and bellowed out at an appropriate volume for the boy's presence. He came from wherever it is boys go, still in his uniform and looking as if he wasn't expecting any particular mood from such a moody and temperamental man. I grabbed and hugged him, pounding on his back until he said, "Ouch!" even though I could plainly tell he was not hurt by it. "Real proud of you, boy," I said.

Then we sat and watched the inevitable basketball game on TV and ate tacos. His trophy sat on the mantel, out toward the ledge, the medallion around its neck. Before I left I pushed it back so it would not be in such a precarious position and put the medallion around the base so the trophy no longer courted top-heaviness. Later, the boy's mother said he didn't take off his gold uniform No. 1 until he went to bed. I understood that. I didn't have time to linger on it very long, because baseball season was coming up. Now I don't have time to coach a team and manage a life too, but if it was me, this would be the batting order:

| | |
|---|---|
| Darius C. | p/of/c |
| Paul R. | 2b/3b/ss |
| Josh A. | 1b/3b/p |
| Cam-Ron J. | c/ss/of |
| Colen W. | 3b/of/p |
| Bobby D. | of/ss/p |
| Mike F. | ss/2b/p |
| Hoby C. | of/1b |
| John M. | 2b |
| Greg | — |

*Wait* a minute. What am I doing here?

Prince Georges County was running a deficit, by the way, of some $108 million, so it was said. In 1995 a ten percent county employee workforce reduction would be implemented;

six libraries would close; a homeless shelter would be eliminated; the public schools would lose $31 million; forty-five police would be cut from the rolls; fire services would be reduced; health clinics would shut down; a rehab program for drunk drivers would phase out. It was said in paranoid whispers that the county Boys and Girls Clubs might be next. For twenty reasons I can think of, I hoped not. There may be too much "I" in this part of the drift. What about you, you may ask. It is a good question. Yes. What *about* you?

## Are Leadership and the NAACP Mutually Exclusive?

The train swung out below the river's mouth, cutting a wide swath in the swirling snow on a bridge over a choppy slate of troubled waters. It seemed we flew over this neck of the bay, and if that window had not been in my way I might have fished on the fly like an eagle. If I seem overly exhilarated by this, it is because I have learned since getting older that nearly everything I enjoy is not good for me except activities involving water. So I've learned to respect the element. I love to imbibe it, and love to bathe in it, and love to drink in the sight of it as I pass over.

Shortly we regained landfall, whisking by idle arms of irrigation equipment that resembled desiccated remains of giant spiders; we went past electric substations (no more lifeless-looking things exist than the apparatus of great power, such as these); the back doors of modest houses, backyards choked up with clutter, posted on concrete foundations set in undulating land now lying fallow beneath the snow cover. Along the track, leafless branches of innumerable trees clawed out in skeletal supplication to the skies. Nothing could appear more beyond help than this.

By April, not two months away, the machines would circle

and spray; the screen doors in the backs of the houses would
be slammed and reslammed to a point of irritation; the clutter would double; and children would be warned, told they'd
"get 'lectrocuted," lit up like Roman candles, "if y'all ain't
careful with them kites near them wires!" The fields would
yield food. The food would taste sweet. It would sell. Trees
would bud and flower in kaleidoscopic variety. Parasites
would set up in the trunks and boughs, using life in and
around the eternal trees to nourish themselves and their help-
less young. And by June, you would not be able to see beyond the lush, opaline arms of trees that once seemed dead.

Seventy-six minutes out of Union Station, the train pulled
up on the elevated track in Wilmington, Delaware, a drab
piece of business that along with February reminded me of
some problems within the National Association for the Ad-
vancement of Colored People. Three years before this I was
invited by the Wilmington branch of the NAACP to speak
and wreck digestion at a dinner. Senator Biden would be
there, but I was told not to let that stop me. Something ominous was in the air and they wanted me to identify it. People
were being avoided on the street, looked off, or laid off, or
ignored, or hit, or shot, or worse—it was a supercharged
atmosphere in general, and would I come and give a funny
name to it? I said I would show, although I would probably
only make it more uncomfortable. They decided to take the
chance.

I went accompanied by the lissome and comely D.K. This
was fortuitous in more than the obvious ways, for if I had
been alone and unescorted I may not have made it out of the
annual awards dinner intact. I was being hunted. Soon after
arrival it dawned on me that maybe the invitation, tendered
by a female undersecretary of the local, had not been given
with upright motives. For openers she said I looked better
than the advance photograph. This is one reason I despise
such photographs. Her agenda became clear as the cocktail

hour advanced. D.K. was not as distressed as I was. Her distress seemed more amusement; she mocked the undersecretary's moves without the latter's knowing it. As the undersecretary batted her eyelashes at a pace that caused one of them to fling itself onto the hors d'oeuvres, D.K. batted hers—over a pair of crossed eyes. Even I laughed when I almost ate some *saumon de Maybelline*. And when the undersecretary stroked the stem of her wineglass, D.K. rubbed hers as though it were a grounded stick and she were a chilly Scout. And when the undersecretary breathed heavily, asthmatically, and drawled, "We've *so* looked forward to working under you," D.K. whispered, "Working you *out*." Then D.K. laughed—though I could not see what was funny by that point, when D.K. *should* have been employing her agile mind in working out an escape route for after the speech.

The president of the local chapter came and spoke to me while regarding me suspiciously, as if I'd not been *his* idea of a good time. I noted his uproarious yet well-worn apparel and knew the local was an unpretentious one. The M.C. for the evening was an Asian-American broadcaster from Philadelphia; a pleasant man, though the look on his face said "God help me." "White" people were there as well, most of them representing various corporate contributors to a cause of fairness—not because life was fair, but because it was good business to keep as many consumers alive as possible. Even "black" ones. *Especially* them, because they knew how to spend unwisely. To many "black" consumers the slogan *caveat emptor* may as well be the brand name of a malt liquor.

One "white" man asked D.K. if he might know her from somewhere, and said that if he didn't, the problem should be rectified. He scratched what should have been a private itch. D.K. and I locked eyes. Though it was my turn to laugh I did not. Nor did D.K. And here we had come, believing it was our minds the NAACP and its followers coveted.

Later Senator Biden dispatched a letter of congratulations on our slipperiness in exiting the premises and on getting out of town unscathed.

At the time, the Wilmington chapter seemed to have little on its mind other than a dangerous climate. Still, on balance it had been an agreeable trip—or was, until the dogged undersecretary inquired if I would be staying the night, since the hotel room was paid for. To which room should she bring the check, a receipt (and, presumably, her remaining rank of eyelash)? Wasn't I sending "that woman"—D.K.—on ahead?

I suggested that the U.S. mails would get the check to me, eventually, though I would be denied plenty of interest in the interim. We stumbled from under the undersecretary's sights. I would have felt safer as a target for Idaho survivalists. These notes are enough to leave a bitter taste in one's mouth, if one lets them. The secret is not to let them very often. On the way back we took the long way, around the windward side of Delmarva. It was a night clear as crystal, miles from the hazes and lights of cities, and the moon was tucked away. I looked over and then up, from whence cometh my much-needed help, and saw the Milky Way in the fullness of its awesome majesty. Ursa Major and Minor were lost in a deluge—an explosion—of stars and heavenly bodies, socking the sky end to end with wonders and moving my soul like song.

When was the last time you rocked back and took in the unencumbered sight of the Milky Way, and silently pondered your insignificance within the larger body? The last time I did was not long after I left the Wilmington NAACP awards dinner. For this I thank that august body, and owe it my eternal debt.

·   ·   ·

The greater NAACP, on the other hand, was becoming known as a thankless, useless appendix on the body politic by some of those same "colored" people it was once bound to serve. Some of them now called for its disbandment. Once it was an effective agency for legal challenges of discriminatory laws. The Legal Defense Fund arm of the NAACP was responsible for that; and for your sake do not confuse the NAACP itself with the NAACP Legal Defense Fund. At one time the lawyers of the Fund would set you straight on that, threatening to exhibit their talents in your direction should you continue making the mistake of lumping them in with the larger body.

Local ranks of the NAACP once had memberships in the hundred thousands; now they were in disarray, although the aggregate membership was still as high as 600,000. The NAACP was running in the red, too, to a tune of about $3.8 million in 1995.

To relieve the malaise, Rev. Ben Chavis, formerly of the Wilmington 10 (North Carolina, not Delaware), had been named the executive director, in 1994. Chavis had been unfairly jailed as part of the Wilmington 10 in the '70s, afterward remained vocal about his commitment to justice, and seemed to know his way around the small end of a bullhorn. It was presumed he might stir the masses to applying for memberships, if not legalities. There had been a whir of excitement—and a brief whir, it was—when Rev. Chavis's ascension was effected. The appointment caused unease in those local quarters atop the neck of yours truly. This was progress, that an organization had gone from Du Bois to the Reverend Ben Chavis as its spokesman in less than a hundred years? Du Bois had "doctor" as the precursor to his name, though his work best articulated his sincerity. Chavis added "Reverend" to his name because some such promotion from

"Mister" seems necessary to those of organizational ambition. It sounds impressive, worthy of genuflection among all of us, the unwashed; "Reverend" presumes an honorable conduct by what follows it—or immunity from conduct appraisals.

Some of us have learned better than to pardon reverends from human frailty. And even if reverends are as good as their words, they still produce sons who bear a close watch. An old NAACP member once told me, "Reverend's an Indian word for 'He Who Speaks from Both Sides of Mouth.' " I chastised him for doubting the clergy, but shouldn't have questioned his wisdom in such matters, since he had on a clerical collar himself. Usually the pronouncements of most reverends, like those of lawyers, members of Congress and authors, resemble the Peace of God only in that each passeth understanding.

This was true in Chavis's case. I admired him as a picture in the paper. When I heard him butcher his positions I thought, "Who's he going to trick?" He walked the walk but couldn't talk the talk, fine if appointed marshal of Hadleyville or forward for the Charlotte Hornets. But not being able to talk predicts destitution for a spokesman. I heard Benjamin Chavis mangling verbs, killing tenses—not that there's anything wrong with *systematic* verb-mangling and tense-murdering. But when you speak in dialect when desperately trying not to, playing your tune in one key, then another, then a third, at any given moment, and not knowing it, while expecting the listener to take to this melody, it puts people on guard—usually the very people you want to trick.

People speak the comfortable forms all the time in private company or casual conversation or in trying to reembody and reenact such company and conversations. In fact, speaking grammatically when in America and trying to appear comfortable about it at the same time is an uncommon conduct that can get you stared at and otherwise noticed in many places. In the Northeast Corridor, as in most venues, one needs to slip into the required gear. There is as much dialect, idiom and vernacular thrown around in the Northeast Corridor as out in the sticks. You know you are on Long Island, for example, if you do a pen-and-ink sketch and someone calls it a "draw-ring." You know you are in Brooklyn if someone refers to the woman who bore him as not "muh-ther" but "muh-vah." That one seems to have caught on elsewhere too. I don't much care for it. It seems to me to have no function. I think it was first in Chicago that I learned being "ready to go" is also known as "red t'go." That one I like. It is quick and makes a point two ways—not only is one "ready to go," one is *red* to do it as well, red implying heat, heat implying movement. "Ain't" is "ain't" everywhere now. Even the most educated will be understood better if they say, "If you learn how to control your temper, ain't *nobody* gonna take your mind away from you." I have also heard doctoral candidates say, "Don't matter." You could be correct, and say that the thing "doesn't matter," but sometimes being correct doesn't show rectitude. The gears of diplomacy are lubricated by language that the people being spoken to can at least act like they understand.

Rev. Chavis had only the one gear, which appeared to be fourth. He could get his point across, eventually, but in order to get him up to speed there was clanking and knocking and no good pickup at all. You longed for a book to read until you got there and had a queasy feeling a wreck was coming along if the engine didn't up and quit on you first. On the country roads among the common people such vehicles of expression would work. But even there mellifluousness and ease of delivery are very much admired. On the crowded turnpikes, beltways, tollways, tunnels, crosstown streets and bridges of the Northeast Corridor, where twenty million people not only drive but seem to be trying to impede you from getting where you have to go, one single gear, a homespun cadence emanating hesitantly and grudgingly will arrest scarce emotion outside of contempt. Rev. Chavis enjoyed his station as director of the NAACP for only a few months.

A surprise? Hardly that.

Rev. Chavis was found to have paid off a woman in the home office in Baltimore with NAACP funds, ostensibly to avoid a sexual harassment beef. Or maybe it was a sexual discrimination case. It was something sexual, that much was clear.

Owing to my Wilmington experiences, I didn't find the conduct odd, let alone grounds for dismissal. I don't know what Rev. Chavis said to the woman, but having heard him I can't imagine him saying anything that would be worth $81,000, the amount she was said to have been allotted.

The former executive head of the United Way charities, one Mr. William Aramony, was found guilty of a similar fiduciary misconduct, but that was done to impress a younger and prettier protégé. Here's how good a strategist Rev. Chavis was: He was guilty of—whatever—with a woman who was not a shadow of his pregnant wife. Rev. Chavis's wife was at least a hundred times lovelier than this woman as well! If he harassed her, it was not because it was inevitable due to her pulchritudinous allure, of which she had none left these eyes could turn up, but because he *could*; practicing up on his ironclad incorruptibility.

Few wanted to dismantle the United Way because Aramony was found out. And that Rev. Chavis could not speak Northeast Corridor jive or exhibit loyalty to his wife or strategize his way out of a hotel hallway did not mean the NAACP had no sterner stuff. I do not like appraising Chavis in this way, particularly, but these are times that try men's patience and make women grumble.

The NAACP carries on historic names like Du Bois, Wells, Garrison, Spingarn and Thurgood Marshall, the way the National Archives carry Washington, Madison and Lincoln. The NAACP *should* serve as a kind of National Archives of all "colored" peoples in America. Jackie Robinson led Freedom Fund Drives for it. And *The New Yorker* critic and playwright Dorothy Parker excused herself from the Algonquin Round Table and Hollywood long enough to bequeath her papers and the publishing rights to them. The essays Du Bois penned for the NAACP magazine *The Crisis* are its legacy. Merely because you don't need the NAACP this minute doesn't mean you might not one day, if only to look something up; or that your sons and daughters might not need it in order to get in touch with the Legal Defense Fund to help overturn pending disaster posing as legislation proposed by angry "white" men who now have their feet up on the congressional furniture. Even in the most obtuse sense, the NAACP might help someone focus who might otherwise wind up massaging your car with a brick.

Sooner or later, discipline must be endured. Since "black" people are running low on fathers for children, for one reason or another, discipline can be found in organizations like the NAACP as well as in the orphanages and jails preferred by new members of Congress. To assume that institutions formed to assist "black" people (outside of orphanages and jails) should be dismantled (except orphanages and jails) because they wobble at the top (including orphanages and jails) is to assume a monumental lot in a time of crisis. Head-in-the-sand logic is unfit for decent folk—even reverends.

To believe "integration" obsolesced institutions like the NAACP, or like financially strapped but alumni-strong

United Negro College Fund universities, is to ignore history as well as the current tilting of the 104th Congress—attractive propositions to ignore, but to do so is foolish. To bray "Anytime institutions suffer setbacks via executive fiat, they should be abolished!" is near the summit of folly. If that "thinking" were accepted, there would be *no* institutions. Christendom would have survived neither the Inquisition nor slavery. Then we would be in a pickle, having to think up honorifics other than "Reverend" to legitimize all the people who would speak to progressive ideas and radical ones like love, fair play and blind justice. Unfortunately, any raving nincompoop can be made legitimate by a right-sounding title. It takes more than a title to move a person beyond self-preservation, self-approval and personal gratification into the *disciplined* realm of blind, well-met justice. People cry for justice as though it is easy to comprehend. It is not. It is difficult to dish up consistently. It does not always favor the same people. There are times when justice wounds you, depending on your prior conduct.

As for Rev. Chavis, he was incompetent only if you found the job where he would be incompetent and put him in it. If you kept a bullhorn in his hands and gave him the charge of a local NAACP chapter, we might have been happy. *He* might not have been happy, but too large an ambition is unbecoming after a certain age. Contrary to what he may now think, the Reverend Ben Chavis did not stir the masses toward justice—his plight stirred them, back when he represented the unjustly jailed in the '70s. His position did the stirring when he was appointed executive director of the NAACP in 1994. Likewise it was not Chavis who was courted and squired by both prominent Jews and Louis Farrakhan—it was the titular head of the NAACP who brought home that unlikely daily double. It was not Chavis who was envied by other reverends; it was the NAACP's executive directorship they singled out. Chavis might not realize these facts until this very day—although probably by now they are beginning to dawn on even him.

Chavis was not incompetent. He was mismanaged. He was short on long-term judgment; he couldn't flaunt Northeast Corridorese without your going "Ow!"; was no great shakes on forming concepts that might discomfit Congress and give youth something to busy their soles. He was what he was: a sergeant who woke up one day and found he'd made general. The question was not "Is the NAACP relevant?" but, "Which of its geniuses commissioned Chavis?"

After my trip through a snowstorm, a new head of the NAACP was named. She was Myrlie Evers-Williams, widow of the civil rights martyr and former NAACP field secretary Medgar Evers. Ms. Evers-Williams had been championed by Ms. Hazel Dukes over muttered objections from Dr. William Gibson, a South Carolina dentist who had helped make Rev. Chavis a general, if briefly, and performed other acts of infamy such as alleged till-tapping as chairman of the board. He was on roller skates as well, replaced by Evers-Williams as the head of the board. A new replacement executive director for Rev. Chavis would soon be found, and rather easily if you ask me. Between Ms. Evers-Williams and Ms. Dukes and whoever they decided would be a good executive director, and the grim situation at hand, an NAACP renaissance might be in the offing. And if I had a psychic hot line I could tell you. But I do not.

As for Wilmington, Delaware, itself, it does not cry out for any more specific examination, at least not by me, so I shall leave it behind and to a better hand. Philadelphia was up ahead.

## Current Events in Fair and Insular
## Philadelphia

As the spires of Philadelphia swung into view, my mood became placid. Ah, Philly, home to Franklin and Robeson, musical home to the songwriters Gamble, Huff and Creed, and now to a new wave called The Roots. It is a fan of green Delaware River Valley within whose folds live sensible, convivial and artistic people, working under a multiplicity of blue collars and other disguises; people who have a cracked bell on display and a sense of calm under fire. In the City of Brotherly Love, one of the first lessons you learn is that you need to know how to fight—but only scientifically.

As the train pulled toward a wye outside of 30th Street Station, we passed the University of Pennsylvania and Franklin Field. I gazed at the fields outside the stadium and saw ghosts of athletes warming up framed by tricolored bunting. They hopped on one leg, impossibly snapped another over a hurdle—it seems impossible now but once did not, isn't that strange?—hoisted javelins, slung hammers into nets, passed batons, stretched into pretzels. This was home of the Penn Relays, America's preeminent outdoor track-and-field meet, run every April. I've spent the afternoon there and been satisfied the time was not wasted. It was reassuring—even more so these days—and disconcerting at the same time. I asked one man why no one there seemed to be angry.

"I ain't had a job in ten years, and I ain't mad," he said.

As I said, disconcerting, but it was good to be in a crowd of friendly people, some with box lunches and other food and drink, willing to share while ogling the enviably taut athletes aging from sixteen to much older. They came from high schools, colleges—small colleges, big universities, Ivy League schools, the United Negro College Fund schools—

from all over the United States, and all of them running, jumping, throwing, in roughly the same manner; *together*, not too resentful in any one way or another, all having in common the camaraderie of being among the comparative few who appreciate the joys and histories of that wonder called track and field.

I like the relay races best. They have such a sense for the dramatic. Drop the stick and the race is over, no matter how steadfast your legs. Teams are brought in from all over the country for the Penn Relays and put on an excellent show. I'll regret to miss it, ever again. Mr. Thomas once took me to the meet and he remains a friend. That alone should say enough about the Penn Relays.

The 30th Street Station in downtown Philadelphia is the most pleasant and utilitarian of all its kind. As opposed to the bustle and commerciality of Union Station or the rathole of Penn Station in New York, Philadelphia's 30th St. Station is the very model of plain function and therefore beauty. It is all one room, basically, an enormous room, as long as any football field and a city block wide. Its ceilings are high—so high pigeons often enter the building and fly up looking for a roost, thinking they are still outdoors. When they find no roost but a ceiling, they land and strut about the floor in high dudgeon. The ceiling is so high an average man could not throw up a baseball and hit the center of it on a bet—if you need an extra dollar, that is one way to get it.

Several excellent emporiums of cuisine deserve your attention, notably Delilah's southern cuisine, where the cornbread is like cake. A bas-relief smooth stone mural on the progress of transportation enlivens a trip to the privy. The 29th Street side is guarded by the sculpture of the Angel of Mercy holding up a victim of a war; its base is etched thusly: *In Memory of the Men and Women of the Pennsylvania Railroad who laid down their lives for their country 1941–1945.* My friend

Thomas had often retrieved me from contemplating this statue, and we had engaged the city of Philadelphia with brazen pleasure, from restaurants to South Street haunts; from cool Lincoln Drive to Wissahickon Park to University City; Mt. Airy to Chestnut Hill to Sugarloaf.

Philadelphia has commoner charms as well. Once I was driving down the street—what street only Thomas knows—and a car sheered off into the front end of mine. I was stunned. Thomas jumped out immediately and began berating the person I thought I had hit in a moment of distraction. Metal had flown off from this wreck of a car, yet mine was unscathed. I'd been hit by a "wreck-chaser," as they are called there—someone trying to procure insurance money by staging an "accident." Thomas, being local, knew it right off. I must have known by instinct—putting instinct on top of the level of volume generated by Thomas's sneering and continuing abuse of the other driver. As soon as I lied and said I didn't have any insurance, the driver of the rattletrap was crestfallen. He retrieved his props, put them away and drove off with Thomas's stream of invective ringing in his ears the whole time.

Thomas is a man of taste, humor and good carriage. He is in his forties now. A lifelong Philadelphian (is there another kind?), he anticipated a move east near the New Jersey line, outside the Philadelphia city limits. Why would he consider relocation, since it was beyond the habit of Philadelphians to consider a move away from their home? They are an insular, contented crowd, and do not brook outsiders well—until outsiders prove their suitability to the proven environment. Judging from what was now going on among outsiders, who could blame the Philadelphians? Thomas anticipated hard times coming for many of his neighbors in downtown Philadelphia, and hungry stomachs were going to eat, even the man who compiled something called the Book of Virtues said so; said virtue had nothing to do with dinner. What with that fact and the other things going on in the government and industry, it seemed best to move from Thomas's piercing Philadelphia view.

Thomas worked in Newark, up the line, in the insurance industry, with bunches of other white shirts. For the last month the range of topical conversation on the commuter trains had been (1) the omnipresent image of murderer Colin Ferguson; (2) timely utterances by the sitting president of Rutgers University; (3) the famed and best beloved O.J. Simpson trial. I considered what Thomas said as the train passed within sight of the leaden zoo and the colorful boathouses, then crossed the Schuylkill River.

Ferguson had pulled out a handgun and in a cold-blooded fashion killed six and wounded many others on a Long Island Railroad train. You'd think he would barely be tried for such an offense before being sent up or down the river forever, but instead he was being featured on television news and called "Mr. Ferguson." Ferguson was from Jamaica, of a privileged class, but when he came to America and couldn't keep his girlfriend or his job with the Long Island Railroad, Ferguson chose not to look in a mirror or examine his dilemmas for a way out of them but to gaze along a gunsight. It is an old story, really, one often told in spite of its age and predictability here at century's close.

Thomas had a friend who worked at the Equal Employment Opportunity Commission in New York. Colin Ferguson had come to him after his employment had been terminated. Thomas's friend told Ferguson most big corporations were "downsizing"—"laying off" in the American language—and that there was nothing much to be done about it. Many "white" men were being told the very same thing in the personnel offices of companies where they worked. Those doing the axing were implying to these "white" workers that "affirmative action" and unfair tax burdens caused by "welfare mothers" were the cause of their pink slips: "Black" people were the problem. Instead of blaming their employers for taking their jobs across the seas, these powerless "white" men took the bait and blamed "niggers."

This is a point where the paranoias intersect. Ferguson said he suspected his employers at the railroad were "racist," involved in a conspiracy to deny his place as railroad scion and purveyor of middle-class values. Thomas's friend responded he had little doubt of it—what else was new? He told Ferguson to cut his losses, train for new skills, make another appointment. Ferguson ended up on a train shooting people. This thin shell who was once a man was now found babbling grammatically on television, serving as his own counsel at trial, being called "Mr. Ferguson." Television commentators marveled at his ability to speak diplomatic, grammatical, liltingly accented English. He sounded more official than Chavis but wasn't tricking anybody either. You could say he was being used to trick others into becoming like him in any cause they believed was "justice."

If people had called him "Mr. Ferguson" in the first place, tragedy may have been avoidable. But as it was, Ferguson was just another homicidal maniac and that was it—the better to be served up daily by scions of the mass media middle class, so that they may keep their rightful, profitable place, as long they don't think too hard.

The snow thickened as the train clove into New Jersey. We passed through Trenton, Princeton Junction—eighteen inches there—and made north toward New Brunswick. Of greater interest than the scenery along this route was a story Thomas told about the president of Rutgers and a protest by students staged a few days before, three months after President Francis L. Lawrence had said this: "The average SAT for

African-Americans is seven hundred and fifty. Do we set standards in the future so that we don't admit anybody with the national test? Or, deal with a disadvantaged population that doesn't have the genetic hereditary background to have a higher average?"

Inspired by this ringing vote of confidence, about one hundred and fifty students—not all of them "black"— interrupted a Rutgers vs. Massachusetts basketball game on the evening of February 7, 1995. This protest was led by a young "black" woman who walked out to half-court and sat down. Others walked out on the court and sat. Some walked around with signs that said, "How do we deal with an intellectually disadvantaged president? We fire him." The protest was effective. The game was suspended—the first game suspension in the history of the National Collegiate Athletic Association. It was what some might call a classic social protest. But then it became a longer bone of contention. Some students insisted Mr. Lawrence be relieved of his post— because *they* had called for it.

"They made the point, now forget about it. Move on," Thomas said. "The man had done some good things at Rutgers. They've got a good-sized minority enrollment now. He said he was sorry. As far as thinking goes, we all know what they've gotta think."

Mr. Lawrence later said he could not "explain a remark that said precisely the opposite of my deeply held beliefs."

Said Thomas, "Even Robeson's son—he went to Rutgers, like his old man—came out supporting whatchamacallit. They did the job to make a protest, chose a ball game to noise it up—nice touch. Now let it go. You made the point. You can't change what people think. These kids think they have that kind of power? Please."

I nodded at the reliability of this Philadelphia brand of scientific logic—but also knew it was their youth that made the students unwilling to let go quite so easily. It was easy for Thomas or me or even you to blow off Lawrence's *faux pas*; we had nothing to prove because we had already proven something. When you are young and haven't had the chance to prove yourself, and people assume you can't ever prove anything, so why give you the opportunity to try, it tends to make you loud, mad or nervous.

"You earned the right to be calm about it, Thomas," I said. "Over some long, hard, memorable years, you earned that right."

Dr. Lawrence's unfortunate train of thought had been trundled out and was running amok. And Thomas was also right in this case; Dr. Lawrence, while not utterly blameless, could not be held accountable for this thought, any more than a wooden marionette can be held accountable for having profanities slung into its mouth-hinge by a hidden voice; any more than you can be blamed for buying the brand of toothpaste you buy. Advertising is a captivating discipline. The words were taken almost verbatim from a certain book. This made it even more frightening—*that Lawrence had not intended to say it, that he felt precisely the opposite, but somehow it still came out that way.* Scientists and college presidents, in their noble quest for truths to make them feel in control and secure, are fine with their minutiae, but the bigger picture seems to blind them. For, "genetically" speaking, I know "black" Americans with solid surnames like Schmidt, Gross, Gould, McCollum, Riley, Rodriguez, Roselli, Campanella, Fauntroy, Abram, Bourgeois, MacDonald, MacEachern and so on, ad infinitum. The names weren't all they received in the kit. The genetic tar pit to which "black" Americans were consigned was the pit of the entire globe. So those who speak to the inadvisability of miscegenation missed the train by a mile. It left four hundred years ago and I wasn't around to greenlight it—though some of my people boarded and brought me along. A casual glance at any gathering illustrates this point ineffably better, but I suppose not to scientists and college presidents whose noses are said to be so close to the grindstone that they cannot see beyond it.

But, again, all that is beside the point.

### Stop Spreading the News:
### A New York Phantasm

Penn Station is a place of such paucity of splendor as this pen can barely describe, so we will not ask too much of it. I made haste up out of the catacombs and headed up and crosstown, toward the Whitney. The snow had stopped and Manhattan's streets were plowed immediately—although the same could not be said for Manhattan's sidewalks, now also bearing the brunt of the grey slush from the streets, which was pushed into hills as high as your eye. I traversed this glacial landscape with utmost care, stopping to join M.L., friend and corporate marketeer. M.L. is ruthless in her work, would not let me be taken hostage en route to our goal by subliminal instructions posing as petty advertising, even as we made our way north and passed by Bloomingdale's. There on a corner, a "white" man with pale blue eyes sat shoeless near the street with a beggar's cup. A "black" woman in braids passed him, placing a dollar in the cup. A short distance away a sallow-faced "black" man with short coiling hair the color of fire on head and chin walked in a state of oblivion, talking to himself, wiping at his Caribbean blue eyes. I wondered if in the end they mattered.

We arrived at the Whitney—surprisingly thick with patrons for a snow recovery day. I was a patron too, though that was not planned. It cost seven dollars to enter the exhibit and since I had asked M.L. to accompany me she looked me squarely in the eye with an expectant glint. I announced to the gatekeeper that I was a longtime member of the press. She told me she sympathized, but that didn't mean I would have to pay more than anybody else. I was out fourteen dollars right there. An artist should've taken a picture of me handing over my money, and put that on exhibit.

We rode an elevator until the doors opened upon the beginnings of the exhibit: a tableau of four headless mannequins, outfitted as security guards and doormen, entitled *Guarded View*, by Fred Wilson. I got it right away. Then a mannequin spoke. This one had a head. He was not part of the exhibit but a real guard. He said, "Got that one, did you?" as the elevator arrived with another load.

The exhibit was well attended; in that way it almost outstripped Penn Station. The security guard with the head told the new arrivals not to touch the exhibits. A Russian dissident struck a match on my sleeve, to light a cigarette and showcase his independence. Another man took a picture of me and commented on my "contrapositive" lines. The guard warned them again, adding this time, they were not to touch me, either. I rounded a corner and saw a mural of misspelled words that seemed to have been written during a child's epileptic seizure. Owing to the O.J. Simpson trial, I got that one, too. So far, each work in the exhibit had a joke—albeit a broad joke—but only one joke per assemblage; a lean ratio for works of art. I was staring so hard at the doggerel-on-canvas that I ran into a fixed wooden bench, probably for patrons left breathless by the wonders of the exhibit. I plopped, consoled my shin and numbly gazed at items of interest while a little girl made a circle of her mouth and pulled on her father's sleeve and pointed at me, then said,

"Daddy, that one moved! Oh, Daddy, I'm scared!"

"It's a mobile exhibit, dear," said her father.

I was about to protest I was no such thing, but then that

would probably start an argument, so I preferred to play dumb.

M.L. called me back up front to consider an explanation printed on a mounted board near the head of the exhibit. Its beginning was from Ralph Ellison's enticement into *Invisible Man:*

> I am an invisible man. No, I am not a spook like those who haunted Edgar Allan Poe; nor am I one of your Hollywood-movie ectoplasms. I am a man of substance, of flesh and bone, fiber and liquids—I might even be said to possess a mind . . .

M.L. continued reading the inscription that announced the exhibit's purpose. She immediately bristled at its identification of the African American male as one of this country's greatest inventions—an invention rooted in a twisted concept of black masculinity. An invention rooted in the fears and projections of the American psyche. It was true—my fears were projecting, toward what people might make of this exhibit. It came recommended, was said to be satirical in part, thus I might be able to translate it. If not, that would be no surprise either. I saw examples of satire and attempts at it, the success of which I leave to you and history, not my unsound judgments. I will go over them with you anyway.

Artist Robert Colescott's 1925 painting *George Washington Carver Crossing the Delaware: Page from American History* had the Alabama scientist and agronomist crudely drawn. Carver stood in colonial military dress and a familiar pose. A caricatured banjo-strummer, a fisherman, a cook, a maid and a jug-drainer, all with painfully caricatured features, sat aboard his longboat; the painting was surely attempting to mock Emanuel Leutze's *Washington Crossing the Delaware.* Seemed to me it was Carver and his fellows who ended up mocked, though Colescott had a good idea to make his caricature look amateurish. I sort of got it. I didn't want to get it quite like this.

Then I thought about what Twain had written in *Life on the Mississippi*, in his chapter "The House Beautiful," where he examined the typical "residence of the principal citizen, all the way from the suburbs of New Orleans to the edge of St. Louis." In minute detail he noted the "pathetic sham" of the pretensions of the house, starting with "imposing fluted columns and Corinthian capitals" in front of a plantation-style home. I'd assumed they were made of marble or granite, and I grew up along that track. No: "white pine, and painted," Twain wrote, from up close. Rudimentary. Inside the house, one aspect of the splendor was described by Twain as follows: "Over middle of mantel, engraving— 'Washington Crossing the Delaware'; on the wall by the door, copy of it done in thunder-and-lightning crewels by one of the young ladies [of the house]—work of art which would have made Washington hesitate about crossing, if he could have foreseen what advantage was going to be taken of it."

Perhaps Colescott had seen similar "artwork" too, and this was his way, in 1925, of making a similar comment.

Robert Arenson's oil-and-acrylic *Special Assistant to the President*, from 1989, was a re-creation of the mug shot of one Willie Horton—the "black" convict who was used in the 1988 presidential election.

Renee Cox's *It Shall Be Named* was a group of eleven gelatin silver prints hanging in the form of a cross, together forming a naked "black" man crucified with his genitals missing. If only genitals were missing from the actual men, I thought, then everyone might cry happy. Lyle Ashton Harris's *Constructs #11* showed a rear view of a black man standing in the dancer's first position, wearing only a blond wig and cotton briefs. This I could have gotten on any edition of *The Ricki Lake Show.* Suddenly it all seemed to be the same droning joke—a cruel one.

Next I came upon a boxing ring constructed with pairs of tap-dancing shoes hanging from the ropes. This would be Gary Simmons's *Step in the Arena (the Essentialist Trap).* It was the best joke in the exhibit so far—I got it and don't see how anyone could not get it.

Pat Ward-Williams's *32 Hours in a Box, and Still Counting* re-created Henry "Box" Brown's escape from slavery, accomplished by shipping himself in a 3′ × 2′ box from below the Mason-Dixon line to Philadelphia. That was good, though I prefer another one of her works—*Accused/Blow Torch/Padlock c. 1986*—a commentary scrawled around the border of a series of *Life* magazine photographs of a burned and chained male lynching victim. It didn't make the cut at the Whitney.

A pair of gilded athletic shoes comprised one work. That should speak for itself, in more ways than one. Some fine china engraved with a large cursive word, *Commemorating,* followed by names like Martin Luther King, Malcolm X, Muhammad Ali, Every Black Man Who Lives to See Twenty-One, etc., etc., was another effort. I got that.

A Richard Pryor joke, lewd and effective, was written in red paint on canvas. I got the joke though I didn't see why anyone other than Pryor would be credited for its invention. Thinking of Pryor brought home the fallacy of the show. Profanity is arresting not simply because it is indelicate. A man can curse in a way so devoid of art it makes you cover your ears and avoid his efforts the next time. But another man can curse in such a rhythmic, descriptive, irreplaceable fashion that you don't hear it as profanity at all, but as meter, pace, authenticity—words best said in that way in order to clinch a story's import.

I turned another corner in this maze. There was a series of

photographs by Robert Mapplethorpe hung at eye level on a wall—a panorama of fire hoses attached to the lower torsos of faceless "black" men. Turns out, as M.L. told me later, they were not fire hoses but penises! I have never seen any such prodigious penises, but then I guess I wouldn't have, having only mine to gauge. I do wonder why only "black" men with elephantine organs are chosen as artistic fodder. That grading system is going to leave a lot of us out of galleries and it makes me wonder what these artists do with these models on break. I tired of the joke's redundancy. I doubted if Mapplethorpe saw those penises as jokes in the first place. If he had been joking, he could have taken a picture of mine, yours or your boyfriend's.

Other than Penises and No Heads, I could see no adhering theme. A critic named Essex Hemphill had complained, "[Mapplethorpe's] eye pays special attention to the penis—at the expense of showing us the subject's face, and thus, a whole person." Edmund White had once noted same. More trustworthy and artistic than Mapplethorpe's homoeroticism was a typical bit of satire about this morbid and fervid preoccupation with dreamy, melanin-stoked genitalia. It cannot be written down with the same efficacy that my neighborhood barber, Moms Mabley or Richard Pryor told it, but that will not stop me.

Two niggers each thought he had the biggest dick in the universe. "Let's see what you're packin'." Didn't want no audience. Went down to the docks and snuck on a steamship. Pulled them out and aimed. One said, "Gah*damn*! This water's cold!" The other one said, "Yeah . . . and it's deep, too."

Another bit of folklore, though in different context, and not profane, is even better: *Snakes . . . make you run into trees.*

Now *those* have it over Mapplethorpe like a tent; not just

any old tent, but a regulation U.S. Army–issue general's bivouac.

Hidden in the exhibit—in plain sight, but hidden somehow—was a small framed picture of a man who looked to be "white" (but wasn't) kneeling on a manicured lawn in front of a house, holding his small daughter who also looked "white." No penises on exhibit here. Not even an outline, though in order to produce this little girl a penis had probably been required at some point. The photo was lost within the exhibit, unaccented, as if anything outside "black" genitalia was beside the point and not worth blowing out of proportion. The exhibit had cohered. Its curator, Thelma Golden, is off the hook, at least with me. I am ignorant, though, and leave complete appreciation of the late Mapplethorpe to heavier minds.

I felt the show was incomplete. This observance of it will also be incomplete so as to be all the more appropriate. There were films in the exhibit and, in fact, it seemed an impeccable film retrospective though I didn't have 120 hours available to see them all. Twenty-nine artists were represented in the art exhibit proper, from painter Leon Golub to the late Jean-Michel Basquiat. Drying inspiration precludes naming them all here. They are good enough on their own merits.

As we left, a class of "black" schoolchildren was being hauled in. The lady leading the tour began her spiel—the same spiel, probably, that she heaped upon the more tweedy types. She went on about how the exhibit was meant to expose the foibles of a public/pubic way of life; to make you think about the "black" men foisted up on a daily basis; how a fool should be able to see the correlation between these wondrous exhibits and the two most widely known "black" men in New York—Colin ("Mister") Ferguson and O.J. Simpson. No doubt as you read this, there are two similar men on more current display. It will make no difference when you read this; it could be 1996, or 2001, or 2020—that sort will be delivered. If they are not delivered and you are in their stead, you are better off. This is what it was like for us, back when. Imagine the horror we endured. But do not weep long for us. We *let* it happen.

The schoolchildren were giggling as schoolchildren are wont to do if embarrassed. They barely heard what the tour guide was saying, for from where they stood they could easily glom on to Mapplethorpe's "contribution" to the discourse. I thought about this as we left. It was not enough for "art" (and what is fobbed off as "art") to confront or define problems—then present more problems as the alternative. The sending up of the wrong must be accompanied by some exposure to the right; or, at minimum, a hint that what is wrong *is* wrong, and not merely the way things are; that is my definition of good satire. Otherwise people keep the wrong idea and you propagate the thing you intended to discredit.

There were bold and innovative absurdities in the Whitney exhibit, but not much timeless beauty—at least none you can't reflect on anytime you take a shower. I would like to say I left the exhibit the larger for it, but fear that was hardly the case. I didn't ask for a refund, but I *thought* about asking. M.L. *did* ask, but was rebuffed. Such is my pitiful overview of the late art exhibition *Black Male: Representations of Masculinity in Contemporary American Art*. It was a success. To the unfortunates who missed it: You'll live.

## The New York Literary Society
## Engages in Harlem

We arrived at the St. James Presbyterian Church at 141st Street and St. Nicholas Avenue early for the 3 P.M. program. The event was the Literary Society's Sixth Annual African-American Read-In, *Celebrating the African American Literary Tradition*. Though some three hundred "black" people were sacrificing good footwear to attend this show, I saw no TV news cameras, no movie moguls; no one in media asked if there was a reasonable explanation for this gathering.

A proclamation from the Mayor of New York was read, then books were opened for silent reading. Meanwhile I stood at the back of the church and met—Yo!—one of the "black" intelligentsia. This one was Derrick Bell, a former professor of law at Harvard U., the composer of two recent books, *Faces at the Bottom of the Well* and *Confronting Authority,* and ever a repository of goodwill and of tort law. I engaged him for a while and he warmed up to me reasonably well—a rare thing for an intellectual to do, off my own experience. Bell didn't have much good to say about certain other intellectuals—that might have helped the warming-up process—especially about some intellectuals yet employed by Harvard U. He left that school a few years before because he got tired of its being the only school he'd ever worked for that didn't have a "black" female law professor. He made way for one by taking leave and then the leave was made permanent, and the spot wasn't taken by a "black" woman law professor, but he'd made a noble sacrifice. As long as sacrifice doesn't evolve into self-righteousness it is good.

Bell complained about what some "black" intellectuals were frenetically overwriting in magazines, berating so-called "black leadership," "black youth," like it was *all* "black" people's fault, these things that were happening in America: "I can't understand why they are writing these things and saying these things. The only thing I can think of is—comfort."

"Whose comfort?"

"Comfort for privilege. What these fellows are doing makes them feel like what is happening is okay—deserved. Right?"

When he said "right" I told him that it had taken me some time to get around to it, but I finally realized some of what Cornel West had walled up inside the brick paragraphs in his books: "He says—at least I think he says—the key is morality."

Never converse with an intellectual and wind it up saying you sort of understand another one. Bell raised an eyebrow.

"Oh? And to think, I thought the key was economics," he said, and then he left me there to chew on my crest for a while, which I did, and contentedly.

The program began. Present were a novelist, Richard Perry; another novelist, Gwen Parker; Mr. Bell; Davida Adedjouma, a young memoirist; Judith and Martin Hamer, literary historians; Eric Copage, a *New York Times* editor and a facile compiler of authentic musings into the book form of *Black Pearls*; Bessie Nickens, a canvas artist who had created a book of photographs of her paintings, accompanied by short, sweet and simple stories (she was around eighty years old); and Terrie Williams, a publicist who had a how-to-succeed book. Yours truly was exhibited last.

I was so enjoying the remarks of others that I was surprised when the hostess, Jane Tillman Irving, said I was obliged to chip in. I went up there shakily and warned the multitude that the trouble was about to begin (another theft of mine. I was determined to make the crowd laugh by any Twain necessary). I often determine to make people laugh. I fail at this determination just as often as not, but this was one of those days when people were inclined to laugh on their own initiative. I said something that I intended to be serious. Tittering came from the crowd. My most momentous points raised a hailstorm of chuckles; my outright admonishments drew guffaws. Finally, I gave in and attempted some hilarity; but this brought down the mood of the congregation, so I went back to dead earnestness and soon even Bell's face was split ear-to-ear with a grin. One woman laughed so hard she shed tears, slipped on the wet spot they made, rolled down the aisle, out the front door, down the concrete steps, into a snowbank, laughing all the way. Even after they dug her out, she was still laughing. When it was pointed out that her hose had suffered runs and snags during her toboggan ride, and that her skin was scraped up some too, what little skin she had remaining, and that the contents of her purse had been scattered to the four winds, and that her car had been broken into, and then stolen, and then wrecked, and that there was a hefty surcharge for rolling down aisles and steps, at least there was at Harlem churches, she said, "Don't you worry 'bout me, I'll get home." Then she reached down and grabbed her ankles and let loose an encore peal of laughter that sent her rolling away again, down the icy street, happily headed to parts unknown.

Nobody would know such agreeable and resourceful "black" people even existed if they got all their information about these "black" people from more conventional modes of communication, other than their eyes, ears, fingertips and good word of mouth.

### Tanner's 1895 Oils Tell on a 1995 Day

The day grew short. I had to attend the Reginald F. Lewis Scholarship Fund Luncheon, sponsored by a fraternity by which I usually and deservedly go unclaimed. It was scheduled for 2:30 P.M. If we got there by five I figured we were doing all right. Five young men from New York public high schools were awarded with partial college scholarships by the New York alumni chapter of this fraternity. If you want to know which fraternity, ask me and I'll tell you sometime; I have come to believe they are all the same when they are giving out scholarships. This was another event that was good news to me but beneath the canvassing of the television stations and press. A teacher from the public schools calcified this point by saying, "No TV cameras are here, but if there is a gun or some other tragedy at a school, then we can't take two steps without bumping into three or four of them."

**M**y last stop was at the Michael Rosenfeld gallery. Unlike the Whitney, there was no big crowd. When the elevator doors opened, I was surprised to find myself in sole proprietorship of the place, not counting the help. "Patron" is not the right word here because I didn't have to pay to enter this exhibit. And here was beauty abounding. Elizabeth Catlett's 1994 sculpture *Woman Walking* was observed by me, alone, without any interruptions, as if I owned it. Now, this was something like. And yet there is an unnerving quality about a grand possession that makes you want to share it off to others so they can confirm its glory—and yours, by association. When you lack the confirmation of others, nagging suspicion nests amid even the purest of joys, saying that the excellence you behold is only a hollow rumor. So there was sadness involved in being all alone in the gallery—but it was a brief, piquant sadness. I walked around the sculpture, touched it, saw how I was made to see a woman walking against a strong wind that tried to blow her dress off her body. The wind and the blown dress defined one direction; her body of determination defined another.

I considered the other works, by Jacob Lawrence, Romare Bearden, et al. Then I was arrested by an oil painting by the Philadelphian Henry O. Tanner. The title of this masterpiece was *The Young Sabot Maker.* Though the exhibit was all sterling, this painting soon garnered my undivided attention. It had been done in that signal year 1895. A sabot, if you don't know (and why should you), is a wooden shoe like those for which the Dutch are famous. The old man and boy in the painting appear Dutch. The man is overseeing the process, watching a boy applying a tool to the forming shoe; shoe held fast by a clamp, boy held tight by the craft. The boy seemed oblivious to the old man's presence. The intense concentration on his face was subtle yet unmistakable to me. The pride on the old man's dour face could have easily been mistaken for impatience—and no doubt the boy had mistaken it for that often, with the old man's blessings. There was so much within that painting: fatherly devotion, familial love; pride of craftsmanship, the passing down of skill from father to son, from one to the other; the nature of craft; art itself, a showcase of all the work and skill involved in even the smallest occupations. As to the quality of the painting: It must stand before you to be appropriately appreciated. For it is a painting, you see.

I gazed at a brass button holding up the boy's overalls and idly thought he must have polished it only yesterday; at the grim old dodger's behest, no doubt. I reached out to touch it and was gently surprised to be brought back to the fact that this was merely hardened oil I touched, not a button. There was no boy, no overalls; there was only a nearly flat surface hanging on a wall in a building on 57th Street, in 1995, one hundred years removed from when the oil was wet and first applied. I stood in front of this piece of human beauty and personal circumspection and was humbled by the skill and determination explored in its creation. From this I drew my own measure of comfort, calm, strength, hope, control and security, which the Whitney exhibit and even the St. James Presbyterian Church—let alone anything else of one-note on TV or in the papers—had been unable or unwilling to provide me. I felt my trip to New York was not in vain. For a brief interlude ignorance had been beaten back. Sadly, it seems resilient.

## This Is Your Brain:
## This Is Your Brain on Television

The return to Washington from New York was uneventful, but my search was not yet done. There was still the knotty problem of getting with the intellectuals. Perhaps we will move on and let them surface as they will in other parts of the drift.

But no; I must throw in here one particular meeting. I heard that a coven of intellectuals was assembling at the Howard Law School to confront the dilemma of affirmative action. After eating plenty of garlic, I went. The meeting was held March 16, 1995, in a moot court room, James A. Cobb Memorial Auditorium, located on the Van Ness campus of the Howard Law School. The occasion was a "teleconference"—an electronic town meeting. The subject was the merits and future of "affirmative action." The coven would be exhibited. On one side of the stage: Maxine Waters, California congresswoman; Art Fletcher, lifelong Republican who helped draw up the plan for "affirmative action" in the Nixon administration; Jesse Jackson; George Curry, editor of *Emerge* magazine; and a man whom I briefly suspected of being Harold Ford, the congressman from Tennessee. I thought this a good long while until someone who was not nearsighted pointed out he wasn't Ford but Arlen Specter, senator from Pennsylvania. On the other side: Phyllis Berry Myers, of no particular office; Armstrong Williams, a radio and TV talk show host, which is nearly the same as being of no office, only worse; Robert Woodson, businessman; Juan Williams, reporter for *The Washington Post*; and, from a remote location, Shelby Steele, professor and well-regarded writer—if "well-regarded writer" is not an oxymoron, like "politically correct."

Some background on "affirmative action" is required here, since by the time you read this it will be a relic of a distant past. "AA" was once a government-implemented system of maintaining, as it was put, "goals and timetables" to ensure African-American participation in the government workforce and in the workforces of the companies who do big contract business with the government. There were three kinds: (1) court-ordered "AA" to remedy past wrongs, (2) contract compliance, and (3) "just 'cause you want to," as Jackson put it. There was a fourth, unspoken kind: sound business sense. If a percentage of your custom comes from "black" people, it stands to reason you will have some of them working to produce, channel, advertise, etc., it. If you don't, then you run a risk of seeming odd, or, worse, old-fashioned, and you are left vulnerable to a possibility of losing big profits.

"AA" had succeeded in getting people some jobs and enrollment into Ivy League and other schools, and some jobs in Fortune 500 companies—indeed, once upon a time "AA" was seen to be effective, and major players like Time-Warner and American Express had "blacks" at the top or near the top of their organizational trees.

If "AA" had existed one hundred years ago, it too would have been abolished, no doubt; but before it was, Dr. Du Bois might have found himself on the faculty at Harvard, and there would not have been enough call for an NAACP.

This progress caused by "AA" had not come without cost. Many times, it seemed the worst "black" candidates were chosen to take jobs—many times in hopes that they would fail, and buttress the theory of superiority always lurking . . . becoming more and more prevalent. People talked about increased productivity's being the goal of business, but often they meant in the personal sense. When others succeeded or produced, they felt lessened, inferiorized or even inferior, angry or let down. Such feelings are human nature, but for a "white" man to feel inferior to a "black" in America causes instant insanity on top of the more pedestrian human envy.

Likewise, many "blacks" felt that the accomplishments they made were tainted by a feeling they had been "given" their position. "Black" people would make timesaving, productive innovations, only to lie awake at night wondering if they deserved to get the credit for inventing them. When the final decade of the twentieth century commenced, the theory was propagated that enough had been done in this regard in the prior thirty years as opposed to what was wrought in the two hundred years before; the current "white" people (even the supremacists, one assumes) had nothing to do with past wrongs and should not have to "pay" for them.

How were they paying? A few of their stragglers felt they had lost or been denied a job because of a preference for "blacks" (see "bank loans," above, for the lucidity of such observations).

It was clear "affirmative action" would be knocked off as soon as the Supreme Court could get its robes over it. That body was about to silently assent to outlaw set-aside scholarship funds for academically deserving but financially strapped "black" college students; Benjamin Banneker scholarships, they were called at the University of Maryland. In the American academy many scholarships were set aside; for students of Greek ancestry, Armenian ancestry—for just about any ancestry a man could invent. There were scholarships for students with certain surnames; there were "legacy" scholarships for the children of alumni, no matter how trifling such offspring turn out to be, and some of them can stretch the far boundaries of idleness; there are many set-aside scholarships, all the way over to those for descendants of Confederate soldiers. But any such set-aside scholarships for "black" potential were beyond the pale.

"Keep in mind—'white' supremacy is a form of preference, a form of entitlement," said Steele. "Affirmative action is our way of buying our way out of real reform. Preferences have become a swindle . . ." Steele had written an article for the "Op-Ed" page of *The New York Times*, suggesting that "affirmative action" be dismantled, and, upon that dismantling, that any sort of discrimination on the basis of race or gender should be considered a felony by law. Steele happily owned up to his novelty.

He was intoning "As I wrote recently in *The New York Times*," but you know the rest. Ms. Waters chimed in: "Shelby, do you know how many discrimination cases are today backed up at the Equal Employment Opportunity Commission—at least ninety thousand of them! We can't even get 'white' people convicted for killing 'black' people and you think we can get convictions for discrimination?"

Rev. Jackson said, "Let us move from anecdote to data." I would prefer anecdote, but I was powerless to affect change. Or is it effect change? No matter. I am powerless either way.

Woodson said, "You're saying, Jesse, that we're only here—that the history and future of the 'black' community is all based on and because of the gifts from 'white' folks?"

Jackson said, "Abso-damn-lutely."

Woodson pounced like a wounded wolverine. "I'm here from my own hard work. Some of us are doing well. Some of us up on this panel aren't doing bad at all." Maxine piped in: "I welcome angry 'white' men, angry 'white' women— there's enough in America for all of us. It is not just for 'white' men anymore. And I'm not about to let this gentleman pull us apart in a class way."

Shelby eventually found time to hit Maxine back, saying, in effect, that she was more concerned with rich housewives in Beverly Hills who contributed to specific political campaigns than she was with the poor people in her own congressional district.

"That's an outrageous statement," said the cool Ms. Waters.

"Take this as an example," said Woodson. "There were one hundred and eighty broadcast licenses given to 'black'-owned companies for radio and TV. At least one hundred and thirty of those were 'flipped'—later sold to 'white'-owned companies. So affirmative action ended up as a personal gain for a very few entrepreneurs. What do you call that?"

"Your 'Republican' friends call it the American way," said Maxine. Needless to say, she was considered a "Democrat."

Fletcher said that he had set up the "affirmative action" programs, overturned the Davis-Bacon act, gone into Philadelphia in the '60s, the Nixon years, and made a proper way for "black" carpenters and other craftsmen and women into the trade unions.

Armstrong Williams cleared his throat, and someone in the crowd shouted, "Strom Thurmond! What about Strom?" Mr. Williams was a protégé of that South Carolina senator and of some other senators as well. This was fortunate for him, for without their patronage, à la Ben Chavis, he could not have made himself heard.

Woodson said, "I would give that one to Jesse. He's the expert on white people." If you are of the opinion that mud-wrestling is a surefire reliever of ennui, take it from me, it is not. Jackson said, "Westinghouse jobs did not go from 'white' to 'black'—they went from the West Side of Chicago to Mexico."

"Gennlemen," said Williams. And then he said some other predictable things against "affirmative action," not realizing, probably, that he was the perfect embodiment of it as it should not be implemented. He rented his office due to his opinions, not by his skills or off his talents. He said all the right things to the privileged and they opened their burgeoning coffers to make sure he was heard. He and Phyllis Berry Myers. And this is no knock against them. They should be known as they are: fearful apologists, not very gifted at math, science, business or art. They may in fact be gifted at one of those endeavors, but until this time have been shy about revealing it. They may spring a surprise on us at some point and, truthfully, we wish they would.

Amid a pause in the argument, Senator Specter said, "There are plenty of sins in the past, but the discrimination is still present today."

No one seemed to hear him or care.

Armstrong Williams mentioned Bob Dole, senator from Kansas, possibly President-to-be. Fletcher sputteringly interrupted to tell Williams that he was a Johnny-come-lately compared to Fletcher himself. "I've known Bob Dole since 1952!" Fletcher said. "The least he could do is return my calls. I've been a 'Republican' all my life . . . but . . ."

But there was no reason he could see to dismantle "affirmative action"—especially not since he was its architect. I was reminded of Colonel Nicholson, the Alec Guinness character from David Lean's epic film *The Bridge on the River Kwai*, based on a novel by Pierre Boulle. Colonel Nicholson oversaw the construction of a bridge under adverse circumstances at a prisoner-of-war camp. The downside was that the bridge was to be used by the "enemy"; in this case, the Japanese army during World War II. Nicholson was mostly concerned that it be a fine bridge, one that people who were not the enemy would be able to use one day, while both the enemy and friend and God in his glory would forever sing hosannas to the heavenly skills and commitment and grace of the men who had made it. After all, Nicholson's men were responsible for building it. I was also reminded of Twain's friend Jerry, the original authority on "cornpone opinions."

Williams did not seem reminded of any such folk. This was his major point, his highlight of the evening, directed toward his elder and senior, Fletcher: "It's obvious I have a different relationship with Senator Dole than you do," Williams sniffed.

Please, whatever you do, do not slander the good name of Uncle Tom by comparing him to Armstrong Williams. Such admissions as the one Williams uttered speak for themselves. Poor Armstrong was nearly hissed out of the building—not for knowing Dole, who, for all the audience knew, was a decent man. Williams was hissed for defining himself as a toady, and for not caring who knew it—least of all some students and jackleg relics from a time fast leaving. All of them had their good piece to say and ax to grind and I have not recorded what all was said in proper order or with much facility. I would have tried to do better by them, for they are not irredeemable, but again the inspiration dried too fast.

Later, as the Supreme Court refused to hear the case about the Benjamin Banneker scholarships that provided tuition for deserving "black" youngsters to go to the University of Maryland, I had mentioned something offhanded in the presence of my son about smart people having short memories. He said, "Well, it doesn't seem fair," to have money set aside for "black" students. Once again the boy eluded me. This was surely no cornpone opinion. This was what he *should* have felt at thirteen—that there should be no preferences outside merit. I was proud he applied logic, and proud that he did not fear me so much that he kept his logic to himself. In a perfect world he would be right. I was older and knew the world was far, far from perfect. His inheritance is incomplete in this way. He has not been left the perfect world. I was still proud of him and entertain hope for his prospects, if the dragon to whom he is to be sacrificed can be slain first.

## Someone's in the Kitchen with Cornel

By acclamation, the king of the "black intelligentsia" was at this juncture a fellow named Cornel West; Brother Cornel, as this self-described "radical democrat" would undoubtedly have it. The occasion of our first meeting was just so: I had been in New York at a public occasion at Lincoln Center and had there run into him. He spoke up, recognizing me. This gave me a start, for the more things you try to do, the more "black" people—most especially the intellectualized ones—will act as though they don't recognize any of it. West actually smiled and said, "Thanks for the text." He meant a book I was guilty of composing. Then he said, "Didn't you also write a memoir that reads like a novel?" Then he accurately named that book. And if his description of it was off, it was to its betterment. It was then the man became brilliant in my mind.

The second time I met him was at the Washington home of Rev. Jesse Jackson. Rev. Jackson had invited West, *The Wash-*

*ington Post* columnist Bill Raspberry and me over for conversation and proselytizing, after West and I had taken part in Jesse's TV show on the Cable News Network. When I arrived, Cornel was already there, at leisure, as were Mr. Raspberry and Mrs. Jackson. Rev. Jackson was talking up about what all he had said at the recent meeting called by the NAACP in Baltimore. And for everything Rev. Jackson *said* he said, Cornel said, "Yes, you did." Jackson said, "I told them this, didn't I, Cornel?" "Yes, you did." "And I told them that other, didn't I, Cornel?" "Yes, Reverend, you did."

Despite the meager evidence of those responses, Cornel exuded intelligence. And he seemed at peace with it even though many periodicals had taken him to task by name and said he was not as smart as they had intimated he was only a year before. Apparently he lost brain cells in the year, at least to them. Not to me, though. Cornel West is the kind of intellectual you can invite over to a clambake or a barbecue and not worry that he will make the other guests ill at ease. If you prod him he will talk about "the sheer capriciousness of our situation," and "the absurdity of 'white' supremacy," and "doubling one's efforts," and polish off the subject by saying, "I am not an optimist—I am a prisoner of hope." I admired his ability not to take over the direction of the conversation and herd it toward himself. It was well within the boundary of his abilities to do so, and in a way that you probably wouldn't notice, though Rev. Jackson probably would notice, especially in his own house.

One Mr. Leon Wieseltier mounted an attack on West in *The New Republic* on March 6, 1995—a volcanic eruption of bile that by its nature bestowed a personal bite to the attack. To paraphrase Shakespeare, the gentleman doth protest too much, methinks.

Wieseltier wrote that he had turned to Cornel, read his books, found them slacking. Actually, he did not say slacking. He said they were "completely worthless," "noisy," "tedious," "slippery," "sectarian," "humorless," "pedantic" and "self-endeared." Some of that was understandable, though I have yet to read a "noisy" book; that in itself was almost enough to make me read more of Cornel's books than I had up until that time.

But I thought this man Wieseltier and others who followed in his wake throwing tomatoes at Cornel hit West but missed the point. West is a man of an almost visible intellect—he often answered Rev. Jackson's questions just before the Reverend asked them—but that has little to do with whether he can *write* amazingly well. I would be trying to agree with all his critics if they only said West's books were as accessible as the peaks of the Himalayas, and equally inviting.

West has written a gross ton of books; ten, I think, or it will be ten by the time you read this. Most of them are written in the nomenclature used by academics. This is probably why he has been passed around the Ivy League like Ota Benga at the zoos. Cornel admits the only book he has ever written that can be read without the machete is *Race Matters*. He *admits* the rest are hard.

West was "defended" in the pages of *The Village Voice* by Ellen Willis, who wrote, "For anyone who has known and talked with West, the presence of a sharp and subtle mind is not in doubt. Yet something disturbing happens between the brain and the page, the private and public conversation, and I'm convinced that disjunction has more than a little to do with the uncritical adulation he's received." Well and so, and so much for defense. Willis has a point here, but it is a point that could be applied to anyone—herself included—who ever faced a blank page with good or bad intentions of filling it up with something amusing or instructive. It takes more than good intent to accomplish that.

So Cornel West is not Mark Twain. Well, I could have told

both of them that. West is not Ralph Ellison; nor Harlan Ellison. I could have told them that too. Cornel West is not even Ralph Wiley. They would not believe that even if I did tell them.

Being smart and being a good writer are like leadership and the NAACP—they may not be mutually exclusive, but the presence of one is no guarantee that the other is tagging along. And just what is "smart" anyway? There are some social dunderheads who are "smart." A "smart" person can't necessarily build a house, unless he has experience in the vagaries of construction. "Smart" people do not automatically make good neighbors, and we have already mentioned the lack in some of them of long-term memory. Nicotine can hook them too.

Mention of the NAACP brings this thought to mind about West: If this were a hundred years ago, the revered American institutions for which he was a marquee name would not have had him on staff—as they did not have his progenitor, Mr. Du Bois. After all, it takes only one book to prove you can write—and for Du Bois, that book was *The Souls of Black Folk*. For Cornel . . . perhaps he has not yet gotten around to composing it. *Race Matters* will have to do in the meantime. I think one day he will top that. But think of this in the interim: The most logical choice for the leadership position of the NAACP today would be Cornel West—the natural progression from Du Bois, one worthy of note, and a comforting thought. But one reason Du Bois helped create the NAACP was that he was denied access to what should have been his natural environments: Harvard and the fair Ivy League.

Cornel suffers no such fairness deprivation, but has new dilemmas. How does one leave the infrastructure of institutional racism behind, consign it to the past, without cooperation of those at the switch? Cornel does not even try. He identifies with Du Bois. He dresses in austere three-pieced suits, it is said in emulation of Du Bois himself. Much of Du Bois is unreadable as well—unreadable by volume if nothing else. It is as the French said of Dumas, who was a writer, though possibly not as smart as West: "Not even Dumas has read all of Dumas!" In West's case there are three ways you can apply that. It is hard to read him because (1) there is too much there to read and (2) some of what is there is served up in the form of academic gobbledygook and (3) Cornel is not trying to hurt anybody's feelings—unlike, say, Charles Murray, who is trying to hurt more than feelings. I'd like to ask the West-bashers this: Who is smarter, West or Murray? How good a writer is Murray? I suppose nobody can tell, especially after reading his writing. Yet there is no rush to write and print a billion articles about *The Decline of the White Intellectual*. No run on that at present. If I were you, I wouldn't hold my breath.

(A few months later, Murray was put on display before me by the Consortium for Graduate Study in Management. He "debated" a man he'd long been trying to avoid, Leon Kamin, head professor of psychology at Harvard. Murray was taken aback that the consortium consisted of perhaps six hundred M.B.A. candidates, many of whom were "black," Hispanic or Asian-American. The moderator was the peripatetic Julianne Malveaux, a "black" economist whose doctorate from M.I.T. presumably carries as much weight as Murray's. Murray should've attended broadcasting school; his presentation was so lifeless that I could barely keep myself awake. I was kept awake by Kamin's splendid rebuttals. He used transparencies and a projector to illustrate the counterfeit nature of Murray's *Bell Curve* statistics—like using test scores of "black" African copper miners instead of schoolchildren. The defining moment (the humorous one) in this debate came when Prof. Kamin overran his appointed

time and apologized—then asked if it was okay if he over-
stepped some more. "You cool," said Malveaux, in a nice
and most appreciated lapse into the relaxed vernacular.
Without looking up, or missing a beat, Kamin, an elfin
"white" scholar, said, "Right on." The room exploded with
much-needed hilarity. Everybody got it, and laughed, no
matter what camp.)

From what I could tell of two meetings with C. West, I
surmised this: His barber is in the poorhouse and his dry
cleaner vacations in Bermuda. Cornel wears a big, packed
Afro coif, and a rugged beard, and wears a watch fob on the
vests of his many dark suits. He is in all likelihood the most
intelligent man I met one particular day; he let me know it
not by what he said, but by his *silences* at the most appropriate times. I saw that Cornel West was a conciliator, a
bridge—precisely the role for him to play in this day and
time, I suppose. Agitation is best left to the writers, a fraternity Cornel might deign to come down and join one day, and
to others with their trusty, rusty bullhorns. The fact of Cornel West's brilliance seems to be quite agitation enough.

Rev. Jackson asked Cornel to move nearby. Anyone could
see that Rev. Jackson had the best house on the block, but
that didn't stop Cornel from being asked. His reply? Agreeable smile. Then silence. Then a glowing affirmation of
the brilliance being displayed by the other occupants of
the room. I had a feeling we were field mice next to him—
not in the realm of public speaking, or the netherworld of
creative writing, but in the clear, cold world-as-it-is of
*recognition*—of being aware what went on around him.
Now, if we couldn't get it out of him, what he thought about
this cold world, that says more about *our* brains than about
Cornel's.

Since the field mice controlled the conversation it turned
toward the O.J. Simpson trial. Mrs. Jackson seemed to make

the most sense about that. I threw in my two cents' worth, which shall be expanded upon later in the drift. Cornel studied us and smiled and displayed such winning and laudatory ways of making us feel adequate, making us feel at home even though he was in a strange house—why, the memory of it takes my breath away until this day.

I offered Cornel West a ride to his hotel and he was smart enough to accept it. We would cross paths later. As we rode, he was most complimentary of me and when I tried to return the favor he merely shook his head briefly and encouraged me to go on with writing. Then he said, "From what you said of Simpson, in a very subterranean way, he was a man who lived with bondage."

"And loved it," I said.

I am still thinking about that exchange.

As he exited the car, I thought of how universal was this human bondage, in one way or another. Smart or dumb, Cornel West is above all a decent man; I got that clearly and straightaway. This is a man who does not like hurting other people's feelings—though if he ever decides to do it, pray they are not yours.

"I envy you," he said, startling me into a moment's silence.

"What . . . w-why?" I stammered.

"For the independence of thought," he said.

And then he walked away, bound to his mission to bring decency and empathy to the sterile and manipulative academy, which without him would be as desolate as any pitiable urban ghetto, and equally rife with decay, because it would be without the totality of human life, skill and decency.

Cornel West is the smartest man I met, one day.

Look what it got him.

## A Boil Bursts in Oklahoma

The bomb finally went off, at 9:02 A.M. on April 19, 1995, outside the Alfred P. Murrah Building in Oklahoma City and 168 people were murdered in cold blood. Four hundred were wounded, 312 buildings were destroyed or damaged. There was the briefest pause in the chicanery of politics. People who labeled themselves "conservatives," or "patriots," had to reexamine their rhetoric—or not. When the President of the U.S., Bill Clinton, pointed this out, he was accused of "playing partisan politics." Rhetoric does not bomb buildings. People bomb buildings. But what rhetoric can do is suggest to "right-wing extremists" the time is ripe if they care to start bombing on their own—and "extremists" can usually be counted on to be consistent with consent in this regard.

And that is what happened in Oklahoma. The "extremists" were there all along. They were waiting, as they have always waited, for their moment. The politicians, radio hosts, TV daytime talk show hosts, news reporters, newspapers, magazines and even the National Rifle Association had told them (or so the waiting legions thought) that the time was ripe. But in their telling, those powers had only been getting elected, making America more "fair" again—fair meaning ad lineage, ratings and new subscribers; yes, then, the time was ripe. Why not? That is all the charlatans were doing. They felt a twinge of sadness (not much of one) that someone had taken their scandalous exhibitions and spoken and unspoken exhortations to heart when they only meant to make a profit from passions and not have anyone act on them, outside of plopping down seven dollars for the feature at the multiplex or thumbing the TV remote control or particular switches in voting booths. They thought it was merely convenient to whip everybody's fragile emotions with the

Royal Nonesuch grift done over in blackface. They did not mean to bring the system down—not *now*, when they are doing so well at it, making such a large profit from it and becoming famous and well-maintained all in a happy confluence.

The bombing threw light on "militias" in different states, showing how those more or less organized entities were being co-opted by "white supremacist" hate groups, how they were infested with men like the "alleged" bomber McVeigh, without their knowing in some cases, without their caring in some others. Paranoia had now moved beyond affirmative action and welfare mothers to include the U.S. government's taking away their guns, planting computer chips in their buttocks, building prison camps for put-upon "white" non-taxpayers who had warned of "black helicopters" of the U.N. about to take over from overhead, led directly into their homes by bar codes on stop signs and scanners printed on U.S. government currency.

The New World Order (which, ironically, was suspected by "left-wing extremists" to be the white supremacists' idea) was said to actually be their great peril—a world where other countries would take over the United States, and Chinese troops and Russian troops and troops from Hong Kong and the Crips and Bloods from L.A. would all come together as one happy force and for reasons unknown or never given, would invade Upper Michigan and Idaho and Montana and take away their guns and (here the paranoias intersect again) herd them onto trains and ferry them to the internment camps for disposal.

Some of this makes the cant of the Nation of Islam sound like Mother Goose. The unacknowledged similarity and thread within both is that the multinational corporations and not the governments now hold sway. But instead of holding the same multinational companies accountable, asking why

159

executives get $10 million bonuses while *they* get pink slips, people blame the most powerless people they can find other than themselves. They feel they can do something about *them*. People who think like that, whose lives are such a tragic dissatisfaction to them, think that once they make their final purge, they shall then become adjutants, and generals, or at least colonels, in this brave new world order of their own fantasy. And they will be respected and exalted and will become wise in ways superior to those who came before.

All that may be—but more likely, whatever they were before their purge, they will remain, no matter what world they happen to miscreate. Mere dissatisfaction in your work does not discharge a bolt from the blue, turning you into Adolf Hitler, or even Franklin Delano Roooosevelt, let alone Thomas Jefferson or James Madison. Perhaps you should be glad. I know we are.

Hitler and the Nazis enjoy a confusing but unmistakable presence in the militia and patriot "movements." They refer to Hitler constantly and compare agents of the U.S. government to Nazis. Even the National Rifle Association did it—"jackbooted thugs," it called those agents. "The Last War is Underway," it said. This from one of its fund-raising letters: "Imagine a knock on your door. It's government agents come to confiscate your guns. Are you in Gorbachev's Lithuania? Think again. It can happen right here. . . . A document secretly delivered to the NRA's executive vice-president reveals frightening evidence that the full-scale war to crush your gun rights has not only begun but is well under way. . . . The FBI has proposed immediate adoption of its manifesto against law-abiding gun owners . . . if they get what they want, gun owners like you will be Public Enemy No. 1."

After he was apprehended, one of the men (Terry Nichols) who was accused of helping construct the bomb in Oklahoma City said he didn't want to answer any pointed questions about it. He said any interrogation about the matter reminded him of "Nazi Germany." He was accused, on considerable evidence, of helping construct the bomb that killed 168 men, women and children in cold blood—but he feared Nazis were after *him*. The neo-Nazis must have laughed. The fool didn't realize how well he was doing their job for them. Half of this "right-wing movement" embraced Hitler and the Nazis openly. The other half believed themselves anti-Hitler and anti-Nazi by being anti–U.S. government. A greater fancy, that. References to "jackbooted thugs" were a *smoke screen*. Such a fascination for the Second Amendment "right to bear arms" was a *smoke screen* (in fact, the Second Amendment is so written as to be a smoke screen, of itself). The sympathy about Waco, Texas, on April 19, 1993, was a *smoke screen*. As patriotic as they claimed to be, few in the militias wanted to admit it was the fascist in them on the rise, prowling, looking to hunt. Hunt what? The end of their woes? Odds were they would only increase them.

Odds have been beaten before. But the house has the edge. That is how it became the house in the first place.

And there was some public sympathy for the bombers— make no mistake about it. Memberships in the militias grew in the months after the bombing, according to police reports. Quite a few agents of the Bureau of Alcohol, Tobacco and Firearms were videotaped frolicking at a picnic in the Tennessee hills, where such signs as "Nigger Checkpoint" and "Any Niggers in That Car?" were hung on trees. And the 1995 graduating class of an upper-crusty high school in Greenwich, Connecticut, thought it was a lark to spell out "Kill All Niggers" in a hidden way in their yearbook. People were fed up. I know I was. Other people, who just shrugged, assumed the people who were fed up were fed up with government, because, immutably, people are *always* fed up with the government. If the militias and hate groups and the jackals who fed off them had left it at that, they would have enjoyed an even broader-swelling membership. This was not the avant-garde here. The jackals had only to read Chapter 20 of Twain's *The Gilded Age, Volume II*, for the finest explanations of the timeless machinations of Congress and the legislatures. Reading that one chapter would have vented plenty of their steam, but, alas, the library too has fallen into disfavor with the "militias." When this phenomenon occurred, we do not know, but it is unfortunate and should be examined.

Without suitable reading materials such as *The Gilded Age* to while away their idle time, these "militias" used the Waco disaster as a recruiting tool. Waco was said to be what drove the bombers over the edge. McVeigh had visited the site where four Bureau of Alcohol, Tobacco and Firearms agents had been gunned to death with assault weapons by members of the Branch Davidian cult, led by self-styled messiah David Koresh. Some seventy-nine people had perished either before or during a tragic fire after a fifty-one-day siege on April 19, 1993. Well-edited videotapes of the incident sold like popcorn at big gun shows and via mail order among the disaffected people who said and possibly even thought they were only fed up with government and not something (someone?) else. A year *before* Waco, McVeigh wrote some rather apocalyptic letters to his hometown newspaper in New York State about a likelihood of civil war.

McVeigh *used* Waco—or it was used on him. All he did was fantasize it was *him* in Waco, not Koresh and his band of poor believers. Such fantasy was useful; when you have been preparing for years for a coming apocalypse that not only never arrives but never gives much hint of itself, not even when you seek it in Idaho and Montana, then you must take what you can get for inspiration. Where were these great

Constitutionalists when the MOVE group was bombed in Philadelphia in 1987? What so inspired their passion for Koresh, a man who said he was Jesus, and his band of "blacks" and "furiners"? The people who said they sympathized with Koresh, then blew up buildings and children to express their grief, also say they are dependable Christians, and then say, therefore, the government blew up its own building just to make them, the Koresh sympathizers, look bad.

Koresh was a cultist of persuasive powers. In his cult were many kinds. Quite a few "black" people were immolated in the Waco compound. Many victims were from Great Britain. Autopsies showed many were shot dead by their own people before their bodies were destroyed in the conflagration at the end of the fifty-one-day siege.

So did these "militiamen" feel sorry for this accused pedophile who slept with the other men's wives while they went celibate and ordered their mass murder to show appreciation, as cultist Jim Jones had done in Guyana? Did the militias feel so deeply for Koresh's throng of divergent followers, including the "blacks," and the descendants of the redcoats? Or did they merely need an *excuse*, a *tangent* from the crux of their matter—that they were being led by the nose by virulent "white" supremacists, and their grim business was about "race," religion and murder? On April 19, 1995, such a racist murderer, named Snell, was executed by lethal injection in Arkansas. There was confusion in the press as to whether he was done up eight hours before the bombing or thirteen hours afterward. That barely matters; it tells you more about some members of the press than about Snell. Normally, a man's being housed on Death Row impinges on his ability to stay abreast of current events. Before Snell was executed, he'd settled into a revealing monologue starting with, "Well, I had a lot to say, but you have me at an inconvenience." Which goes to show you, a man can murder a Jewish shopkeeper because he was a Jew and a "black" state trooper because he wasn't "white" and still get off a whip line even when facing the inevitable by-product of his trade.

"Governor Tucker, look over your shoulder. Justice is on the way. I wouldn't trade places with you or any of your political cronies. Hell has victory. I am at peace," Snell said. Those were his last words and an interesting selection of words it was. If you are in Arkansas, facing the bluffs of the Mississippi to the east, and look over your shoulder—there's Oklahoma. "Justice is on the way" tells you the man had dubious ideas on justice that do not coincide with yours or mine. The part about not wanting to trade places with politicians indicates a knowledge of a quandary they might soon be in—such as cleaning up bomb debris. "Hell has victory" is good. That sums up his goals and the situation of the day fairly well. It may be that Snell didn't know anything about that bombing in Oklahoma City, but it sounds to me like he might have, just saying for instance. Call me a good American lunatic conspiracy theorist if you like, but it sure sounds like he knew something. It's either that or the state of Arkansas had executed not only a double-murderer, but also one of the world's leading mentalists. If Snell knew, and he was on Death Row, others knew. Others like him. Others who admire him, the way you and I admire Mark Twain.

Snell and McVeigh thought themselves good "white" supremacists. They should see the day. Shoot a couple of people, bomb a couple hundred more—that isn't any decent kind of "white" supremacy. I've seen some "white" supremacy, and what they did doesn't cut it at all for panache or creativity. Now, importing a couple hundred thousand skilled workers from Eastern Europe and giving them jobs while cutting education funds away from American children, in-

cluding "black" ones but not necessarily limited to them—
that's what I'd call decent "white" supremacy right there.

As for the Oklahoma bombing, the media fixated from it
back to Waco—falling for the okee-doke—and to Ruby
Ridge, in Idaho, where a man named Randy Weaver, another self-described "white supremacist," now living in
Kansas, lost a wife and son to rifle fire from U.S. marshals
on April 19, 1992. Less noted here was the fact that Weaver
and his cronies killed one marshal before his wife and son
were shot, and were trying to kill even more with rifle fire
when they were shot. His fire was what drew fire in the first
place. And to take some further note of his actions, what
were his wife and son doing in the line of fire when he knew
these marshals and FBI agents were likely to shoot back?
Why weren't they hidden out? The FBI said one renegade
was shot and the bullet passed though him and struck poor
Mrs. Weaver, who probably hadn't anticipated that when
she took her vows. Weaver's son was killed in a shoot-out
with U.S. marshals before the FBI arrived on the scene. Yet
people besides neo-Nazis, for their own purposes, said,
"Remember Ruby Ridge!" on the radio. I, for one, cannot
forget it.

Just to compensate for it, I'm for letting these "revolution-
aries" *have* Montana and Idaho. Part of me will feel a pang.
I had planned on visiting Montana at one time or another
and doing a little fishing there, thereby preserving the ecolog-
ical balance of the area, for safer fish have never been
spawned than the ones I angle for. But I am prepared to
make some sacrifices. I am practiced at it. If they want to
have Idaho and Montana, so be it. You'll get no kick from
me. I'll even try to convince the government to trade with
them and bear up under the brunt of the coming U.N. on-
slaught. But somehow I get the uneasy feeling they won't be
satisfied with Montana and Idaho. I get the feeling that

wherever I am—that's the land they are not going to be able
to do without. And that's a whole other conversation.

The radio and TV talk show hosts made a federal case out
of Ruby Ridge merely to get *ratings*; the "dukes" and
"kings" and "earls" of talk radio may have even got to believing what they preached. One such luminary—the halfway
intelligent one—deserves naming: Rush Limbaugh. He is
named because he all but told people that what he was doing
was his version of satire. When he attacked the government,
which he did daily, it was a profitable enterprise for him. Ad-
vocacy can easily become an industry, and that is usually
when advocates bear close scrutiny. And Limbaugh more
than anyone else was responsible for the results of national
elections the prior fall, when the Senate and House became
"Republican"-dominated for the first time in forty years. He
allowed credit to be showered upon him then, but wanted to
stay dry where Oklahoma was concerned. To give him even
more credit, after the bombing, he wrote in *Newsweek*,
under the double heading of "Why I'm Not to Blame" and
"Blame the Bombers—Only":

> Make no mistake: What we have in Oklahoma City, very sim-
> ply, is a gaggle of bad people who did a bad thing.
> Now let me be clear and let us be civil. People who advo-
> cate the violent overthrow of the U.S. government are not
> right-wing anything; they're anarchists (*Newsweek*, May 8,
> 1995).

This outburst won Limbaugh no new friends in the "militias." They felt betrayed—betrayed that they had been given
the signal, and now everybody was trying to take it back and
say there had been none and the "militias" were acting on
their own. Some time before the partial sanity Rush displayed in *Newsweek*—sanity up to a point, for Rush said his
audience was mainstream America, yet at the same time he

was down on mainstream media, even though *Newsweek* and six hundred radio stations nationwide were not exactly backwater—Limbaugh said, "We are this close to a violent revolution in this country." It was noted Limbaugh is a political satirist and makes money at it and everyone should be aware of that. A little old lady from Arkansas named Elders made that notation; she knew everyone wasn't aware.

What was it the President said that so horrified the radio talk-show hosts and certain newspaper columnists with cornpone crumbs all over their chins? Here are some examples:

> People are encouraging conduct that will undermine the fabric of this country. It should be spoken against whether it comes from the left or the right, whether it comes on radio, television or the movies, whether it comes in the schoolyard or, yes, even on the college campus . . .
>
> . . . we must be careful or we will end up in a dark place.
>
> [There are] loud and angry voices whose sole goal seems to be to try and keep some people as paranoid as possible and the rest of us all torn up and upset with each other. They spread hate, they leave the impression that, by their very words, that violence is acceptable . . . It is time we all stood up and spoke against that kind of reckless speech and behavior . . .
>
> When they talk of hatred, we must stand against them. When they talk of violence, we must stand against them. When they say things that are irresponsible, that may have egregious consequences, we must call them on it . . .
>
> [The bombing] was not just an attack on individuals. It was an attack on our democracy, on our way of life, on our house—
>
> There is nothing patriotic about hating your country, or pretending that you can love your country but hate your government. How dare you suggest that we in the freest nation on earth live in tyranny? How dare you call yourselves patriots and heroes . . . I say this to all the militias and all others

who believe that the greatest threat to freedom comes from the government instead of those who would take away our freedom. If you say violence is an acceptable way to make change, you are wrong . . . If you appropriate our sacred symbols for paranoid purposes and compare yourselves to colonial militias who fought for the democracy you now rail against, you are wrong.

. . . The exercise of their freedom of speech makes our silence all the more unforgivable; so exercise yours, my fellow Americans. Our country, our future, our way of life is at stake. I never want to look into the faces of another set of family members like I saw yesterday. And you can help to stop it . . .

It seemed this Clinton fellow had finally said something presidential. The "conservatives" howled that he couldn't gore their ox and then leave it on their hands. It was wrong to link them with the events, they said. That they did not want to face the link doesn't mean the link was wrong. Once, a person's threat against the sitting U.S. President was considered sedition. It probably would still be, if you or I did it; but a Senator Helms from North Carolina had warned the President not to come to North Carolina, "unless he has a bulletproof vest." Of course, he later said that was satire, probably figuring no one would know the difference, and perhaps not even knowing the difference himself.

Another "white" man, kite-high on crack cocaine, crashed a light airplane into the White House. And yet another man, of vaguely described Hispanic descent, fired an assault rifle at the White House, pockmarking the building; and another man climbed the fence with an unloaded gun saying he wanted to see the President. But after the Oklahoma City bombing, the politicians said it was Clinton who "played politics," even as some people they hinted were "jackbooted thugs" (they actually had turned out to be women, children and the aged) were being buried in Oklahoma. Clinton figured they'd sing a different tune if they were the ones being shot at.

What Limbaugh wrote was correct. What Clinton said showed rectitude. To say it was wrong for Clinton to say violence was wrong was to identify one's self not with the First Amendment, or even with the Second, or with anything else outside homicidal mania.

The people who had bombed the Murrah building weren't interested in any political landscape either—only their own cornpone, their own self-approval, stemming from the approval of others they know and depend on for livelihood. "Conservatives" had won control of both houses of Congress precisely on the votes of such disenchanted men. They had already won, in the democratic sense.

So whether those who set the bomb or who didn't apologize for it admitted this or not, the bombing was about "race," "religion" and the thrill of so-called patriotism. Cyrano might not admit having a nose, but that doesn't mean it's not there.

The bombing in Oklahoma City was similar almost to the point of being identical to a bombing described in detail in a "book" called *The Turner Diaries*—a popular book among the denizens of the militia.

More pertinent to their cause and a more evocative and accurate study of life in a citizens' militia can be found in Twain's "A Private History of a Campaign That Failed," from his book *The American Claimant*. But that does come up short as inspirational propaganda to stoke the fires of Mars and keep the troops in place.

What *The Clansman* was to 1895, *The Turner Diaries* was to 1995. The ammonium nitrate bomb used in Oklahoma was described in these "diaries." In the "book," and in reality, the bomb was used against a well-populated federal building. In the "diaries" it was the FBI building in Washington. In reality, it was the Murrah building, which, one assumes, was less fortified. The bombing in the book occurs at 9:15 A.M. The bombing that took 168 lives occurred at 9:02 A.M. I suppose those thirteen minutes were enough to distance it from the fictional happenings of the "diaries." It is *clear*: The bombers sought to make the "diaries" come true.

In the "book," the ending is the "liberation" of California, via nuclear bomb, and a giddy festooning of lampposts with hanging piñatas. They are not piñatas? No, they are "blacks," "Jews," "Mexicans" and "white" women who have slept with them—especially those who have slept with "blacks." All that would be left would be "real American" men, and women those men did not suspect of faithlessness, which should make it nearly a stag affair. And all 22,784 of them would live happily ever after. Such a wonderful ending! I could write for a hundred years and never come up with an ending so popular. For even I am not immune to this ongoing public stimulus. There are times I want to kill certain "black" people myself. I usually get over it in a matter of hours—a week, at most. I want to wipe the slate clean of them myself—or at least as they are portrayed on the screen, described on radio, in newspapers and art. But sometimes I buckle when I hear what "black" people actually *say*, notice how they actually *act*, as *individuals*, and realize how essential to my peace of mind is their fate. I hear how their young invariably play music too loud—unlike the way we did when we were young. I know the truth is not what people loudly pronounce that it is. The truth is usually nearer to what people are trying to hide—and unsuccessfully trying to hide it because the truth has a glow of its own, and it seems to burn brightest between the lines.

Of what little I have learned the hard way, I believe that

not the "black," "white," "Jew," "Muslim," "conservative," "liberal," "Catholic," "Protestant," "Republican," "Democrat," "militia," "government" or any other manifestation of "us vs. them" will win out. I think decent people will win out—or at least write more books. And if the decent do not win out, I hope they lose in such a way that the winners aren't looking for them the next day.

What's an epoch or two anyway? A week after the bombing, a report from the Associated Press revealed that two scientists from George Washington University had found and properly dated spear points carved from animal bones in eastern Zaire, near the border of Uganda. These ancient tools had grooved rings at one end, the better to lash them to the end of a staff. They were used for fishing expeditions that apparently were more successful than any I have mounted: The anthropologists had also found the bones of a six-foot catfish along with the spear points. They did not find any remains of hush puppies and coleslaw, but then it was found these barbed spear points were so old, carbon-14 dating was pretty much wasted on them. They predated hush puppies. Similar carved bone spear points had been found in Europe and dated from 14,000 years ago. And 14,000 years later, here we sit bickering. The barbed spear points found near the Ugandan border (have you ever been to Uganda? It is one of the fairest, greenest lands on the good Earth; but there, as here, it is the people who are the problem), those spear points, as I was saying, were believed to be *90,000 years old*! So we are talking about *six additional epochs in between*!

Is it our role in history to help bring about a new epoch of hanging gardens of dead bodies? I wonder if neo-fascists think they can manage this slaughter and then become respected fathers, listening to Wagner, dandling grandchildren on a knee, praying to a just God on Sunday? And this slaughtering is not going to come easy. For how does one know whom to kill first? In America, when you kill en masse, you are killing some of everybody. One would-be Goebbels from the Great Northwest said, "This place [America] is going to look like Bosnia! . . . [The color of] your skin is your uniform!"

That is a good one—to begin to slide a coming apocalypse toward Bosnia. U.N. troops on the soil. Civil War. The imagery works—only this ain't Bosnia. Some people would have it be that way, though, and they are not "black" people—or at least, not the people with darker skin. So now *Bosnia* will be used by the "militias" and their burgeoning underground, so they can have a reason to live and fantasize that *they* are the ones being fired upon. Here is where the infantile denial rises up to bite them on the redass. Just how will *color* help you identify "black" Americans? Your saying that all the "white" blood in "black" America is beside the point makes you all the less likely to recognize hundred-percent-pure "white" blood on the hoof. If you kill everyone you suspect of being "black," then you are going to kill *everybody*, because you suspect *everybody*, because that is the nature of paranoia. Some Jews have the same uniform too. How are you going to tell them apart—particularly those married to Gentiles and with children? The murderer Snell killed a pawnshop owner because he was a Jew—only the man *wasn't* a Jew. And he was a retired policeman. How do you tell whom it is women have slept with before? You could get rich quick without slaughtering if you would bottle that mystery and put it on the open market. And what about decent "white" people? Are they going to align themselves with those who would bomb innocent children to smithereens then rationalize that civilian noncombatants must be sacrificed? Is there still right and wrong? Who do you think is on the right side in this epoch? Let us personify the dilemma for them, for they are unlikely to on their own. Let's say they want to go after Shaquille O'Neal's head. Will they kill Hulk Hogan, O'Neal's friend, first or last? Oh, O'Neal will move Hogan out of the way to meet them. They might get him first. But he's so strong and *smart* he might offer up greetings of his own even if they do. How do they ever turn their backs to Hulk Hogan again after that? What have *they* ever done for Hulk? Or anybody else? The paranoids in and out of the "militias" will call *each other* government agents, in a heartbeat, and call their best friends traitors because they might not care for the government but stop short of putting the face of this inevitability on dead children. So the friends must go too. So when does this slaughtering stop?

The answer, I think, is never.

I suppose "patriots" would not ponder such questions. They don't seem to be ones for pondering. They'd commence slaughtering and sort out who later. But after the slaughter is done and the people in America are the privileged color and women are all back in line—then what? What is the nobler nature of these "men"?

As to this nature, Mark Twain was on the record, from his time as a young prospector and budding journalist in the Nevada territory, mid–nineteenth century, "the good old days." While it is incontestably true that at the time some "red" people were in Nevada, "yellow" people cooked, cleaned and built the railroads, and none of them would have been there at all if the "black" pioneer Beckwourth hadn't found safe passage through the Sierras, the official society of the new Nevada territory was in the shape that current "militias," "patriots" and "survivalists" would return it to today. As far as the eye could see, there were only "white" men all about, living under no aegis of any federal government, wearing guns in open, you might even say conspicuous, ways. So this test-case society consisting solely of armed "white" men freed of the long arm of the law has already existed on this continent. You say there is reason to pine for it? How was it better, superior, more morally upright? Thrall us if you can with tales of its compelling, overwhelming magnificence. Would there be no more hatred, blood feuds, pain, jealousy, sloth, suffering, mendacity, crime, stupidity or ignorance? Did it come upon a more reliable way to catch a fish? Mark Twain, who was there, in person, found time to take crisp, neat notes in *Roughing It*:

> The first twenty-six graves in the Virginia [City] cemetery were occupied by *murdered* men ... The reason why there was so much slaughtering done was that in a new mining district the rough element predominates, and a person is not respected until he has "killed his man." That was the very expression used ...
>
> In Nevada, for a time, the lawyer, the editor, the banker, the chief desperado, the chief gambler and the saloon-keeper occupied the same level in society, and it was the highest ...
>
> Vice flourished luxuriantly during the heyday of our "flush times." The saloons were overburdened with custom; so were the police courts, the gambling dens, the brothels, and the jails—unfailing signs of high prosperity in a mining region—in any region, for that matter. Is it not so? A crowded police-court docket is the surest of all signs that trade is brisk and money plenty. Still, there is one other sign; it comes last, but when it does come it establishes beyond cavil that the "flush times" are at the flood. This is the birth of the "literary" paper ...

## Not the End

The next afternoon the sky turned slate grey then nearly pitch black. A rumbling squall line came through the area. A funnel cloud touched down three blocks from where my son lives, six blocks from the park where he commits baseball and basketball in his spare time. A few hours later I drove by the shattered business fronts, the bricks that were once their facades lying in piles; they had been toppled by a tornado. The sky had cleared as quickly as it had darkened, though vestigial winds remained. A boy whose face I knew came running down the street from the direction of the park. The boy yelled toward me. I couldn't hear him at first—nor did I want to, considering what boys are in the habit of yelling. I was calm, distracted, aloof, withdrawn—until I made out what he was saying over the wind. Suddenly I could not see anything but him or hear anything but this: "Colen's shot! Colen's shot up at the park!"

I never knew what the expression "my blood ran cold" meant until that moment. I surely know what it means now. My son was at the park. My car was behind a road-block fashioned to keep traffic away from the destroyed building fronts. I vaulted from the car, sprinting in limping, desperate fashion toward the park. Within a few dozen steps my breath came in ragged gasps, my legs burned like the fires of perdition and my surgical knee locked up—and all that only made me run faster. I dashed into the park and there was my son on the cement court, on one knee, the front of his grey sweatshirt flecked with crimson bloodstains.

"NOOOO!" I screamed, racing over to pull him off his knee. The other boys gave way, which is not their method anymore; it must have been something in my eyes. His eyes were still open, and if his eyes were open he had a chance. I am not a strong man but I lifted him as if he were a newborn child and was about to sprint back to the car and head for the hospital when through a reddish haze I heard him protesting, then felt his muscles bunch as he broke from my desperate grip and landed lightly on his own two feet. It is hard to hold back a thirteen-year-old boy who doesn't want to be held, and sometimes it's best not to even try.

"What's wrong?!" he said.

"Are you shot?! ARE YOU SHOT!?" I said, frisking him.

"What? . . . Dad . . . quit it."

"The blood on your shirt!"

"Had a bad hangnail. It tore off and bled pretty good and I didn't have anything else to use. Nothing else available."

My relief? Indescribable. When I thought about it, I knew the boy had not been yelling, "Colen's shot up at the park!" He had been yelling, "Colen's *hot* up at the park!" The wind had whistled through the frame of the stripped buildings and distorted what I'd heard; I had not read him properly. The wind had taken his words and changed them, without the benefit of any ears and mouths in between to do the work instead. I had misunderstood.

As the other boys looked on at their playmate and his disturbed father, I tried to assume a posture of normalcy.

"So. Heard you were hot up here."

". . . little warm, I guess," he said.

I apologized . . . ". . . sorry . . ." and sat as if in a dream and watched him play a while longer, but his mind was no longer on the game. We rode home together and not much was said. I was sheepish (but not much embarrassed, not much at all). He was embarrassed for me. "I'll be all right," he said finally. "I can take care of myself. I'll handle it." He looked at me so to be sure I knew that he meant what he said next: "I'll *hannel* it."

I trust him. It is the rest of the world I do not trust. Knowing what you now know, having spent with me a day on exhibit—can you blame me? Oh, sure, certainly, you can *say* you blame me. But can you *mean* it? No need to answer. I think I been there before.

# 4

# The Necessary Illusion

*Before there was a* Final Solution, *there was a first one . . .
[then] a second, and . . . a third. [T]he descent into a final
solution is not a jump. It's one step, and then another. . . .
Construct an interior "enemy" and use that "enemy" as
both focus and diversion . . . [Use] overt and coded name-
calling, verbal abuse . . . [R]eward mindlessness and apa-
thy . . . [G]ather from the "enemy" collaborators who agree
with and sanitize the process of dispossession . . . [P]atholo-
gize the enemy . . . [R]ecycle "scientific racism" and the
myth of racial superiority . . . [Then] "criminalize" the enemy, [allowing you to] prepare, budget for and rationalize the
building of holding arenas, especially [for] the males and absolutely [for] the children. Last, maintain at all costs
silence . . .*

    —TONI MORRISON
       Charter Day Convocation Speech at Howard University
       March 3, 1995

"Luke . . . eento my eyezzz," said Madame Z.

"My name is not Luke," I replied. I had come into Madame Z.'s rooms for a reading. She is a seer known far and wide for her magical powers—and also for being far and wide. The body of her wisdom was buried beneath a Bedouin tent of black broadcloth. It settled over the room much as night falls over Egypt; to say she was a big woman would deny her full due. I came to ask about relationships between "black" people and religion. I desired my fortune told as well, and wouldn't turn my back on any pleasant revelations concerning myself and the afterlife. But first I had to unscramble her speech so that I might understand and translate it, as needed, to lessen your burden here.

"Not *Luk*," she said. "*Luke*."

"Oh, *look*," I said. "Where is that accent from?"

"Eet's univairsal. Gzherman. Russzian. Japaneze. Spanich. Slaffick. Nigzerian. Freunch. Arabeeck. Eetalian. Svaheelee. Mandahrin. Eenglish. And American. Veddy."

"American? . . . I see."

"*Do* you?" she said. "Do you see ze Necessary Eelooshun?"

"No, to tell the truth. Maybe if you'd open the drapes. Oh, those are not drapes. That is a sleeve of your dress. Lovely material. Madame, could I ask you to answer this question? Can religion save my son from an earthly perdition? I want to know, and will double your fee to include a good fortune for me . . . Any thoughts you have in transmittable form on another subject would be accepta— Oh all right, I'll take the so-called illusion too, if there's no extra charge."

"Come," said Madame Z.

A twitching of broadcloth, a creak, and the great pile moved of its own accord. I followed this thundercloud into a darkened parlor. It was a well-lit parlor until she entered it.

"Ees there enough room?" she asked.

"There would be if I was a wire hanger."

"Can you see me?"

"You, and little else."

She removed her shawl, and pitch darkness became navigable. She sat surrounding a crystal ball. I will do my best to translate, keeping in mind the limitations of the alphabet and of my ability to transcribe a shaky memory with it. "You must see the Illusion," she said. "Then the rest will be clear." Her big eyes rolled up into white. I heard her voice though her lips did not move. I've seen ventriloquists do this and did not come back for seconds.

*"Ommmm . . . In America, the 'whites' must see the 'blecks' as irredeemable . . . ommmm, and the 'blecks' must see the 'whites' as able to be redeemed . . . Ommmm."*

I opened negotiations immediately. "That's boiled nonsense. Neither statement is true," I protested. "Though I do admire how you throw your voice and roll your eyes around. I knew a skinny, knock-kneed girl once who could take her eyelids and—"

"Of course it is not true," she said. "That's why it's an illusion. It's what you must see for the prophecy to come true."

"If you don't mind, could we skip to the prophecy part?"

"Very well . . . you shall die."

". . . You must do a lot of repeat business, giving out prescriptions like that. Be for real. Who *won't* die, Madame?"

She and her Voice ignored me and my attempted sarcasm. She now spoke for herself again. No need for parlor tricks. "You will die with a pomp. You will be executed—hanged." She uttered the last word with an outrushing of breath. When she said "hanged," I knew she had not missed lunch; I wished with all my heart for the disembodied Voice's return. I did not take the news well either.

"What will I do to buy that fate?"

"Nothing."

". . . Forgive me if I don't take it, then. It's too sad."

"Sad? A celebration! You shall be a murderer, a despoiler of women, an imbecile, and once established and famous, you shall twist. Your remains shall burn. Children shall dig graves—"

"Stop! That's terrible! Worse than that dress!"

"Not so very terrible. Before you are ex-e-cu-ted"—she lingered over the word, making it a sentence—"you shall be on television. The finest interviewers will treep over themselves to beat a path to your cell; people who never met you shall explain what makes you tick; your name will be on every lip; your visage on each screen; picketers shall hold candlelight wigils; lonely women shall write billets-doux proposing marriage, fil-ums shall be made about you; you shall be more notorious than a person has any right to eck-*Spect*. You will haff a kingly leisure until the day you ha-a-a-ng." (Lunch included garlic.) "As for hang-ging,"—and bacon—"as you say, you are going to die anyway. What matter the method?"

"I might kick some about the method."

"You are sure to."

"I mean kick *before* the hanging, Madame. I might want to know why I am being accused of a hanging offense. Why hang me?"

"I can only talk about your past, and how you came to such a turn." She angled her face to and fro like a bird's as she said this, waving her fingers sinuously in the air, laughing in a throaty, ominous rumble—all this theater, as if knowing the past implied the same set of obscure talents as knowing the future.

". . . You have always been of a criminal nature. When you were thirteen you resented hard work and escaped it as often as possible. As a sixteen-year-old you stole bologn-ya only because you were hungry. At twenty-one you met a woman and wondered what it would be like to help her test mattress springs. Demon uff life! You made her like it?!! At twenty-five, you committed speeding wiolations. At thirty, inured to a life of crime, you became an editor. You missed only being elected to Congress to complete your reign of terror."

At this (and no projectiles accompanying it) I brightened. "You mean if I run for Congress I will be spared the noose?"

"No," she clucked. "You will still hang. You will hang last but you will still hang. The hanging part is not optional."

"Madame, please, you are taking up all the air and it is getting harder for me to draw breath in here. And as far as the h—execution goes, I don't believe it. I have not hurt anyone."

"If you are religious, you might be saved."

"So, then! I am a good Christian! So I will not hang?"

"I did not say you would not h—why do you move away?—hang. I said you might have salvation. That will come after you hang."

With my face now at the bottom of the door in search of some fresh air I loudly insisted, "Then I am no religious zealot!"

"Not yet . . . Why do you talk to the door?"

"It answers me in a way I can live with . . . Does it matter what religion I am?"

"Not to me or your executioner. But if you were Muslim or agnostic or even a true Christian, it would go easier on you."

"How's that?"

"You'd hang quicker."

"I wish you wouldn't say hang. I wish you would say I'll be shot, or broadsided by a bus, or bitten by snakes, or stung by jellyfish, or pecked by ducks and geese—anything but hang."

"You do not wish to hang?"

"Almost as much as I wish not to hear you say it again."

I could parry no further. She left me bereft of repartee and low on oxygen. Undaunted, she prattled on: "You know of the April 19, 1995, bombing of the Alfred P. Murrah Federal Building in Oklahoma City[1] where many American children, 'bleck,' 'white,' 'brown,' 'red' and 'yellow,' plus combinations, were injured or keeled? When the bomb was reported and everyone rushed to the site, were not the watchwords 'Islamic fundamentalists'? Did not everyone whose business it is to know say this was the work of 'Islamic fundamentalists'? And when it came out that they were fundamentalists of a more Christian variety, were they called 'Christian fundamentalists' or 'evil monsters' or 'terrorists'? No. They became 'an ad hoc group of tax protestors.' Everyone said, 'Let us go back to church.' A minute before, church had been the last thing on their minds. They wanted to go to war. You did too. So if you would consider becoming a Muslim—not forever, but long enough for the idea to take hold around you—combining that with being a nig—being urbane, I guarantee an early departure for you."

"In that case, I was born Christian and will die Christian and in between I'd just as soon not be anything—"

"Too bad. Men are quick to kill over the proper way to worship God. What denomination are—were—will you be?"

"Oh, I kind of float. I don't mind good proselytizing of any stripe when I hear it. I stand willing to be converted—I just wish you wouldn't convert me with a bullet or a noose. In my youth I admired the sense of timing and the musical swaying of the Baptists but was made senseless by the interminability of their encroachments upon the Sabbath. I think it was my snoring during the two o'clock sermon that gave me away, and caused them to cast me out from Beulahland. I was led in orthodoxy by Methodists in my youth and have not gotten over what I read in the Bibles they keep over there. I hoped they were not *all* like that; there had to be more encouraging Bibles than those kept close by the Methodists. So then I checked into the Presbyterians. But their Bibles too laid responsibility for their editing on some fellow named King James. If I were him, I would try to lay it someplace else. No child of mine would be frightened witless by any supernatural tales, without me around to provide my own explanations. I searched on for a denomination that would not require as much of it. I jumped up and down with the Pentecostals, but the Holy Ghost did not visit me when it was propitious, seeming most distant as the plate passed. My fervor was less than expected even on occasions I thought the spirit did invade. The Pentecostals recommended me back to the Presbyterians with a shove I thought a bit hard. On my way, I smelled incense and listened to incantations from the Catholics but couldn't get the dialect down. The hymns all sounded as if they were written for wakes. The jolliest ones barely drew two pats out of my foot."

"Well. In order to hang you we can always fall back on religion, but maybe— Don't I know your face from somewhere?"

"I've never met you before."

"But I haff met you. On television. An artist sketched a picture of you and it appeared on television and in the quality newspapers in connection with the Smith case[2]—that poor woman! You carjack her car, rip her Michael and Alex from her arms!"

"I did not! I was nowhere in the vicinity!"

"Do you want prophecy or must you spit? You didn't keel them but it's better if you take it. Otherwise it's un-American."

"I can live with that! I'm already seen as un-American by plenty of patriotic Americans!"

"You haff no choice."

"So I'm ruined, then?!"

"No! This is natural—that you will be inferior, criminal, sacrilegious, then hang. First you will be celebrated. Men will defend you, women will weep, children will know your name—such children as the bomber and the Smith woman haff left alive."

"Yes! She drowned them! He bombed them!"

"What hay can be shtacked by that? It would cause a self-examination, make people question their televisions, listen to their children and even treat their neighbors kindly. It will all go better and be much easier to swallow if you admit the crime."

"No one would believe me!"

"*Au contraire*—everyone would believe you. Not in their subconscious minds, in the mind of their loving God, but in the conscious minds of self-approval. Subconsciously, everyone—'white,' 'black,' 'TV show producer,' 'host,' 'detective,' 'sheriff,' 'reporter,' 'accused,' 'preacher'—everyone knew by the fourth day of the nine-day search that something was wrong with her story."

"I knew it before that!"

"But you said nothing, even though the woman continued to appear on television with her story and the sketch of you—"

"That wasn't me!"

"—whatever—even when everyone knew she was lying, she was allowed to continue a televised performance. You are so shtupid. Everyone knows 'blecks' are too shtupid to know anything. That book, *The Ding-Dong*, it states 'white' people are smarter—"

"It's not *The Ding-Dong*, it's *The Bell Curve*, and both it and you are preposterous! The Smith woman was mad! *In*-sane!"

"... Yes, the Smith woman may haff been driven mad after what she had suffered. It was said she was sexually initiated by her stepfather. Yet she was a friendly, well-liked girl in high school in spite of it, not making her life's miseries public. She was no whiner. She loved her husband, father of her two boys. He was unfaithful. And to her, of all people. She was twenty-three years old in an uncertain time when it would have been better to be fourteen, or eighteen, or forty-four, or sixty-four, or thirty—any age but the dreaded twenty-three. We have all been twenty-three. We know how painful it is. She was a woman divorced—a pain so exquisite only married people can endure it. She had two sons to care for, which can drive you insane in short order unless you are committed to it, and even then ... Her new lover was the son of a wealthy man. He broke off with her. She thought he would ask her to marry him. He did not bite— To top it off, she had roof, car, health, job—but what is that to a woman who needs a man to show off? What kind of self-respecting woman suffering such deprivation would *not* go insane, *not* drown her children?"

When Madame began her litany about the Smith woman I had felt pity. Toward the middle of the list I wept and was ready to take the rap, even prepared to pay her way through college. By the middle I mentally saved myself the tuition, and toward the end, I had dried up considerably. By the finale, I was choked with a gleeful roar of a strangely good-humored indignation.

"It is the image we are talking about," said Madame Z., politely ignoring my mood swings. "The image of one color of villainy is one we need. As for you, well ... it would be easier to bear if there was a corpse of a 'bleck' man in the driver's seat of that car in the bottom of the lake in South Carolina."

I stood on unsteady legs. "She may have been mad, Madame," I said, "but mad or not she knew who to blame to throw the scent off her trail. I cannot avoid my fate. Though the people couldn't be stupid enough to believe this, it was publicized, and they did believe it. Even when they stopped believing it, they still publicized it. Since children were being abused and even murdered by parents every day (or vice versa) the only reason this case became so prominent was my presence in the scenario!"

"At last you catch on quick," said Madame Z. "You make the thing work as an entertainment, 'bleck' man! You are a shtar! Revel in it!"

"I pass! How can you tell me of inherent inferiority of the minds of 'bleck,' I mean, 'black' people, and then, ha-ha, at the same time announce on television that a 'black' carjacker, ha-ha-ha, the dumbest of the dumb, eludes capture by the intelligence of combined law enforcement agencies for nine days, ha-ha-ha-ha! How can it be believed during the midst of the publicity campaign for your *Ding-Dong* that one of the dumbest 'blacks' could appear in a small town in South Carolina in broad daylight without being seen, 'jack' a lone car stopped at a stoplight, a stoplight that never turned red to make a car stop unless another car was at the intersection; believe that he could tell a mother to get out of a car and forget her children, and believe that her fear of him would be so deep it would outweigh the maternal instinct; believe she would leave her children in that car, and that the carjacker would take the time to tell her he didn't have time to put the children out, though he had time to put her out, then tell her how much time he was short on; then believe he could evade a constellation of law enforcement in all its intelligent glory, with two hungry, rambunctious boys in tow, for eight solid days!

"People not only believed this, they *embellished* it, in the true if not the best American style! One woman said 'the "black" man drove the car up a ramp into a waiting semitrailer and them kids are gone for sure.' She is up for a literary award now. People had added their own creativity to the Smith woman's story, like first-time novelists making gumbo by committee!

"Smith welcomed the national cameras every morning, like clockwork, to get everybody going better than coffee. The cameras were there to be let in, willing to use and be used in the cause and decoy of caring about children—although other children had been abused and murdered (or vice versa) during the eight days' time. There was something special about the Smith case. People were fascinated by it. That was how television producers framed their greed. The Smith woman cried, such as she could muster it, pleaded for the return of her children until her own brother-in-law said to the camera, gazing into the carjacker mirage and the looking glass, 'If you have any morals, don't hurt those children!'

"How could she have you believing it, wanting and needing to believe it? The television cameras even sought out the boys' paternal grandmother and stayed on her because she was photogenic and spoke well about anguish involved in kidnapped grandchildren. After it came out that the Smith woman drowned her children, a woman with a microphone standing in front of a camera broke into even such a private moment of despair and asked the grandmother, 'Don't you hope there's some kind of explanation for this?' The grandmother looked into the callous eye—God bless her sanity—and said, 'Explanation?' She did not call the woman a blasphemous name—God bless her patience. She said, 'There is no explanation for murder!'

"Outside of her, why, you are *all* insane, and I'm in the car with you! Ha-ha-HA-ha! Yes, I *do* have the boys. They're in the backseat! We just drove up here from South Carolina! They *asked* to come along. They said, 'Please take us with you, mister. Mama's been acting funny lately. Can we stop off at McDonald's?' "

"You're getting the hang of it, all right," said Madame Z. "You will be famous soon, well-defensed, you will liff well . . ."

"And then hang," I said somberly.

"Why dote on that? Tell me. Do you remember the anger at the beginning of the Smith case and after the Oklahoma bombing? The righteous indeegnation? The fervor for justice?"

"Yes."

"What happened to it? After the Smith killer was found not to be a mentally deficient 'black' carjacker but Smith herself, why then was there no measurement of brains and 'morals'? After the Oklahoma bomber was said to be McVeigh, why did he not stay a 'terrorist' or 'evil monster,' but became a member of an 'ad hoc group of tax resisters representing militias concerned with the Second Amendment'? Why did the anger go away? Why was it that all people could do with the horror, fear, anger and passion over the crimes was to translate those responses into religion and say Let us pray?"

". . . Because, Madame Z., in prayer there is a moral salvation. The paradox is that by praying Americans go right back to where they started. For if they were not hypocritical in their prayers in the first place this kind of immoral conduct could not continue. The only way out morally is for 'whites' to see 'blacks' as less human—incapable of morality and thus unbound by its constraints, not subject to its causes and effects. Only if I were thought of in this way could I be executed for no reason but to clear the name of a criminal who wouldn't fit the profile—executed without remorse, culpability or sense of indelible sin attached. That is why 'blacks,' and 'whites' most of all, cling desperately to this illusion of yours; why they need to believe, and not in religion, but in this illusion. The 'religion' has become money. Product. Personal gain. Material wealth. The trappings of such wealth. Those are the idol gods of this repugnant illusion of yours.

"As you say, Madame, the end result—of 'whites' believing all 'blacks' are inhuman, and of 'blacks' believing not all 'whites' would *act* on this belief that they were inhuman—is my own execution."

"You haff done well," said Madame Z. "Now go."

"By saying I've done well, I take it, you mean you do not want money for services rendered in allotting me this 'fortune'?"

Madame Z. scowled, then said, "Next Christmas, if you have not been hung before then, bring me by a goose or a turkey."

That was fine with me, because it was only June then, and . . . But that would be a whole other story . . . wouldn't it?


**S**eriously, is it right to inflate murders for "commercial" purposes because a "black" person committed them? Is it right to lionize murderers of any stripe? Is it right to kill when we do it in God's name? Is it right to ignore killing, even that done in the name of God? Is it right to profit from murder in the unspoken name of politics, or journalism, or any other of the more profitable entertainments? Is it wise to do this? Is it safe?

No amount of hymn-hurling, polling or check-cashing exempts us from knowing between right and wrong. There is no explanation for murder and no excuse for profiting from it. We learned that first in church unless we were held hostage in a proper home first. The lamest excuses for murder are "religion" and "patriotism," with "passion and love" a hard-charging third. We shan't speak of the "patriots" among us. They will be heard from often enough. To the others I ask: If God wanted folks to kill folks, wouldn't God have given out sharper claws, poison sacs, bigger incisors, or no good conscience? If God did bestow consciences, who is responsible for removing them? Dare we cite "zealots"? Dare we mention "lovers"? Dare we indict "patriots" and risk being hanged? Or dare we not?

# 5

## Wynton Marsalis and the Tyranny of Genius in a 12-Bar Form

*The 12 notes in each octave and the varieties of rhythm of-fer me opportunities that all of human genius will never exhaust.*

—IGOR STRAVINSKY

Zero hour, hip-hop nation time, in a Doggy Dogg, post–Cold War world of entropy where the enemy is us,[1] to let the six o'clock bad news tell it. Consumer perishables are hawked on television and radio to relentless and monotonous beats; sold on billboards with slogans like "Serve, Then Chill," and "Two Cold." And that would be the most pleasant information you get. You are informed quickly and loudly when an abused eleven-year-old Chicago boy with a necklace and a belt of cigarette burn scars named Robert Sandifer shoots a fourteen-year-old girl in the head, then is shot in the head himself by his gang member surrogate fathers and then put on the cover of national magazines. The boy's mother, second-generation welfare illiterate with a taste for the crack pipe, couldn't have cared less, and you can see it in her attitude. A song is about to debut on the R&B charts titled *Your Love Is a 187*. You know 187 is police code for homicide. But *how* do you know? Thirty-eight thousand pairs of shoes are delivered to the Mall in Washington, D.C. They once belonged to gunshot murder victims. Wild, wild West. Handgun made every thirty seconds; at the movies, Oliver Stone's violent *Natural Born Killers* more in keeping than the formulaic idealism of *Forrest Gump*. Drowning in a sea of images of chaos. It is August of 1994, the heat is thick and stifling, the living anything but easy. A dis-ease is in the air. Outside 59th Street subway station in Manhattan, bent men in ragged clothes with matted hair shuffle about holding paper bags around cans of potable napalm boasting enough alcohol content to barbecue livers in short order. These men are of all complexions. But your eye is somehow captivated only by the darker ones. Some shirtless young "black" men, the more enterprising ones, drum out a racket of mad polyrhythms on overturned plastic buckets, hoping loose change is tossed their way. One appears to be an idiot savant, showing only the whites of his eyes. His beats are the most wildly intricate.

Well within earshot, the trumpet virtuoso and composer Wynton Learson Marsalis cleaves undetected through the stiff waves of August heat toward nearby Lincoln Center, off Broadway. He is the silvery brown dorsal fin, indicative of something far more substantial than what appears on a seemingly uniform surface of craven images being jammed down your throat.

On August 7, Marsalis strides into Lincoln Center to debate James Lincoln Collier, author of *Jazz: The American Theme Song*. The debate results from a note Marsalis sent to *The New York Times*. In the letter, published December 19, 1993, Marsalis wrote Collier was "a poseur . . . who attempts to elevate himself above his subject matter . . . [Y]ou won't see [Collier] at any public gathering of musicians debating or discussing specifics of jazz." Collier picked up the gauntlet, responding in a letter published in *The Times* in February 1994, saying Marsalis "has never done any scholarship and does not understand the scholarly method."

Marsalis is "black," Collier is "white"—as if you hadn't guessed. Marsalis is the purveyor of some of the most perfect man-made sounds outside Aaron Neville's larynx. Marsalis is also co-founder and artistic director of the Jazz at Lincoln Center series, and conductor of the Lincoln Center Jazz Orchestra, which, according to its own publicity for the 1994–95 season, "has over the past ten years provided the most exciting succession of events in American performing art." Marsalis took the position of artistic director in 1993, brought in new musicians and his own ideas, and insisted the program be run in a manner he saw fit. He was as immediately challenged in the New York press by "jazz critics," and now in particular, beginning in this second year of his regime, in an informal debate with James Lincoln Collier. You would think Marsalis needs all this like a hole in the head. Traditions of WASP ascendancy and institutional control are one thing, art is another. But it is August 1994; the country is headed toward a dark place. When you ask how long he will stay on as artistic director of the Jazz at Lincoln Center series and the Lincoln Center Jazz Orchestra, he smiles and says, "Forever."

You think he is being naive or overconfident or humorous when he says this, and you choose to assume it is the latter.

You have already knocked at his apartment near Lincoln Center, using the familiar pattern of the opening Allegro from Mozart's *Eine kleine Nachtmusik*:

Knock . . . knock/Knock . . . knock/Knock/knock/Knock/KnocK/KNOCK.

You hear him chuckling as he opens the door, offering a slight bow and a knowing smile. Marsalis played the Brandenburg Concerto No. 2 with his hometown New Orleans Symphony at sixteen, and auditioned for the Tanglewood Festival in Massachusetts at seventeen (he made the grade); he finds his audition's adjudicator, conductor Gunther Schuller, still seeking him out for all-night talks on a yearly basis. Marsalis went to Juilliard at eighteen, played with Art Blakey and the Jazz Messengers at nineteen; by twenty-five he had been awarded eight Grammys for jazz and classical recordings; by thirty-two he had released thirty-two album-length recordings, eleven classical, twenty-one jazz, including '94's release *In This House, On This Morning*, whose theme is a Sunday church service. The final four cuts, beginning with *Recessional* and ending with *Pot Blessed Dinner*, are (to your ear) as original, sinuous and melodic as any music Louis Armstrong ever played. (Marsalis would consider that evaluation sacrilegious.) Marsalis is also said to have twenty more original compositions, including the Lincoln Center–commissioned work *Blood on the Fields*, polished and banked, waiting for a market that does not appear to be there.

Thus you expect to meet a genius, but a brooding one. So it is a pleasant surprise when what you first notice about Marsalis is that he seems *happy*. You are to find he is most especially happy when he can do battle. The battles he's "chosen," especially Wynton vs. craven images of hip-hop, or "rap music," seem unwinnable for anyone short of mythic proportion. Ulysses bested Cyclops, Quixote won hearts, Ali beat Liston. But will Marsalis outlast hip-hop?

And why, and to whom, is that even a question?

Marsalis—Skayne to his friends—fingers the seven-pound trumpet with the built-in mouthpiece, the Raja, designed for him by Dave Monette. He doesn't play. Sound, like color, cannot be adequately described by words. Marsalis has determined to try.

"It's a Doggy Dogg world, Wynton." You say it in a teasing, seductive, challenging way, speaking of "Snoop Doggy Dogg," who along with his producer, "Dr. Dre," is a purveyor of a form of hip-hop called "gangsta rap." "You know it's a Doggy Dogg World."

"I don't believe that. I'm sorry Miles Davis died, because I wanted him to see the transformation. The transformation is going to take place. It's going to be a breaking away from extreme vulgarity and ignorance and violence as a statement of soul."

You say, "Is that the only statement hip-hop music makes?" but he's already well into his glory and can hardly hear you at all.

"I believe that's going to happen. I don't know when. It's going to happen. This is the theme of the whole. There's too many great things that have taken place for them to be washed away and be replaced by what's being shoved into its position . . . It's ascending. It doesn't descend. It's about soul, joy, even love. Transcendence. Beethoven, Bach, Picasso, Duke Ellington, who was on the throne. Albert Einstein. If you read what they had to say, in the center, it always ascends. Martin King. King said, 'The arc of the moral universe bends toward justice.' That power, that optimism, cannot be destroyed. It's not a matter of philosophical argument of the avant-garde. For me it's playing trumpet. It's playing what you have. When you have a trumpet, the light in your sound, once that leaves . . ."

"What are your weapons?" you ask.

"Swing . . . and the blues."

First, though, there is the small matter of helping to decide the canon of the Western world. Not exactly a piece of cake.


Kaplan Penthouse in Lincoln Center is filled to overflowing. The still air carries a tension, a hum like an electric current—the sound of two hundred engaged, excited and intrigued people, SRO in the middle of August, no less. By comparison, two years before, jazz critic Stanley Dance lectured on the legacy of Earl "Fatha" Hines in the same room, and twenty people showed up.

Debate is verbal boxing. Even the face of the ticket encourages the metaphor: *Jazz Talk: Marsalis vs. Collier, Kaplan Penthouse, August 7, Lincoln Center Productions.* In this vein, Marsalis could be an Ali. The proper adjectives apply: handsome to the borderline of prettiness, possessor of supreme confidence and absolute mastery of his chosen craft; verbal suasion and personal magnetism that seem to draw in any surrounding humanity. Often, when he and his septet play on the road, Marsalis leads entire audiences out of the venue and onto the streets, forming a happy processional from his New Orleans roots. Audiences follow, amazed at their conduct even as they go.

"Intensity without volume," he says when you ask "What is your secret?" "Sustained intensity equals ecstasy," he says. Marsalis is on a mission, and people seem to sense it. He brings heat and light to a subject you claim not to understand or care about, a subject with inexorable pull on your life, defining you, whether "understood" or not. Are we talking here about boxing, or history, or music, or "race," or religion? All of them. If we hear beyond the noise, a new bell is sounding. And yet there are no new things. So what is this new bell? Does Marsalis himself even know? No time left to ponder. The battle has been joined without regard for rhyme or reason.

Marsalis believes Collier portrays Duke Ellington and Louis Armstrong as Rousseau's noble savages, producing the sound the way you produce intestinal gas. It had little to do with form, technique or a grinding work ethic driven by inspiration; theirs was not *true* genius. It was just in them and had to come out. Marsalis believes such assessments might eventually be applied to him. He can't allow *that*. He can't allow a line running from Buddy Bolden to Bunk Johnson to Freddie Keppard to King Oliver to Armstrong (you do not know the names, but he does) to himself to be written off as anything less than fine and considered art.

Marsalis mounts the stage dressed in warm earth tones: buttoned-down shirt, vest, tan slacks, brown suede saddle oxfords. He is confident. But the transparencies have been put together out of order, the PA system does not have the recordings tracked in the right sequence, and he doesn't have any copies of Collier's books in order to read from them and refute conclusions. Marsalis has to ask Collier to borrow his books. Collier graciously agrees. Marsalis looks out over the audience, toward his own technical people, and sighs:

"We don't want to be *too* organized around here."

You nearly choke, holding back a howl of glee. That is not just satire, that is *dread* satire—the kind to make the people who get it think about doing things better next time. The debate is soon on. Looking at a slide of Armstrong playing, Marsalis challenges Collier's published assertion that Armstrong's "embouchure" was improper, that he played therefore improperly, on the "red" of his lips:

> MARSALIS: The real reason Mr. Armstrong had problems with his embouchure is he played in a heroic fashion and endured a pain no other trumpet player . . . would play with. Things that Armstrong played, no one can play . . . feats of endurance . . . four or five shows a day in the upper register with a big fat sound. The true reason for his problems with his embouchure is he was like a boxer who just would endure incredible amounts of pain.

Collier says Duke Ellington didn't have much of a library:

> COLLIER: How many books would there have been at this time for Duke Ellington to read on "black" history? There

were not many around. And . . . if he had a library of 10 or 20 or 50 books, that's not a lot of books to read. Anybody out there who thinks 50 books is a lot of books to read, I feel sorry for. Duke Ellington, there is no evidence . . . that he had a lot of intellectual sophistication . . . Anybody who considers himself intellectually sophisticated is certainly going to have a library of several thousand volumes, there's no question about that.

What this has to do with Ellington's book of over 1,100 original songs is difficult for you to fathom, but then that is not at all surprising since you do not have the requisite several thousand volumes to qualify for intellectual sophistication, not to mention for bullshit detection. In his book, Collier posits that Ellington came upon one harmonic progression by looking down at the keyboard and seeing his fingers spread a certain distance:

> MARSALIS: Mr. Collier, you don't *see* harmony, you *hear* harmony.

This draws applause and, really, should end the debate. But the tension in the crowd comes not from any discussion of music. They are waiting for the fireworks—"race" arguments. Meanwhile, Marsalis keeps asking, "May I look this up in your book?" which is like a boxer asking his opponent, "May I punch now?" After Marsalis demonstrates his ear on piano to refute another Collier speculation, he puts Raja to his lips. Collier rolls his eyes. Marsalis puts the trumpet down. It wouldn't be fair for him to play in a debate over music. His playing tends to end debate.

> MARSALIS: I called you forward to discuss technical issues, then everybody says oh, let's talk about race. Well, let's talk about race later, let's talk about music for a little while . . .
> COLLIER: You have had three basic criticisms pointed to you . . . One of them has been that you have used primarily

"black" players and that you never really celebrated . . . a "white" musician . . . You've never done anything on Bix Beiderbecke . . .

Beiderbecke is the late jazz trumpeter from Davenport, Iowa, who happened to be "white" and is undoubtedly one of the superb jazzmen, not because you or anybody else *says* so, but because anybody who heard (and hears) him realizes through anything north of tone-deaf ears that the man could play. Just as undoubtedly, it is not solely for his skill with the cornet that Collier now mentions him. The fairly direct accusation is, Marsalis has not scheduled a program honoring Beiderbecke because he was "white."

"You come to jazz to get away from this kind of stuff," says Gene Seymour, a frenetic reporter from the recently departed *New York Newsday* and *Emerge* magazine. It was Gene Seymour who first published the question about Beiderbecke, in an attempt to bring perceived balance to his reporting. (If, for some reason, you are trying to sort out surface identity, Seymour is a "black" American, in the sense of "race." His skin is the color of sand.) In this way, both Seymour and Collier are right: We are unwise to say "classic" American literature is an exclusive province of "whites"; we are unwise to insist "classic" American music is an exclusive dominion of "blacks." If, indeed, we are trying to say either thing in the first place. Marsalis is trapped by this unveiled "race" question. The audience, God help us, is galvanized by it.

> MARSALIS: . . . I want everybody to hear this answer because race is the crucible of our entire nation. Everything comes down to that . . . I'm the artistic director of Jazz at Lincoln Center. I am hired for my taste . . . [to] determine what the shape of this program should be . . . I have a hiring record. I've been a part of hiring of every musician and of the

director of our program [Rob Gibson], who is "white" . . .
Three conductors have been "white" . . . for anyone to accuse
me of racism because I don't feel Bix Beiderbecke is on the
level of Louis Armstrong—we haven't even put on Louis
Armstrong. It's incorrect, it's unjust . . .

An Armstrong program is scheduled by the Jazz series
LCJO (denoting the Lincoln Center Jazz Orchestra) in December 1994, as Marsalis's book, *Sweet Swing Blues on the
Road*, with photographer Frank Stewart, is released by the
W. W. Norton Company. Armstrong hadn't been pro-
grammed earlier because Bolden & Co. had to come first in
just the sort of orderly process of scholarship Collier is on
the one hand espousing. On the other hand, what Collier is
saying is, *Don't leave me out, I'm important in this*; it seems
the "classic" boot is on a different neck. Marsalis has no
doubt said the same before, in a different context. They are
inextricably bound up in their fight. You are reminded of the
painting of two boxers engaged, one "black," the other
"white," by fin de siècle painter-lithographer George Bellows, titled *Both Members of This Club*. You know what is
most intriguing about the painting is Bellows's impressionis-
tic renderings of the faces and emotions of the patrons at
ringside. That is the *real* fight.

Soon Collier cites a study on the jazz audience, title un-
memorable, enunciates the author's name loudly, as a plea:
"In such-and-such, by HOROWITZ." He later repeats,
"Such-and-such, by HOROWITZ." Does he hope to split the
judges by their own bigotry? It's in you, a race-gender-
religion/advocacy-industry. You're being played like a reed.
Get in trouble, lose on merit, scream racism, sexism, reverse
racism, homophobia. Want to shift focus, inject anti-Semitism.
Let people who really suffer from racism, sexism or anti-
Semitism be portrayed as crying wolf. There is no recognition

from the audience. The plea evaporates. You grunt. You know it's a con. It's hard to con somebody who isn't greedy in the first place. Later, Marsalis will say he didn't notice.

*You: How do you feel when you are circumscribed by race?*

*WM: That's not an interesting discussion in music. That's sociology. And the greater issue is music. People make excuses for why Beethoven was the way he was, or Bach. Bach said, "If somebody worked as hard as me, they would be like me." I don't put that in a racial context. Do you know what happens next Wednesday? Do you? I don't. The artists never do. Picasso, whatever, they never do . . .*

> MARSALIS: Jazz . . . comes out of United States Negro culture. It does not mean that "white" people are excluded from it . . .
>
> COLLIER: . . . You said jazz came out of the Negro culture, the "black" culture, whatever term you want to use . . .
>
> MARSALIS: No I didn't say "black," I said the United States Negro culture, which . . . includes all Americans. Now, I don't mean Negro in a way of no "white" people because "white" is part of Negro. That's what the definition of Negro in America is, one drop of Negro blood. So that leaves a lot of room for "white."

The debate winds down. Marsalis shows a slide of his Uncle Alphonse and Aunt Marguerite, who helped raise him and his five brothers in New Orleans. How fair and tan his aunt and uncle are. "The American Negro culture is a mulatto culture," Marsalis says. Collier professes ignorance. He looks at the slide and says, "I don't know what this means." No? Why, even now in 1994, even Ismail Merchant–James Ivory–Ruth Prawer-Jhabvala, the holy trinity of Anglophile film who brought you *Howards End* and *Remains of the Day*, are working on *Jefferson in Paris*, focusing on Jefferson's relationship with Sally Hemings, the mulatto "alleged" mistress he was supposed to *not* have had four children by. No, you guess the widower Jefferson would've *never* made love to a nubile young woman who looked like a cross between Dorothy Dandridge and Halle Berry, who called him master and who, for all we know, professed her undying love. But her "blackness" would preclude his humanity, preempt hers. *He* could not love *her*. Nobody but the scum of Europe would think of lying with a "black." You think, "Was Jefferson a man or not?"

Marsalis wins the informal debate by wide, clear, unanimous decision on your card. No knockout. Overtrained.

Questions are allowed. Cornel West rises and says: "If we had a novel by Balzac . . . we need to either go back to [Collier's] reading of Balzac or to radically call into question why you're not on the inside of his world . . . this is music but unfortunately in America, music and race are inseparable, not identical . . . there's a history in America of intellectuals talking about African-American cultural practices, not having done enough homework . . . when we look at who blows and who doesn't blow, it's not racial, it's how much work you've done, discipline, what kind of subtlety you've been able to procure . . ."

"Who is that guy?" says an audience member, a "white" man.

"He's an intellectual," you say.

"Oh. *That's* why I can't understand what he's saying."

"Exactly," you say. Only then do you smile.

Collier is later described by a friend of yours, who is "white," as a lackluster writer and a terrible historian of jazz, a pretentious man with not much to be pretentious about. But then the same could be said of some "black" literary scholars. This questionable pretentiousness does not mean that every point they raise does not require some thought or attention. There does seem to be too much neatness to America, that "classic" American music remains a "black" phenomenon and "classic" American literature remains a "white" one. That's a little too cut-and-dried for America. And it is small potatoes, because Marsalis's primary battle is said to be on the front lines as the alternative to "hip-hop" or "rap" music.

Cornel West, speaking to writer Jervis Anderson, had broken a code here: "The old music can no longer sustain the rituals of everyday life among young inner-city people. Rap, a form of the new music, does. It's an extension of the improvisational tradition in jazz—a union of the rhetorical and the musical. And it's a form the young can commune with in their own way . . ."

A young man in dreadlocks from Philadelphia who goes to Morehouse College has told you about a new wave, one that spills over from music into art into language into fashion, that even West and Marsalis are only dimly aware of at the time—a new genre, melding jazz and rap, led by the likes of groups like the Roots and the Fugees, and J. Spencer, featuring vocalists-lyricists, vocalists-instrumentalists and fine instrumental musicians, all together in one band. The young man made it clear that from fashion to language to music to art, this language of hip-hop was not going away. A new bell keeps sounding, yet people keep insisting it is but the gong between rounds of the prizefight.

Marsalis seems to like the word "Negro," prefers it to "black": "Negro, I like it, because, what is it?" he says.

It is true that the negative connotations of the word "black" are easily manipulated. You've done it yourself. "Colored"? Yes, but then, who isn't? The timeless endearment "nigger" has been rendered pointless by would-be comics and others who use it the way police wield nightsticks, so to bully you into laughing. "African American" works in a strictest formal sense, like "European American"—at least the American part is in there; whatever these unnamable people are, they are American, whether you like it or not—but the hyphenated form has too many syllables for anything resembling smooth conversational patter. But "Negro"? That appellation is at least two generations removed from the here and now. So where on God's green earth did Wynton Learson Marsalis get that?

Ah. Stanley Crouch and Albert Murray are productive American authors, superb wordsmiths, artistic consultants to Marsalis. In relation to Marsalis's debates against the likes of both James Lincoln Collier and Snoop Doggy Dogg, they could be compared to boxing trainers, oracles, or even the witches from *Macbeth*. It would depend on how you see it. Let us merely say that to Marsalis they are influential. They are also "black" men, though you doubt that is how they would define themselves, and nobody can blame them for attempting to define themselves. They might also say nobody else can define them as "black," and categorize them, and limit them, and there you would doubt them very much. They sat front row center watching their man battle Collier.

Crouch is formerly a writer at *The Village Voice*, recipient of a MacArthur "genius" grant, author of three volumes, including a stimulating set-to called *Notes of a Hanging Judge*, and a work-in-progress biography of Charlie Parker. Before the debate, Crouch was introduced to you by Cornel West. "I know you, Stanley," you said, smiling. "You hate everything." Whereupon Crouch sneered aristocratically, then invited you to come in and "watch this massacre."

Crouch's mentor, the all-purpose literary professor Albert Murray, is the seventy-eight-year-old contemporary of Ralph

Ellison and author of eight books, including *South to a Very Old Place*, *Stomping the Blues*, *Train Whistle Guitar*, *The Spyglass Tree* and *The Seven League Boots*.

First you are allowed to question Crouch:

> CROUCH: Do I think we're being positioned [by critics in the press] as Afrocentric bigots, and is that ironic? No. It is paranoia. To say if you don't care for something, it has to be for "racial" reasons—this results from what's going on in trash culture. We're living in times we would've rather read about. The initial negative New York press reaction to what Wynton is doing at Lincoln Center has to do with intellectual cowardice of the "black" intelligentsia, "black" silence in the face of nuts like [Al] Sharpton, [Leonard] Jeffries, Farrakhan, Khallid [Muhammad]. Paranoia stems from the irrational, cowardly actions of too many "black" intellectuals. That creates an atmosphere of distrust. But from the changing tone of the New York press, quality is winning over rhetoric.

Crouch met Marsalis after hearing him with Art Blakey at The Bottom Line in the Village. Crouch took Marsalis home, hit him with some Duke, laid some Pops on him and talked about his country arse. That was fifteen years ago. "Without a doubt, I learned a pile of shit from Stanley Crouch," says Marsalis. "But before I met him I'd already made an A in almost every class I'd taken. Don't like to say it. Sounds like bragging. Never listened to Duke Ellington coming up. To me, he was somebody old people played in a ballroom. Taking Geritol so they could dance to some music. Older musicians told me—wasn't the first time I'd heard it, but they tell you in music. Crouch, Murray, they tell you with words. Words are different. Anybody can understand that."

That this trinity of Marsalis-Crouch-Murray would ever be portrayed as "race"-exclusionary or even particularly "race"-loyal *is* ironic. Crouch made his bones by all but literally torching "black" American artists at precisely their hour of triumph, lambasting Spike Lee for shortsightedness in the wake of *Do the Right Thing*, saying, "[It] was a little man's fantasy, twisted up with a confused morality that justifies itself in the name of racial pride . . . for all its unity, it is the sort of rancid fairy tale one expects of the racist, whether or not Lee actually is one"; eviscerating the oeuvre of Toni Morrison on the very day she was announced winner of the Nobel Prize for literature, saying, among other things, that in her magnum opus, *Beloved*, Morrison should have noted "black" Africans were complicit in the slave trade. Crouch dismissed Morrison's body of work with this comment: "I see nothing." Crouch also found a way to draw an analogy between Lee and mass murderer John Wayne Gacy. "Intellectually, Lee is like John Wayne Gacy in his clown suit, entertaining those who cannot believe the bodies buried under his house." Crouch has cogent points and can make them eye-catchingly well. At the same time, he is viewed with suspicion by some "black" artisans who consider his critiques overarching, dictatorial toward them and overly accommodating of the status quo with his I'm Reconciled riffs. But Status Quo, him give up the heap big grant action.

> CROUCH: They are attempting to deny their birthright. The confusion of middle-class "blacks" who want to be victims. They're messing up "black" youth . . . Real rebels are not people with their pants falling down and caps on sideways. The Negro is Americana. Everybody knows it. To an extent all Americans are part Negro.

This theory emanates from Murray, and from minds like that of Murray's high school teacher, Benjamin F. Baker, at Mobile (Alabama) County Training School, who sixty years ago said to twelve eager charges, "Booker T. Washington sacrificed too much to expediency. Dr. [W. E. B.] Du Bois, in his up-north bitterness, spends too much time complaining. The youth of today must find the golden mean." For Murray, part of that golden mean was his late friend Ellison. Part of that mean is now Wynton Marsalis.

Historian C. Vann Woodward ("white," for those who are scoring) had long ago said, "So far as culture is concerned all Americans are part-Negro . . . I include Afro-Americans. They are part Negro, but only part." Murray wrote that down (alongside many other interesting things) a quarter-century ago in *South to a Very Old Place*, a nonfiction volume nominated for a National Book Award in 1971. Murray is Marsalis's most honored mentor. He has no patience with Afrocentrism, saying America and the world are Eurocentric, and that's not a good or bad thing—it's *the* thing. After all, Murray says, we are on Greenwich Mean Time. After all, we are speaking English—Americanized, no doubt, but English.

"Albert Murray? Ooo, shit. Didn't know they had nobody out here thinking like that, seeing how all the culture was one, the 'black' is 'white' and the 'white' is 'black,' " says Marsalis. "Albert Murray, he made me think. If the U.S. would realize we are part of the nation. But we keep trying to fight to not be part of the nation. And that's who gets the ink, that's who gets it, and the ink affects how people think. Be *part* of this motherfucker, man."

You are allowed to question Murray:

MURRAY: Wynton has a sense of context, seeing against richest possible backdrop. That backdrop is, I'm not West Indian, I'm not African, I'm from the plantation, the auction block. The Middle Passage is where my tradition begins. It is a tradition of confrontation and inspirational improvisation. Equal-protection government meant the most to "black" slaves and the scum of Europe. It wasn't a divine right of kings, some kind of aristocracy. Wynton is setting canon. To do that, you enable one to define what he is learning. In jazz, you study how Coleman Hawkins refined reed, then Lester Young, then Charlie Parker, then Coltrane . . .

By this measure, then, it makes sense that the Jazz Series would have already honored Buddy Bolden and King Oliver and is now getting to Louis Armstrong. So if the Colliers of the world would keep their pants on, then the (if you will excuse the expression) scholarly process would lead to and then through the like of Bix Beiderbecke. "It's not celebrating achievement by terms of popular success," says Murray, finessing the point. "It is defining form as fine art." Murray then theorizes that there are three legitimate art categories. He uses food as his allegory.

*Folk Art* is a gumbo made with a smidgen of this, a pinch of that. It is different in one part of the landscape than another. It's provincial, largely inexportable, the crudest way of forming an aesthetic statement. It's peasant art, but not primitive or savage. It is sincere (Hongry? Let us fix you something *good* to eat). It can move you to goose bumps, but has the smallest range.

*Pop Art* is a McDonald's hamburger. It has a broader range, but is much cheapened, self-indulgent, opportunistic (Hungry? Here's something to eat. It's only $1), insincere, unfulfilling.

*Fine Art* is, say, Chateaubriand, or American Thanksgiving roasted turkey dinner with the trimmings. It has the greatest range, the greatest control of the aesthetic statement, and it sharpens the perception of audience, viewer, reader, consumer.

"We're trying to conserve our consciousness," Murray says. "You can't embrace chaos. And that's what's out there right now. But the dragon is what evokes heroic action. The greater irony is this: It is the dragon—be it slavery, entropy, white supremacy, whatever—it is the dragon that influences you to heroic action."

So then the most telling fight is Wynton vs. hip-hop?

"Yes," Murray says. "Wynton *is* a genius. He must be, to be a protégé of mine. I don't have time to waste. You can ship these other motherfuckers back to Africa."

His laughter is warm, effusive, so you join in.

But later, Branford Marsalis, Wynton's gifted older brother, does not concur. For years, Branford and Wynton were estranged, at least musically, for Wynton was a classicist and Branford leaned toward the contemporary. They were in different camps. Wynton was upset when Branford left his bandstand to open for Sting and, later, for Jay Leno. "You know, Crouch writes stuff like 'Wynton's band mounted the stage like knights in shining armor, defending their tradition,' all that. To me, that is just . . . bullshit. It's just music, man. That's all it is. Just music." Branford Marsalis left the *Tonight* show early in 1995 on the strength of the release of *Buckshot LeFonque*. In a burlesque, unpretentious, contemporary and utterly undeniable way, it is as evocative as *In This House, On This Morning*.

*Buckshot* wends through an opening theme into a vibrant, brassy jazz scheme, *Blackwidow Blues*; through Maya Angelou's spoken poem *I Know Why the Caged Bird Sings* augmented by catchy South African rhythms; through a rhythm-and-bluesy *Mona Lisa*; through a languid, reflective track overlaid by Branford's plaintive sax and a Jamaican "dancehall" rap spin-off, *Wonders & Signs*; through a ballad *Ain't It Funny (What Love Can Do)*, sung by Tammy Townsend; through the ultra-ryhthmic *Some Cow Funk*; through a reverberating brass refrain reflecting the record-scratching techniques popular at the beginning of the hip-hop age, *Some Shit, @ 78 RPM (The Scratch Opera)*, where Branford's solo turns repetition into something decidedly not repetitive; through a Caribbean-flavored *Hotter Than Hot*;

into a Jay Leno joke, leading into *Breakfast @ Denny's*, a rhythmic dirge combining instrumentation and vocals emanating from the throats of human beings. It's all oral tradition. Even when you read a book silently, you are hearing it. This is the new wave of the Roots and the Fugees and others; onward now, through track twelve, *No Pain, No Gain*, where screaming electrical guitars and a pulsing metallic beat are followed (in what at first seems to be an incongruent manner) by a jazz horn melody; that is followed by a hard-edged rap; then a piece in which Branford stumbles through an emotionless piano ditty before giving up and then, or so it is implied by sound, shooting himself—the track is called *Sorry, Elton*; the finale, *And We Out*, begins with the languid river-like theme of *Buckshot*, then morphs new wave—rap overlaying bursting echos of jazz horns. The forms merge in the end (at this end, at any rate). It is work thoughtfully done.

Obviously this is not work for fools. Does Branford think his brother has been unduly influenced by the classicists Crouch and Murray? "No, not really," he says. "In the end you decide for yourself." Is it further and appropriately ironic if it would be Branford who is doing the better battle, by attempting to bring a synthesis out of the present cacophony? Or is it Wynton who does better battle by announcing one, via proxy or not, and then excluding, for whatever reason, those who have something to say, their only necessary credential being that they are sincere, and American? Can it be that even blood brothers cannot see eye-to-eye?

**Y**ou are told to look up an old man who knows all there is to know about music. He tells you some things you question and we will get to them later in the drift. But he seems to have a good feel for the Marsalis family history. To wit:

"Book 'n' Skayne? Why them two rose up 'round Big

Easy. Book and Skayne the oldest of Dolores and Ellis Senior's six hardlegged tackheads. Book and Skayne, that's
Branford and Wynton. Then it's Ellis Junior and Delfayeo,
then Mboya, then Jason. They paired off in sets of two; well,
Book and Skayne paired off. One set might stay at times
with their grandma in the St. Baernard's projects. At times a
set stayed with Uncle Alphonse and Aunt Marguerite over on
Governor Nichols Avenue. Skayne likely as not don't remember livin' in Breauxbridge, down by Lafayette. Or he oughter
not, young as he was at the time. They moved around. Here
and there. Spots and places. When they was living in Kenner,
him and Book missed the last Number Twenty-one bus after
one of theirs or Ellis's gigs. Had to walk through Metairie to
get home. David Duke from Metairie, so wasn't no surprise
when they got called: 'What 'chu naiggers doin' heah?' And,
wasn't no surprise when they responded neither. Got chased,
but they didn't get caught, and they was on foot, and them
chasing was in a car. Yeah, it's funny now. It was funny then,
'cause they didn't get caught.

"Skayne went to a mostly 'white' elementary school. One
'white' girl didn't automatically turn up her nose at him.
That made him curious. He asked her why she didn't turn up
her nose. She said 'I'm from Montana. We hate the Indians
there.'

"Book was older than Skayne. Ellis got him a clarinet and
set him at the pie-ana. Ellis was far too cool to press music
on them boys. Ellis respected work and silence. Ellis knew
what Book did, the others might want to do. Dolores said,
'Get Wynton something, too.' She didn't want Skayne left
out. Skayne got the trumpet. Give Skayne that hard mudda.
They always had instruments, but music didn't seem like a
big part of growing up. Played ball, ogled girls. Ellis was a
musician and he scruggled. It was hard being a modern jazz
musician even in Big Easy. Public didn't 'cept it. Ellis didn't

have no money. Best-paying gig he had was when he played with Al Hirt and made good money for like, two three years. Big Al give Skayne a trumpet, but it wasn't like no manna from heaven. Al was being nice to a fella on the bandstand looking for ways to cut into his sons. Skayne was sev'n. Who knew? Country boy. Couldn't even see why nobody would wanna be sophisticated. So serous 'bout that trumpet that he used to try and catch small animals with it. Put grass all up in the bell. Make up thangs, him and Book, with a Sears 'n' Roebuck chemistry set, put that in 'nere, blow hard, see if the whole thang'd blow up. Dolores made sure they had something hot to eat when they came in, made sure they had a certain vibe. Made sure they knew the value of education. She went to Grambling, told Skayne not to think much of them A's he got in high school after they moved to Hickory Street. She got A's with her eyes closed.

"Skayne got to thinking one night at Lew 'n' Charlie's down on Rappaport, and started looking at that trumpet and not frowning so hard. He learnt the Sound not from the music but from them that played it. They was scruggling, but Skayne saw the soul. That was it for Skayne—be like 'em. Part of it wasn't playing. Just wanted to be like 'em. Didn't want to practice no trumpet. Didn't want no ring around his lip like Pops Armstrong. Skayne thought the girls wouldn't like him with that lip, that he wouldn't be able to impress no women. Skayne wanted to be. Not play. Be. Get it? He thought, 'Damn, Skayne, you got to be able to play first.' Didn't miss a day of practice for sev'n years. When he was fifteen he met Clark Terry, first one he saw he felt was playing great, showed him wasn't doing nothing. Skayne hung out with him. Terry heard Skayne play, got real quiet, called Skayne 'the Demon.' Terry gigged one night until 2 A.M., then rose up early the next morning to hear Skayne play that Brandenboig with the symphony.

"Skayne wasn't into jazz nor classical. He did what he hadda do to get good on that horn. Him and Book, they hooked up a funk band called The Creators and pushed the funk hard, man. Playing horn from the most rhythmic R and B—Parliament and Funkadelic with the Brecker Brothers, James Brown's J.B.'s horns, that's what Skayne got off on. Kool and the Gang's *Hollywood Swanging*. Skayne'd rather play horn from *Poppa's Got a Brand New Bag* or *Mother Popcorn* than a Brandenboig. For true. 'Sides, back then, him and Book got one hundred dollars a night playing funk. If Ellis got fiddy dollars, he'as lucky.

"Skayne can scat the opening of Stevie Wonder's *Sir Duke*, in on-tomato-pee-a, scat dead on it from jump street on through. Book can do it, too. S'all oral tradition. Comes out the head, past the voice hole and then through the sax, the trumpet, the fingers, whatever you got available. Skayne might can scat better than Book by a little. Book, he older. Skayne, he had to be the one. Always challengin' folks. Book once told him, 'Man, if you'd just shut your mouth, we'd be cool.'

"Before that, Skayne got passed around more than a li'l bit. John Fernandez, who was band director at Xavier University, told him, 'You don't want to practice, don't come back.' Skayne didn't go back, neither. So Fernandez would come by 8318 for some gumbo and to check on the Demon. Sent him to Bill Clifford. John Longo was Skayne's teacher too. Only took five dollars a lesson. Said it was a privilege. Bill Fielder came to the house and gave Skayne a piccolo trumpet for fiddy dollars—five hundred dollar trumpet, and he give it to Skayne for fiddy. Skayne said when Fielder came back, he'd be able to play it. First week, he couldn't even get a decent sound out of it. Just 'brppp-brpp.' But the vibe was there. Once the cats see you serious they would open up and give you what you need. George Jansen was 'white,' one of the only 'white' men who could or would show 'black' how to play down that way where everything is 'black' or 'white' or mostly in between. Seem like all of it was just yesterday. Skayne says the family ain't all that close. Boys is boys. Ain't like having a bunch'a sisters. Don't get together on holidays. Don't talk much. Dolores say she got a problem with all that 'men will be men' stuff. She used to worry 'bout him. She got a problem with this so-called genius. Said it was like peanut butter. Said you put a gob of it on bread you got to spread it around some. You need jelly. Peanut butter and jelly—now, that's genius. Then she let go, realized that whatever else genius is, it is definitely a blessing and a curse first.

"Ellis was the kind other men in the barbershop listened to when he finally did say something. Skayne's barber now is Cherry. Cherry, he say, 'Skayne asked, Man, you think my brother's happy playin' with Jay Leno on *The Tonight Show*? Why Book leave my bandstand to open for Sting, man?' Rattled Skayne's confidence when Book left back in eighty-four; without Book, it was like he had nobody to play off. He couldn't see what to do without Book. Blind Marcus Roberts, J Master, who couldn't see at all, told Skayne he'd lost his nerve. Two-fifths of his band, the strongest two-fifths by his own idea, Book and Kenny Kirkland, was history. But that's life, and what happens in it. The blues say, deal. Skayne thought about Book when he wrote *Blood on the Fields* and played *In This House, On This Morning*. Skayne knew Book would'a took up that tenor and torn that shit up.

"It's all right now, twix Book and Skayne. They dealt."

"**T**wain . . . Humpf." With those two expressions within one burst of breath carefully metered for the desired result on the listener, Mr. Albert Murray described paragraphs that were left unsaid. You are now in his small Harlem apartment, gazing at his rows of books—Malraux, Hemingway, Thomas Mann, Faulkner, first editions, mint condition, most of them signed at Murray's behest. He has perhaps five hundred volumes on display—something less than the requisite several thousand, but enough to solidify this point: Murray is of that school in literature. Music is something else. Canvas art is yet another.

In your crisscrossing of America, you had come across the legacy of a native Mexican painter named Alfredo Ramon Martinez. As a child, he was discovered somewhere down in the Yucatán—"discovered," for his was a brilliant if native or "folk" skill for painting. He was born in 1871, and in 1880, at the ripe age of nine, he went as a student to the National Academy of Art in Mexico City, with one of the Hearsts, Phoebe, as benefactress. He was sent to Paris to study at fifteen. And he stayed in Europe for fourteen years, studying the classic form of the "masters." Fourteen years later he returned to Mexico City, and was then installed as the director of the National Academy of Art. On his return, he looked at one of his old paintings, and he wept, saying, "How is it possible that the fourteen years which I have dedicated to study have destroyed this simplicity and originality of design? This is what I had sought there; this is what I longed to paint. But all the great masters whom I admired so much completely absorbed me and destroyed my personality." This knowledge of displacement allowed him to reclaim his own personality, and with that, along with his study of other classic form, he created a new "classic" form, such as *India Con Cesat*, c. 1929 and *Cargador de Lena*, c. 1943. Study of the "classics" is an encourageable endeavor (and it is an endeavor to study some of them, a crushing one to study some others). The people who constructed "classics" were only people, subject, as we are, to the vicissitudes of life and form around them. To re-create one's own experiences in the exact form of some other person's life is dishonest, and the dishonesty will show. You think this was what Alfredo Martinez was saying. You once wondered on it when your "black" teachers told you that in order to live up to your scant native abilities you would have to study the form of "classics." Their way of saying it was, "You have to know the rules in order to break them." From the prior forms, you had to incorporate what was appropriate—but only when you saw it went better that way to illuminate your own experiences.

Classic vs. contemporary. That is the real Culture war, and always is. From out of that war, unheard at first, always sounds the new bell. With the one burst of breath, Murray was intimating that Twain, who wrote, but not bookishly, was not of a "classic" form he preferred, like Faulkner or Mann or Malraux and many more of his favorites. Twain was near crudity itself. You don't know if that's so, but you hope it is, because you have always felt crude yourself, deep down. You know that Murray was charged one way in school, went to Tuskegee with Ralph Ellison, and read and admired Malraux, Faulkner and Mann, then taught for many years on college campuses, teaching the "classics," proud to be a "Negro" without being captive of the latest public pathology. When he had dined years before with Richard Wright's wife, Ellen, she had become upset. She was a "white" woman, and wondered why Murray was smiling, convivial, not always brooding, bitter and suffering, like her husband, Richard. But aren't you a Negro? she asked. Yes, said Murray. Duke Ellington Division, though.

Murray was now working on a scholarly recipe involving Hemingway. And that fits.

Is it possible, or even preferable, to do or be both? So, to be of a school, be it classic or unclassic—is that enough? Schools teach form, but then so does life. Form must then be reshaped, outfitted. It comes down to leaving the best record *you* can leave, according to *your* life, according to *your* means, *your* own methods. The more wisely you choose your methods in relation to your personal circumstances, the more successful you will be at finding people who understand your form. They don't have to know the form themselves. They merely feel its legitimate urgency.

"**I** said to Mr. Murray, 'We let you down, didn't we?' " recalls Marsalis, as you and he pass the reception desk in his building. "He kinda lowered his head. He said, 'Yeah.' "

An immense young Irish-American hails Marsalis. This robust fellow plays hoop for Baruch College. He tells you Wynton has a cute little lefty jumper and to be wary. Marsalis wants to play you in some one-on-one basketball. He is serious about this. You are serious about not scuffing your new black bucks. But it's important to him for you to know he's "got game," that he is *connected*, that it's not all yesterdays with him. On your way out a diabetic derelict black amputee in a wheelchair stops Marsalis. Wynton slips him a bill, keeping it out of sight. Later, as he snaps green bean pods in a sushi bar, the illustrator Peter Max compliments him on his LCJO programs, performed before large, appreciative audiences in Avery Fisher Hall, home also to the New York Philharmonic. On our way back, a white teenager from New Jersey with a trumpet ring forming on his lips shyly promises Wynton an original Ellington recording he's found.

All along, Marsalis runs a commentary:

"The question is posed by the blues. How are you going to deal with what you're given? Are you going to deal with some dignity and some soul, or are you going to whine about it, let it defeat you so much you see pain in everything? . . . I can't sleep. I have like, this *energy*, man. I can be tired and still have this *energy*. I sleep three to four hours. When I'm working on music, I don't sleep or eat much. I work everywhere, even on airplanes and I'm terrified of flying. Something like *Blood on the Fields* took two months to create. I don't like to be off, I'm like my daddy in that way. I don't mind working. I will procrastinate, though, wait until the last minute. *In This House*, I had no idea it would be that long. *Blood on the Fields*, had no idea it'd be three hours. Thought it'd be an hour, but it's three . . ."

The tyranny of genius is that it never goes away. It never lets you rest. It *burns*. The vessel genius inhabits is flesh and blood. Genius drives this deteriorating, finite vessel of flesh and eventually incinerates it. But the burning gives off a bright and lovely light. Marsalis is on the road three hundred days of the year, to Japan, Germany, Brazil, from symphony halls to bandstands at small jazz clubs like the Iridium (across from Lincoln Center), to high schools all over America. Wynton concentrates on the high schools. His exterior motivation is Wynton vs. hip-hop, but that match was made by Crouch and Murray and could be Cervantesian in logic—the proverbial tilting at windmills. Sometimes in a debate or a fight you are asked to attack something you sort of believe in and defend something you sort of don't. He was once younger.

"I do go out to schools, but mostly I play," Marsalis says almost defensively. "I write, compose . . . Mostly, I play." Plays and composes. *Joe Cool's Blues* was released in the summer of 1995—at the same time the actress and model Victoria Rowell announced she was pregnant with Marsalis's third child.

You speculate that his inner motivation for going to high schools and trying to reach young students is at least partly this: His brother Mboya is autistic. When Wynton was a boy, he teased Dolores Marsalis about Mboya. He's got to make up for that. He has two sons, Wynton (Li'l Skayne), six, and Simeon, four, by his longtime companion Candace Stanley.

"When I was nine, my brother Mboya was born," says Marsalis, "and that was the biggest event within my family, much more so than anything about music. I used to kind of tease my momma . . . 'Somethin's wrong with this boy.' You know, I was teasing. He started talking. Then he stopped."

Dolores isn't buying your speculation. "I don't know if Wynton knew at the time how much pain I was in," she says. "His father and environment gave him his motivation.

"People sat right here in this very house and said jazz was dying. I think Wynton thought, 'How could music with so much life die?' He felt this was worth a fight."

Marsalis says, "I go to schools. A lot are still segregated unofficially. Black kids are playing; some are sounding terrible. Can't play at all. I say, 'You think y'all sound better than school bands where the "white" kids are playing?' They say, 'Yeah, we sound better.' I ask why. They say, ' 'cause we're black.' I say, 'You don't. You don't sound anywhere near as good as they do because you don't know anything about music. We can argue racism; but first let's argue about you not being able to read.' They say, 'Who's this dude? You play jazz? I think I know. He's on the Jay Leno Show.' So they don't know. But then I once didn't know either. I like to touch them, put my hand on their shoulders and talk to them. They don't like the touch at first, but they get used to it. And I believe deep down they know they need it."

You speculate that eleven-year-old Robert Sandifer, if he'd not been shot, if he'd become a rapper, if he'd talked about bitches and hos, he wouldn't be talking about Dolores Marsalis, or your mother, but his own. The spoken word reflects on the *speaker*, not on the subject. You speculate Snoop Dogg is the preeminent rapper because of producer Dr. Dre's mix of rhythm tracks from the reliable old school—infectious rhythms of Parliament/Funkadelic and James Brown.

Snoop's syrupy drawl is straight out of the Mississippi Delta. It is very much folk art *cum* pop art, for there are no doubt some rappers in black skullcaps, sunglasses and scowls running around talking about bitches and hos whose mothers always made sure they had hot dinners and tried to get them to go to church after they became too big to carry. But it's the only trumpet Snoop had. And he doesn't decide what gets the contracts, distribution, what goes on the cover of *Rolling Stone*.

*WM: I love me some competition.*

Marsalis is competitive by nature. If there were no dragons, he'd have to invent them. If there were no older men like Crouch and Murray to advise him and look to be vindicated through him, he'd have to go find them. That was how he came to jazz in the first place. He wanted to be like those wise men. And most of all, he wanted to be the best.

"Sometimes it seems he was born with that competitive streak," says Dolores Marsalis. "I attribute it to early toilet training. No, I do. The desire to control. 'I'll please Mother if I can control.' He was toilet-trained by the time he was eighteen months. If I had it to do all over again, I might not do it the same way."

Marsalis was nineteen, in a forgotten park, wearing a shiny grey polyester three-piece suit with a derby when he met Miles Davis. Davis looked at him and rasped, "So you the po-lice."

Marsalis didn't know what he meant, thought he was crazy, asked Herbie Hancock what in the hell Miles was talking about. Hancock laughed and said, "He means he knows you're coming out here to clean everything up." But it wasn't until 1985, a year after Branford left his bandstand, that Wynton sought out Miles on the bandstand in Vancouver. "For me and Miles it was a strange thing," he says. "It was like we knew each other in a certain kind of way. I jumped on him once, but the only reason why was because the cats in my band put me up to it. He was on the radio talking about how I wasn't shit, my whole family wasn't shit. The cats started teasing me. 'Miles said your whole family ain't shit. I dare you to go up on his bandstand.' Even J Master Marcus Roberts said, 'You *should* go up on Davis's bandstand.'

"I said, 'Man, I'm not gonna go up there.' They said, 'You scared? We ain't never thought we'd see you be scared.' I went, waited for him to play something I could play on. Once he played the blues, I went out there. I started playing. He tried to cut the band off. They couldn't handle me. I played a little while longer, then I stopped. He said something. I cussed him out. I put my horn in his face. He said, 'Come back tomorrow night.' I said, 'I'm here tonight.' I walked off. He knew what the point was. After I left, he started playing something really wild. I could hear it. It sounded like an elephant dying or something."

But was Miles Davis being more true to the idea of art than Marsalis—or Murray or Crouch—would give him credit for? After all, one of Davis's final recordings was *Doo-Bop*, which merged his jazz trumpet with a rapper's monology. Davis was maligned and challenged for that recording. Come to think of it, how better for artists to tell they're on the right track? If you're not being maligned and challenged, *then* you're ineffectual.

You tell Marsalis what you think: More than being a man on a mission to challenge hip-hoppers, or high-minded Western canonizers, or Miles, or Branford, he is a part of an ongoing artistic search to create harmony from dissonance, integrity from chaos, the blues from black and white. He can't be circumscribed by race, for archaic American definitions of race—always blind in one eye—cannot contain him.

The lines are blurred. They always were. We aren't ready. We never are. It's easy to debate the obvious demerits of black and white. Art does not come so easy. Never has. Never will. America isn't as simple as "black" or "white," us or them, and it never was so simple, not even in the good old days.

Time to work. Time to play. Time to swing. Wynton Marsalis must play what he feels he has to play. That is the only way to go. He will come to this in his own time, and in his own way. A baby grand piano dominates one corner of his apartment. Three horns lie about: a piccolo trumpet, a battered, crooked trumpet, and the Raja, that seven-pound horn the color of gold that he plays for hours every day until his lip bleeds or the scar tissue holds and becomes stronger. He picks up a straw hat to use as a mute. How can he hold the heavy Raja with one hand so steadily for so long? "You have to *want* to hold it," Marsalis says. "You have to play that trumpet, man, or that trumpet will play you."

You are leaving now. He plays you right out of the door. *Do Wop Do Wop Do Wop Do Wop Do Wop Do Wop Do Wop Do Wo WWW Wwwww.*

The sound is hypnotic, pure, a stream of clear water poured from a crystal pitcher into a parched desert throat. A day later you realize Marsalis had played the last measures of the refrain from Ellington's *It Don't Mean a Thing If It Ain't Got That Swing* . . . *Do Wop Do Wop Do Wop Do Wop Do Wop Do Wop Do Wop Do Wo WWW Wwwww* . . .

Maybe you'll knock that way from now on. Maybe not.

# 6

## Where Negroes Get All That Rhythm

*Music is, first of all, motion; after that, emotion. I like movement, rhythmical variety, polyphonic life.*

— JAMES HUNEKER

**O**ne of my previous benefactors (it was M——, as I recall) reached me by telephone wire and informed me that if I wanted to be a serious scholar about music, and not merely the untutored dilettante, I should make an appointment with Dr. Vada P. MacAfee, formerly of Atlanta, now residing in Oakland, California, who was the foremost authority on many things, especially on the subject of rhythm and its origins. M—— said I should tell MacAfee who sent me, and that would unlock him. If I wanted to clear up these matters for myself and perhaps then for posterity, I should take heed of the old man's words.

Not stopping to consider M——'s opinion of me or my time, I went to Oakland and found "Dr." MacAfee sitting on a slate porch in front of a lime-colored stucco house off Grand Avenue near Lake Merritt. He was asleep in a glider groaning in perfect pitch with his snoring. I tried to rouse him with calls of "Dr. MacAfee!" but had no effect, so I stepped onto the porch and one of his eyes opened. "Dr. MacAfee?" I asked. "Who wants to know?" he said. "M—— sent me," I said. "He said you could tell me the origins of rhythm." "The which?" he said. I repeated my request, and M——'s name for emphasis. MacAfee pondered it for a while, then spooled out the following yarn. He told it without hesitation, pausing at times but usually maintaining the gravest of tones so on those counts I would not for a moment doubt the story's veracity as he told it. First he asked me to "cop a squat." I sat down as ordered. MacAfee then cleared his throat, hooked his thumbs behind his suspenders and gave them what seemed to be a satisfying tug outward. Then he told me this tale, with but a single interruption on my part:

"It's a serous matter, where rhythm comes from. Nobody knows about all rhythm, and you got to go a good ways back to even know about the kind I know about. I'll tell it to you exactly as it was told me. You have to do your own judging off of that. Some of it'll seem fantastic, and it might of growed in the re-issue before it even got to me, but if you change the names around to suit you, she'll fit. It'll sound fantastic but I'll lay you it could'a happened and prob'ly did, and it's the names that throw you off, 'cause what in life ain't nigh on to fantastic anyway? Happened a while back, when the world was a mite wetter behind the ears, air was clean and peoples was more humble than they is today. Death went out for a walk back then, as Death's always been liable to do. Don't buck your eyes. Death's just a name. Usually it come in the shape of a fella, and the fella's given name at the time was—well, I don't know, exactly, but I was *told* they called him "Bay-Bruh," and one day when Bay-Bruh went out of his house for a walk, Blind Jack Hin-ton made his move.

"Back in them days all the rhythm in the world belonged

to Death and what didn't belonged to Mother Nature. Death wad'n in no mood to share rhythm with peoples and Mother Nature's supply was allocated for the seasons, plants, other animals and so forth. So peoples was walking around without any rhythm—or very much that was apparent while they tried to get around on two legs with the same fluiditry other creatures got around on four, less'n they went up on two for a minute just to mock peoples. At this point peoples was unaccomplished in rhythmic movement. Being so stiff, they was pretty easy to mark. Death could catch 'em five at a time, and did.

"In them days, Death (or Bruh, as he was calling himself), he wud'n as feared as today. Peoples could get so bad off until they 'preciated Death. Blind Jack was not so inclined, but he *was* to be married that day and, if anything, the prospect was, in his mind, scarier than Death. Took his mind right off it. In this way Jack was not unusual. If you want to distract a man, mention marriage.

"But, fate got a different look from the side than from head-on. Other mens wished they was in Jack's shoes, for they saw his bride-to-be, name of Hatshepsut, was prime for the position from their vantage point. She was a fit example of a woman—graceful, nothing shrill in her, clear and forgiving eyes, didn't pay mind to fools' flattery, neat as a cat, chock full o' help. She'd always given Jack plenty of room and she walked with a sense of something yet was so down to earth nobody ever called her by her formal name that fit how she looked and the way she walked. Everybody called her Peaches. She was patient, kind; possessed the most luxuriantly luscious set of lips in the known world; lips down-soft and pillowy, and bowed just so, just right; lips resilient, beautiful; lips so wonderful that most men believed she could melt the steeliest manhood down to parade rest with no trouble at all.

"These facts did not dry the sweat on Blind Jack's brow none on that day. Blind Jack was called Blind Jack because that man didn't miss nothing. Had an eye like a hawk's— only thing was, he rarely applied it to a mirror, so he couldn't see himself worth a damn, though he could tell you all about your business straight on through, so folks took to calling him Blind Jack, and it set.

"Jack had been to wedd'ns, and what he seen up in there was not restful. Why, he ust'a wonder, during wedd'n processions, did they take those baby steps, like they didn't want to get where they was going, leaving a body standing there sweating bullets at the altar while they took their own sweet time, making a man suffer and turning him stock-still, an easier mark for Death?

"Now, you and I know all wedd'ns need co-ordinatin', or they come off flat, if not worse, if they come off at all. But, according to Jack, this wedd'n coordinatin' was also a problem; there was always some frustrated female in charge of the wedd'n who was more distracting than the bride, let Jack tell it; a'picking at the veil, a'pulling on the train of the dress, a'jabbering away as though without her there would be no accredited wedd'n at all, acting like she had more to do with the festivities than the bride but it had been the bride's strategy that come away the winner, not hers—leastways that was how Jack seen it. From what Jack gethered, the woman in charge of the wedd'n better not be in the wedd'n party or she'd be right up there with the minister and out-talking him, repositioning folks and staring down the groom and a'picking at the bridal train a little more and centering herself on all photographs, which, by her mind, there were never enough of. So, Blind Jack thought, why didn't *she* get married, save everybody else the trouble? Jack was cruel that way.

"Blind Jack figured the 'vows' to be curious as well. Why make vows in the first place when everybody knew vows are never noticed unless somebody broke them? Why not vow to be human and to come home at the end of the day? This was Jack's way of thinking, or so it was told me. Then there was the matter of the minister, who says what to Jack were such ridiculous things as: 'If either of you know of any impediments to why you should be joined, say so now.' Blind Jack figured both the groom and bride knew plenty 'pediments, but did they ever own up at the time? No they didn't. Blind Jack knew Peaches's mother's mouth ran like a waterfall while he was a man who enjoyed peace and quiet. Peaches knew Blind Jack blew his nose at the dinner table while she was a woman who'd grown up with manners. And so on and so forth. Impediments? Roadblocks, was more like it.

"Then there was the admonition, 'What God has joined together, let no man put asunder.' Which was about the most hypocritical statement Blind Jack ever heard repeated in a church, which was saying something strong, right there.

"In the first place, just about all peoples ever did was put asunder what God had put together. Blind Jack and Peaches and most of their friends was Negro peoples, like you and me, so it is just another name for human beings. Yet they was told they was not to stray far outside their neighborhoods over to where other human beings were, unless they was coming to work and not get paid then leave quick. Now there was some putting asunder right there. Killing somebody was putting life asunder from the body, and there was plenty of that going on, even back then. Sometimes Death didn't have to hit a lick at a snake because people seemed to enjoy doing his job for him. And as far as marriages go, according to Jack, wouldn't take nobody else to put it asunder; the groom or bride or both together would likely put it asunder themselves, and have it seem as natural as waking up in the morning.

"Jack had also noticed this statement: 'If there is anyone

present who knows of any reason why these two people should not be joined together, let him speak now or forever hold their peace.' And nobody says nothing! But as soon as the ceremony was over, before the reception got started good, everything that could go wrong and had gone wrong and might go wrong and should go wrong and always goes wrong would be discussed, even hoped for, starting with the flaws of the wedd'n itself. Everyone would say it would have been such a beautiful wedd'n, if only: Then they would continue with the 'if onlys' for a good half hour if you was fool enough to sit and listen. At one wedd'n, Jack had heard this old woman answer under her breath when the minister said something about, 'One man, one woman.' 'Yes, Lord,' said the old woman, 'one was enough for me.'

"It was the way that she said it that made Blind Jack laugh—and then stop laughing.

"Blind Jack looked thirty, felt forty and was nearing fifty in actual chronological age on this, his wedd'n day, the day he decided to steal rhythm from Death, in the person of Bay-Bruh, so he could put off marrying Peaches. Now, Jack figured marrying Peaches would be the death of their choice to be together. He always told her as long as she came to him because she wanted to, and not because she had to, they would be ah'ight, and fine as May wine. What he didn't realize as he slipped into Bruh's house to borry some rhythm was that Death had gone out looking for *him*, and four more like him. Jack slipped through a window and into Bruh's hallway, and there it was, hanging on the coatrack. Rhythm itself—kind of a reddish-colored stole. Jack grabbed it off real neat and was busy admiring it when he kicked the base of the coatrack with them extra-long dogs of his, and even though Bruh was blocks away, he heard all the commotion and shot on back to the house just as Blind Jack was putting rhythm over his shoulders.

"Just as soon as Jack got it on, he felt better and his head began to bob and his shoulders began to move back and forth of they own accord, one at the time, but together, so it seemed, and Jack felt the pleasantest kind of tingling inside, just beneath the skin.

" 'Now, this is something like something!' Jack said to himself. 'This is like being alive twice!' He didn't have time to dwell on the feeling long because just then Bruh swung open the door. Without rhythm, Jack would'a been had right there, but with rhythm along, he dove out of the window, and Bruh was left with an *idea* he'd seen somebody in his house but he couldn't be sure. Then Death noticed that rhythm was missing from the coatrack. And Death sent up a howl that curled the hair of anybody who heard it, and most of the Negroes around there did, so that explains why they hair remains so curly until this very day. (Some say it is 'higher evolutionary process' that makes their hair like that, more compacted, but don't you pay them no mind, young feller; they wouldn't know what color a blue jay might be unless they saw one.) Now, you may have been told Death is a thin, skelacious thing in a black cowl and shroud holding a long scythe on the end of a hoe handle. Well, it's true about the hoe-handle scythe, Death wouldn't be seen out and about without it, but other than that the description is all off. Death, at the time when it was going by Bay-Bruh, was a big, fleshy man, with folds around his waist and the back of his neck and gigantic sensitive feet and hairy toes he couldn't see unless he bent way over, which he couldn't on account of the rolls of fat.

"No, Bruh Death didn't move too good at all. Without the monopoly on rhythm, Bruh was easy to spot and could be slipped. Death knew it had to get rhythm back to lessen its load, since he wasn't going to be confused with no jackrabbit; Death also figured to make quota by getting Jack and

four more like him. Death also had a good sense of smell and
the nose to prove it. So though rhythm helped Jack escape,
Bruh's olfactory sense told him Jack and rhythm might be in
the same place. So Bruh Death went to where the wedd'n
was to be held.

"The wedd'n was held at the Metropolitan Inter-
Denominational Hall, and all the Negroes for miles around
were there, because just about everybody knew Peaches's
family, or they had simply come to hear the hundred-member
Blind Gospel Faith choir, which was scheduled to perform.
The church was filled up with these Negroes, and even some
non-Negroes were there, in spite of the laws against it, because they had their own feelings about the laws, and also
liked Peaches.

"Blind Jack bopped on in as Peaches stood patient and
quiet at the altar. Normally everyone would'a been
a'murmuring and a'clucking about Jack's being a little late
for his own wedd'n, but Jack moved with such—what *was*
that he was moving with? Well, whatever it was, it sure
pleased the eye, to no small degree or apparent end, and all
the Negroes and non-Negroes at the wedd'n found themselves a'gazing at Jack in a kind of a high admiration, even
though he was a little late. They didn't know it was Jack's
plan to sweep Peaches up and away from the wedd'n and
give her some rhythm and tell her that's all they needed to
get by in life—wedd'ns was window dressing, and they
wadn't the sort to have to prove how they felt about each
other to nobody else.

"So Jack sidled up to Peaches and was a'cracking same in
her ear while a'noticing how beautiful she was, but somehow
not a'mentioning that part of it to her. He thought he was
convincing, as grooms late for their own wedd'ns go, but
Peaches still looked kinder disappointed. Just then Bruh
Death opened the door. No usher stepped in to ask whether

he had an invite. Death looked at Blind Jack. Normally Jack would'a been scared but rhythm made him brave. Bruh knew this.

" 'Might not be able to git you today, Jack,' said Bruh, 'but these five on the back row'll do me right smart until such time as I catch you missing, which I will.'

"Now, the five in the back row of the church were none other than Hapshepsut's family—Peaches's mother, brother, father, her sister-in-law and nephew. Them five had gone from the front row of the church back into the back once Jack had turned up late. They was back there a'plotting what they would do with Jack's skin after they'd flayed it all off'a him for leaving their beloved Peaches a'waiting at the altar. They might tan Jack's skin, and make sandals out of it, or belts; or maybe they'd grind the skin up, and mix it with meal, and sell it for horse feed—and just as they was heating up this discussion, Death walked in and they was as surprised as anybody else, and they didn't have no rhythm, obviously, so they was a'sitting like frogs on asphalt as Death raised up his big ham of a fist with the hoe-handle scythe and looked to add 'em on in.

"Death, in the person of Bay-Bruh, prob'ly would'a took their measure then and there if it hadn'a been for Peaches. You can call what she did quick thinking, only she didn't think. Warn't no time. She pulled rhythm 'way from 'round Jack's shoulders, flung it up in the air, then screamed at it. She screamed, 'Life!' And if she hadn'a screamed that exact word, what happened next would *not*'a happened, and we'd live in a different kind'a world today. If she had'a screamed, 'Stop it!' or 'Naw!' or 'Get away from my folks!' or 'Baltimore Elite Giants!' or anything else, rhythm would'a just floated harmless down to the ground and no one would'a had the nerve to pick it up right in front of Death, and Death would'a took five at one blow and got rhythm back on the same day, which would'a made it a good day for Death.

"But that ain't what happened. When Peaches said, 'Life!' the red stole broke into a billion threads and settled over the crowd like—well, like confetti at a wedd'n. A little got on Bruh too, but not enough to give him the edge on all them Negroes and few non-Negroes at the church that day. Bruh swung his hoe-handle scythe like he meant business, but Hatshepsut's family ducked or dodged and Death hit nothing but air and Hatshepsut's folks did not allow for seconds. Death was caught missing and everybody in church felt alive twice. The choir not only was a'singing but a'clapping and a'swaying out of nowhere. Bruh knew he had no customers, so he left. If Death can't sneak in on you, he's treed.

"And then Blind Jack and Peaches was married up all nice and right and proper and everything because even Jack could see by now that Peaches was not one to let walk around un-claimed, and so even Jack looked pleased about the proceed-ings afterward. Later, at the reception, everybody sang and danced and were all 'on the one.' Bruh came too, and moved about 'em, but couldn't gain no grip, and finally caved on in and tried to dance too, and everybody laughed at him be-cause Death wouldn't know the beat if it was standing on his chest. Some Negroes and even one non-Negro danced with Death and smiled at him confident, and Death didn't even take a swing at them because it was no use with the way they was a'moving. They was always one beat ahead.

"And till this day today, if you see a ballroom full of Ne-groes dancing to a beat, they will all seem to be moving as if compelled by a single force. And everybody, including all non-Negroes, would also be this way if long ago their fore-bears had not b'lieved themselves to be too good or too smart to attend the wedd'n of Blind Jack and Hatshepsut 'Peaches' Hin-ton. For once rhythm landed, it was passed into the blood, a permanent thing that keeps a good watch out. That's why Robert Nestor 'Bob' Marley didn't die when a man shot at him from point-blank range at his house in Jamaica one night. Marley saw the flash, rhythm beat the bullet, turned him sideways; bullet just grazed his chest. And he was able to record some more rhythms for the peoples to put over their shoulders before Death finally did catch him missing a couple of years after that.

"Georgie Clinton, you must'a heard'a him. Why, some of his peoples was all up in that wedd'n. Place was a'crawling with Clintons. His peoples got a double-dose of rhythm because they swept up after everybody left. That's why today that boy, old as he is, can't even write a decent love ballad meant for slow dancing like without putting all these different rhythmic effects in there. Even my sister had one of that boy's songs played at her wedd'n reception just last spring; and in case you b'lieve this ain't on authority and is all made up, lemme tell you what happened. Her fiancé was called Light Bulb, on account of he was fair-skinned, but do you think she cared? No sir. She was a fine girl. Any man would'a been proud to have her. Any man but Light Bulb on that day—"

Here I interrupted MacAfee:

"But what happened to Jack and Peaches?" I asked.

"You know," said MacAfee, "peoples often ask me if the man who told me this story also told me what happened to Blind Jack and Peaches after that. Well, yes he *did* tell me, but I can never keep it exactly straight. I think what he told me was, about twenty-odd years after the wedd'n, Death caught Blind Jack missing and was hauling him in while Peaches was getting back in from her ma's. But in twenty years of having rhythm, Jack and Peaches lived a lifetime's worth. They had three children natural born with rhythm, and Peaches and Blind Jack raised them right otherwise, which is about the best thing you can do in this yer life. Blind Jack was in 'em, so Death didn't get all he came for. It was just before Jack took his last breath, as Peaches held his head and looked into his eyes, that he told her, 'Now I get it, Peach; we did it so we could make life.' Peaches looked at him with wet eyes and said, 'Always did have to bring you in out of the rain.'

"So, I said all that to say this: Next time some rhythm catches you up, remember, you wouldn't have such fancies if Blind Jack Hin-ton hadn'a been brought in out of the rain, and *speaking* of rain, it was raining pots and pans that day when Light Bulb was a'sweating bul—"

At that point, Providence intervened. The phone rang. MacAfee asked me to stay squatted and I did while he answered the call. He looked over his shoulder at me and said, "Why sure, M——. Got him right here," before turning away. Soon his back heaved with what appeared to me to be racking sobs of grief—although to you they might have appeared to be spasms of laughter and ridicule at my expense because he had put one over on me so effortlessly. However I chose to believe a sudden new tragedy had entered the man's life. I didn't want to be a burden to him, so I left and headed south toward Los Angeles, a wiser man.

# 7

## Whoopi-Do and Hugheses 2

*My hair was dyed so it would "read correctly on film." At first my hair was absolutely red, flaming red. The next dyeing made it blonde. I was beginning to break out in hives. Then it was dyed completely black, until it was without life ...*

— HARRY BELAFONTE

Langston Hughes has a riff he runs about rivers. Hughes is a poet. His poetry causes us to speak of him in the present tense even though he is dead. Hughes may have accomplished other things when he was alive—wonderful, ordinary, crazy, regrettable things—but they all can be rounded up under the past tense now. His poetry cannot. This is the riff he runs in "The Negro Speaks of Rivers":

I've known rivers:
I've known rivers ancient as the world and older than the
    flow of human blood in human veins.

My soul has grown deep like the rivers.

I bathed in the Euphrates when dawns were young.
I built my hut near the Congo and it lulled me to sleep.
I looked upon the Nile and raised the pyramids above it.
I heard the singing of the Mississippi when Abe Lincoln went
  down to New Orleans, and I've seen its muddy bosom
  turn all golden in the sunset.

I've known rivers:
Ancient dusky rivers.

My soul has grown deep like the rivers.

At the end of the twentieth century in America, if you change
the word "rivers" to "movies" in that poem, you will have
summed up my own current and regrettable state of affairs:

I've known movies
I've known movies ancient as Hollywood relics and older
  than varicose veins.
My soul has grown deep like the movies
I bathed in the neighborhood theater when dawns were
  young.
I built my hut near the multiplex and it lulled me to sleep.
I looked upon the video store and raised the profits above it.
I heard the singing of cable when Spike Lee went up to
  Brooklyn and I've seen its muddy bosom turn much too
  expensive in the utter darkness.
I've known movies
Ancient dusky movies
My soul has grown deep like the movies . . .

Everyone knows that after Clark Gable took off his shirt and
revealed his undershirt in *It Happened One Night* in 1934
there was a new, unprecedented demand for undershirts,
making the manufacturers of them very happy. True advertising was born. Brain implantation of whatever those persons

behind the camera desire. There is a reason it costs $1 million per half-minute to advertise on television during the Super Bowl. Your mind is the reason. There's one thing more addictive than crack cocaine: television. No study has been done to measure the mind's response to the televised images it is shown. No study worth the paper it is printed on *could* be done, for the workings of the brain are immeasurable. Consider then the power of film, where the screen is bigger, observed in a huge, dark room called a theater, which is much like a sensory-deprivation chamber. Films are etched in-brain sans challenge. No interruptions, unless you're lucky enough to be accompanied by a "black" person talking back to the screen in a vain attempt to keep his mind.

These days, if you want to plant a particular undershirt or a tube of toothpaste or a pair of sneakers into a movie or have a character mention a brand name, you have to pay big. This is called "product placement," wherein a manufacturer pays a movie's producers to have a product placed in a scene, off to one side, of no particular interest or utility, just as in real life. Meanwhile, the recurring images, the close-ups, are of men who seemingly have never known undershirts, but have heard of guns, really huge guns, too; and knives; and bombs of all categories (preferably nuclear); and nonstop profanity: men who know how to apply them all effectively—all but the latter.

People who make movies say they are only reflecting society. None of them seems destined to replace Mark Twain in the society-reflecting business. It has gone beyond reflecting society. Now, film and society feed off each other—two grizzlies eyeballing each other up for weakness, sex or perhaps dinner. One film showed young athletes drinking beer and then lying down in front of vehicular traffic to amuse themselves and amaze us. Shortly after that movie was offered nationwide, young athletes in different places in America drank beer then went out and lay down in front of traffic. Some weren't hit by cars and trucks; some were. No further comment about film's impact is needed. As to guns and violent behavior, it seems that "black" people are limited to these portrayals, with no content around to explain them, or to yuk-yukking for no good reason.

"Behind every great fortune is a crime." That is certainly true of fortunes made by some "black" movie directors. The hip-hop b-boy shoot-'em-up drug movie was the staple of movies closing in on the turn of the twenty-first century, including *New Jack City*, directed by Mario Van Peebles; *Boyz in the Hood*, by John Singleton; *Menace II Society*, by Allen and Albert Hughes; *Juice*, by Ernest Dickerson; and *Clockers*, by Spike Lee. Those five were not all of the genre, not by any means, but they are the only five that came close in some way to transcending its limitations.

Thanks in no small part to a couple of these movies, the term "drive-by" came to be seen as out of the "black" culture—a surprise to me, because I had seen plenty of "drive-bys" while watching a television series called *The Untouchables* in my youth. That, to my mind, is where "drive-bys" got started, as well as the sale of an illegal drug (in this case, alcohol) for profit, with murder as extracurricular activity. And, as I recall from black-and-white television, James Cagney might make Tupac Shakur look like a piker in the thug business and probably rap with and outdance him.

In Dickerson's *Juice*, the two are interfaced, as Shakur's character gleefully watches Cagney's finale in *White Heat*. "Top o' the world, Ma!" Dickerson's film transcended genre in visual effect, which follows, for he was originally a cinematographer, and shot the first five films Spike Lee made. *Juice* also made me remember *Angels with Dirty Faces*, where Cagney, portraying a murderer facing capital punishment, fakes cowardice on his way to the electric chair so the young boys who revere him will not think so much of him anymore and not follow in his footsteps. Cagney, the quintessential tough guy, celluloid personification of "thug life," was one-up on Tupac because Cagney, all along, or at least from nearer the beginning, knew it was all an *act*.

*New Jack City* transcended the genre in that Van Peebles got off first—it was done in '90, and was an unsubtle homage to *Scarface*, not nearly as well done, but several actors—including Wesley Snipes and Allen Payne—emerged from it unscathed and even somewhat enhanced.

Lee's 1995 *Clockers* transcended genre in that it was no glorification and once again exhibited Spike's unerring sense for the charming vicissitudes of Brooklyn and his stark visual sense. His opening montage of murder victims evoked the middle passage of stills in *The Godfather*. But by fall 1995, when *Clockers* was released, the genre had begun to exhaust itself in its current incarnation. Lee had avoided it like the plague, and hoped to put a pin in it right here. He could have jumped in years earlier but resisted, in fact resisted shooting *Clockers*, but was convinced by the entreaties of the director he most admires, Martin Scorsese.

But the film that transcended the genre in the purest filmmaking sense was, undoubtedly, the Hugheses' *Menace II Society*. "Black" filmmakers have squeezed all the juice and cut the pulp out of the lemon when it comes to that genre. It will be interesting to see if they can now tell other stories better. I for one would not underestimate them.


It would be impossible to overestimate Allen and Albert Hughes after viewing their second motion picture, *Dead Presidents*. You have to watch it twice to get all of it, and can watch it again and pick up something new and different each time. With each viewing its worlds enlarge, as do the boundaries of those worlds and their inhabitants. It is one of those rarities of artistic endeavor. It simply does what it sets out to do. In that way, it is excellent. In fact, it is marked by greatness—a shocking greatness, even to one who is accustomed to seeing "black" people accomplishing great things.

The Hughes brothers and one of the stars of their latest film, Chris Tucker, and an edgy publicist subcontracted by Disney, the studio that signed the Hugheses to a contract to make pictures, came into grungy radio station offices to promote the rollout of their fall 1995 release. I waited in ambush, much as I suppose a young baseball fanatic awaits the arrival of a great baseball player (even though in this case I am twenty years the players' senior) in hopes of—what, an autograph? No, the knowledge of how they do what they do in *Dead Presidents*. It seems like the best thing in the world, to communicate, and appears as nothing but fun from the relative safety of the bleacher seats. The movie had been shown at the Avalon Theater in Washington, D.C. I had not known what to expect from it. I had by then seen *Menace II Society*, but had been in no great rush to see that, thinking of *what* I was told it supposedly was, not considering the issue of *how* it was done until I saw for myself. Allen said the brothers had been "bored" by the content of *Menace* by the time they got to shoot it. They'd had that story a long time.

In book publishing, there is an axiom: Watch the author's *second* book. It will give you a window into his latent abilities and creative intent. *Dead Presidents* was the Hugheses' second film. There are pictures you get up and walk out of, or switch stations to avoid, or sleep through the third acts of; there are pictures you can see once and have that be enough, good or bad; *Dead Presidents* is not one of those. It was taken from a small, twelve-page story from the Wallace Terry book, *Bloods*, about "black" Vietnam War veterans and their experiences in the theater of war, and before and after, in the theater of America. The story they chose was inspired by a D.C. veteran's tale.

In the picture, the young protagonist is named Anthony Curtis and is played by Larenz Tate, who portrayed the nihilistic O-Dog in *Menace*. Anthony and two friends, Skip and José (Chris Tucker and Freddy Rodriguez), graduate from high school, and the three cement friendships with each other and their young female peers, then go off to war. Their time in this war is reenacted in the brief, powerful second act. In the third act, after their return to "the world," their lives are troubled, and they do psychic wrestling with the genocidal human carnage they have seen and in many cases initiated. Walking away from war is not the same as putting an end to it. So far, the intent of the film seems similar to 1978's *The Deer Hunter*, a sumptuous and expensive production that received five Academy Awards, including Best Picture, Best Director and Best Supporting Actor, all deservedly so, if anything needs or deserves an academy to honor it. But, in the third act, the two films diverge. *Dead Presidents* rode a different kind of comet to its eventuality, "the heist."

One reviewer in *The Washington Post* wrote of *Dead Presidents*: "... *the Hughes[es] may want to indict the white power elite that sends black men off to do their fighting for them and then gives them nothing in return. But they don't make their case ...*"

*The Deer Hunter* made precisely the same point, but without the racial references the *Post* reviewer could not get past: "... *It indicted the [privileged] power elite that sends [unprivileged] men off to do their [dying] for them and then gives them nothing in return.*"

In *Dead Presidents*, the climactic heist is performed, for the most part, with the robbers made up in the most morbid and disfiguring sort of *whiteface*. That, to me, was a striking and subtle stroke. This was the antithesis of the minstrel show: The grinning, happy, eye-rolling, lazy, stupid "black-face" had become the murdering, feral, money-loving, gun-toting criminal "whiteface." Need some get-back, Von Stroheim.

"Need some get-back" is a line from "The Big Payback," an infectious James Brown on-the-one rhythm track from the early '70s that the Hughes brothers use to underscore some of the third act. I asked the brothers the obvious; and they were aware that "The Big Payback" (like nearly all other songs on the sound track) was being used, "sampled" and re-mixed in all kinds of creative and uncreative ways by today's rap artists. They said they had tried a thousand songs from that era until they came up with the ones that best enhanced the visual. "We wanted [the audience and in some cases the musicians themselves] to know where the music comes from," Allen said. Between that, their mounting of the story, their coaxing from the actors of bravura performances, their sound design and sound track, their bizarre "whiteface": Why, such dense texturing and multiple layering of expression is supposed to be reserved for "classic" creative literature. Isn't it?

The Hugheses enjoy a future of brilliant possibilities. They have creative control and things to say. They are humble, at least in the face of the work. When one viewer said to them, "I think you've made a flawless film," they scoffed: "We know better than that." They don't put themselves in their pictures. "Our noses are too big," they say, laughing. But Albert does appear in the background of a scene in *Dead Presidents*. The end frame. He's on the prison bus too.

It takes only one meeting to know how these brothers have allocated their forces. Allen is the people person, the actors' sounding board, the point man who interacts most easily with the public, the publicists, the screenwriters, the agents, the executives, etc. Albert is the tech guy, i-dotter and t-crosser of the hard filmmaking aspects.

After the initial screening I asked them about sound design. I had noticed in *Menace* that they overaccentuated the cock of a 12-gauge shotgun over a grainy, documentary-style visual of one such gun being trained; or how they came close-up upon an eye on a gas range, and haunted the sound with a background of plucked strings as the eye burst into flame. *Pwhump.* The heat is on, baby. So I asked if they thought the curve of their sound design had ascended along with the curve of the rest of their technique. It was a tech question, and the more reticent Albert spoke up, for this was his meat.

"Oh, they tried to use the 'nigger knobs' on us," he said. Tech guys are not known for their diplomacy. Albert was saying that some sound technician had tried to lower the quality of the sound, and thus diminish the effect of the movie overall, simply by using a particularly wrong set of knobs in some control board aspects of the work. But Albert knew the control boards like the backs of his hands; he could say, in essence, "Don't be using *them* knobs on me. Use them A knobs." Allen's way of putting it was this: "We wanted to be moving upward in every phase. *Menace* cost only three million dollars. And some people wanted us to stay a low level of quality." But they did not allow it, and had come up with what Chris Tucker would call the *shit* in *Dead Presidents*. They were out to promote and attempt to bring this coup to the attention of an unsuspecting public. This was occurring at a time when *The New Republic* was publishing an article by a twenty-four-year-old "white" female journalist named Ruth Shalit (she would have had to have been "white" for who else but she could have kept her job after a couple cases of sloppy plagiarism; also, at this juncture there were only "white" journalists and editors in the offices of *The New Republic*). Shalit's article stated the premise that "diversity" (niggers in the newsroom) was causing a general decline in quality of *The Washington Post* and was fueling a venomous resentment between "black" and "white" staffers of that newspaper—which did have some "black" reporters and columnists working for it, and was both as readable and as unreadable as ever, as far as I could tell. Since *The New Republic* had no "black" journalists in its offices, you might harbor suspicions they were just trying to say how right they were to have it like that over there. I think *The Post* is more widely read and more profitable, even though "black" people at *The Post* supposedly kept it from working at the highest levels of production possible. All this malarkey from *The New Republic* was at least enough to make one glad one did not work either there or at *The Post*, but it does elicit sympathy for those who do.

Still, this article and premise were established: Diversity meant an inevitable decline in the quality of the product. Yeah, right, especially if you're going to use the "nigger knobs" on me—knobs like Dinesh D'Souza, whose "book" *The End of Racism* (the most ironic title for a book in the history of words) was also being hyped at the same time as *Dead Presidents*. D'Souza wrote—well, why bother? Let me shorten it to: Niggers ain't shit. In this, his second book, Dinesh explained the historical certainty of this original theory, said slavery was not all *that* bad, a good thing, actually; said that racism and segregation were only natural, desirable, even; said that "black" culture was in precipitous, irrevocable decline. He seemed ignorant to the fact that in America, people get "mainstream" culture in large measure from what he was calling "black" culture. Dinesh got his U.S. citizenship papers way back in 1991, was a native of Bombay, India, and all of thirty-three. Perhaps he had passed his citizenship test, as Richard Pryor once described, by knowing all the negative and loud and rapid ways of saying "nigger." Nigger-nigger-nigger. Good boy, Dinesh. Considering his abilities, how could Dinesh even get a book published with such fanfare and a first run of 100,000 copies? Was there any other subject that he could've tackled with such optimistic backing? Highly doubtful. Only by writing terrible things about "niggers" and only by using the very editor who loved and nurtured *The Bell Curve* could he go unchallenged in his stupefying ignorance; only by "using the nigger knobs." In this case, D'Souza was the knob in question. Out of the mouth of Albert Hughes, a line speaking volumes, and even describing some of them, was born: *"They tried to use the nigger knobs on us."* I'm tempted to call it a dictum, but this is not so much about what the Hugheses say as what they do. For dictums (and answers to problems such as D'Souza proposes), we return to Frederick Douglass:

> When men oppress their fellow man, the oppressor ever finds in the character of the oppressed a full justification for his oppression. Ignorance and depravity and the inability to rise from degradation to civilization and respectability are the most usual allegations against the oppressed. The evils most fostered by slavery and oppression are precisely those which slave-holders and oppressors would transfer from their system to the inherent character of their victims. Thus, the very crimes of slavery become slavery's best defense. By making the enslaved a character fit only for slavery, they excuse themselves for refusing to make the slave a free man. A wholesale method of accomplishing this result is to overthrow the instinctive consciousness of the common brotherhood of man. For let it be once granted that the human race are of multitudinous origins, naturally different in the moral, physical and intellectual capacities, and at once you make a plausible demand for classes, grades and conditions for different methods

of culture, different moral, political and religious institutions and a chance is left for slavery as a necessary institution.

As we waited to hype their film on the air, I noticed Allen trying to engage people (like me) in airy conversation, while Albert moved quietly around on the threadbare carpeting, lightly touching the prehistoric and inactive recording equipment, thinking only God knew what. Allen went over to him after a while and asked, "You ah'right?" And Albert nodded serenely. He merely killed time until he could get his hands on some more interesting technology. Together, I thought, they have a chance to do it. Not only are they brothers, they are twins, so each will always have at least one person he has to listen to. When I asked if they could avoid the megalomania and concomitant irrelevance and dysfunction that go hand-in-hand with being a director embraced by Hollywood, like Cimino, or directors who are the Hugheses' contemporaries, and "black," Allen said that they relied on each other in precisely this way to stay level, humble (at least in the face of the work) and connected to that which they had so far successfully attempted to re-create. By this late date, only an identical twin could grab his brother around the neck and say, "Wait a minute, you and things are getting crazy up in here," and have it be taken as a helpful ballast instead of high insult.

It was Allen who worked with the cast on nuances. Tate, a man searching for himself, found he was that rarity—he could function coolly under stress of war. He became the totem of all survivors upon his return to a world that had changed greatly; returned to a woman he was not sure loved him. Not sure he even deserved to be loved.

Rose Jackson played Juanita, whom we meet as a seventeen-year-old who is winning in her own way. She is an electrifying actress because she seems so perfectly natural. Allen first saw Rose in Rusty Cundieff's movie satire of rap, *Fear of a Black Hat*, taken from the Public Enemy disc called *Fear of a Black Planet*. Keith David portrays Kirby with a vengeance. His character epitomizes the decline of the chosen surroundings, the Bronx, where he runs a small pool hall and has a far corner on the numbers racket before the war and the civil rights movement and "white" flight and twisted nigger knobs and crooked cops and the state lotteries run him toward a less misdemeanorish take on his survival.

The Hugheses even get some dramatic moments out of Tucker, when he would've served well only as comic relief. Tucker is a humorist in the tradition of Pryor, noted not only from your laughter and subsequent loss of breath anytime he launches a soliloquy in the film, but also from his comments to the radio show host as he was interviewed as part of the film's promotion. " 'Black' people have been making each other laugh ever since we were out in the fields in slavery," he said. "The tradition goes on up to Richard Pryor, on and on . . ." The radio talk show host mentions profanity in comedy. She can't stand *Def Comedy Jam*. Tucker says he understands that, some of Russell Simmons's show consists of untalented people given a mike. It is a profane and loutish karaoke, but, then again, some of it isn't, so why focus on the negative? The host, not having a good day, demanded that Tucker "tell me a joke." She repeated the demand. Wisely, Tucker, for one of the few times in his life, clammed up. I did not say what was on my mind, what I learned from Twain: It takes no talent to repeat a joke. Any fool can do it. Tucker was a humorist; his skill lay in *how*, the *manner* he told a story.

Once off Tucker and the placebo of humor, there was plenty of movie left. Allen was slightly surprised that the Vietnam footage had allure, or perhaps that anyone from the general public would think so—and that is good, that *sur-*

*prise* that someone likes a thing you have done. It implies you are still doing work to please your own standards. Those scenes surpassed nearly all since the Russian roulette POW shots of *The Deer Hunter,* nearly equaled those of Oliver Stone's *Platoon* and did equal and in many cases outstrip Francis Coppola's *Apocalpyse Now.*

"Black" film is not a genre, but I was still asked if I could compare *Dead Presidents* with another 1995 Vietnam War film, *The Walking Dead,* produced and directed by African-Americans. I said of course I could compare them, but if I did, the producers of *The Walking Dead* might not appreciate it, because it would be like comparing World Series–level major league baseball to company picnic–level slow-pitch softball. In comparing *Dead Presidents* to *The Deer Hunter, Platoon, Apocalypse Now* (or even to heist movies like *Dog Day Afternoon*), making allowance for the differences in budget, it *could* be that I simply identify more with the characters—simple dramaturgy having its way. After all, this was one of the first times I'd seen characters I'd been introduced to and liked, "black" men, thrown into cinematic combat in the re-created jungles of Vietnam, who did not then immediately all come apart at the same seams. Most might come apart in reality, most everybody would in war, but not all at the same seams. That is what I was accustomed to seeing in film, uncomfortably so; some of this allure is only personal. But some favorable comparisons go beyond that.

When a recon point man steps on a mine and looks back, his stricken face must be just as it is in *Dead Presidents;* both surprised and horrified. He must know that's his ass, putting it bluntly. And if he is blown to bits, then that's what I should see, since that is what happened—it was not a staged explosion with a stuntman jumping off a trampoline in the foreground. The man was blown to bits, and the Hugheses were good enough to re-create it that way—make it seem that way, even though I do not think they actually blew a man to bits, but they certainly fool you.

I'm sure there are messages I missed amid all the rampant entertainment and the things that I didn't know and the good people doing bad things and bad people doing good things, and I hope to get hold of these other stimuli on subsequent viewings. *Dead Presidents* is a feast for the mind. Later on, I marveled less over their picture than over this fact about the Hugheses:

They were *twenty-three years old*!

"When Spike came out [with '86's *She's Gotta Have It*] we had our cameras too. We're not all the same, but then you know that. Of course he inspired us. But while he was working out the bugs up on the screen, we were doing it behind closed doors," says Allen. He nods when the point is made that *Clockers* was perhaps a bit behind the cultural curve. He calls it like he sees it. The universal American baseball analogy keeps its useful application. Lee was writing *The Jackie Robinson Story*. In many ways, Spike Lee *is* Jackie Robinson, and one can completely understand his passion for the project. Robinson, a college-educated man, became a Brooklyn provincial hero, and a national icon; the intense player who overpowered baseball as much as played it, played on will and cunning as much as with physical gifts, much more than fiddled with the game's nuances. Who had time for nuances? He was on a mission. Robinson is known foremost, even aside from being the great ballplayer he was, as the Man Who Broke the Color Line in the Big Leagues. Is that not the lot of Spike Lee? That sword cuts both ways. When, amid the hundreds of "black" ballplayers that followed Jackie Robinson into the major leagues, Willie Mays and Henry Aaron came along, they were known for playing baseball *so well*. They had that luxury. As did Carl Franklin, auteur of *One False Move* and the brilliantly mounted *Devil in a Blue Dress.* What is it better to be known for, in the end? It probably depends on who you are and what you are driven by. With the Hugheses, it is as if Mays and Aaron were identical twins playing on the same team. Would you not follow and respect if not openly root for such a team? Of course you would, if you had any sense.

I'll tell you what is hopeless. Anybody trying to limit these brothers is hopeless. A "Million Man March" was scheduled for October 16—a month following the Hugheses' trip to the capital. The gathering was to be headed by two perennials, the otherwise unemployable old master sergeant Rev. Ben Chavis, and the underestimated Minister Louis Farrakhan. I would go over and evaluate it, not because of them, but because of *you,* because some other brothers would be there, not all of them the same, or related, not all there for the same reasons, but nearly all feeling a pervasive dread that they were being used, set up, measured, fitted for a suit they did not want, a box they were not ready to fill. A few like the Hughes brothers would be there representing their various disciplines. I would've bet you on the spot, then and there, that much more impact on art, science, society, history, a million "black" men, and the definitions of "functional" and "classic," would ultimately be delivered by the likes of the relatively quiet Two-Man March of Albert and Allen Hughes. What they do, we should watch. What they see, seek out. God being always right on time, these are some *smart* boys. It's too late to bet you about this, because now you know.

The children of Israel run the movie industry. It is their industry. Much in the same way that professional football and basketball are industries of "black" people—only not really. The children of Israel write, produce, direct and use their names when they do. But when they act, and become movie stars, the idea is to get as many people in the hinterlands to relate as possible, and so the stars change their names from those said to be befitting for the children of Israel to those more manly and Saxony. Not only do actors who are children of Israel do it, other actors do too. It is called "assimilation" and not "lying to yourself and the general public." This "assimilation" may give the more thoughtful children of Israel pause late at night, sometimes, but it is the only glitch in an otherwise humming industry.

Now take the case of one Caryn Johnson. Caryn is an African-American woman who by force of circumstance once lived in Section 8 government housing as a teenaged single mother. By no means does that fact imply any other. Caryn was also smart. At the age of twenty-three, she had appeared in no movies and did not seem likely to be "discovered," certainly not in the way or to the degree she was; not according to her early circumstances. But Caryn had a way of telling a humorous story with some art. And she had a sudden stroke of genius, one having to do with assimilation, in the movie sense, which is a tough trick for a "black" person, for reasons that are fairly obvious and written all over his/her face; reasons that put everything on the table up front and cut down on suspicions. If Caryn couldn't assimilate her chocolate face and naturally curly hair, she could at least assimilate her name. She renamed herself Whoopi Goldberg. Movie stars and executives who had lost the tiniest bit of sleep over avoiding their heritage embraced her to their hearts. Here was a performer who openly embraced a name said to be befitting of the children of Israel. And so Whoopi was "discovered," given roles in movies. That she brought them off is no surprise, not to us. That she was given a chance, the "vehicles," was the surprise.

Later on, after Whoopi had proven how smart and resilient she was and had acted in the movies and been well compensated for it (though she was never kissed), she fell head over heels in love with one of the children of Israel, who called himself Ted Danson, the better to be ambiguous. And they were so deeply in love that they decided to tell a humorous story about it publicly. They decided it should be a satirical story. Whoopi and Ted laughed to themselves about it during their private light rehearsals; they made up lines they liked, but lines they neglected to get the timing down on properly. They were lines that supposedly skewered the public's attitude about the perceived incongruity of their relationship—it wasn't incongruent to them, in fact, it seemed to them to be the antithesis of incongruity, and they were intent on bringing people around to seeing their side of it. But some people just won't be brought around—especially by underbaked efforts with messy timing.

What happened was this: Whoopi was being "roasted" by the Friars' Club up around New York City. She had Ted come out and affect a Negro dialect and tell ribald jokes about their life together. Ribald jokes usually work at a roast. And Negro dialect usually works anywhere. But Ted came out in "blackface" to do his jokes.

What would have been wrong with coming out and telling the ribald jokes and mounting the Negro dialect, however clumsily, as *Ted*? Wouldn't that be novel? Why, if you were going to talk about sex in such raw fashion, do you have to put on "blackface"? If you are going to say, "Oh, don't nigger-lip me, baby" isn't "whiteface" more appropriate? I have never heard a "black" person speak such words, in dialect or out. I have never seen a "black" actress with collagen injected into her lips, and rarely have I seen a "white" actress without it. So what was it that Ted Danson was hiding from at the Friars' Club? I'll bet Ted never once put on "blackface" when he and Whoopi were in private, getting ready to do the do. Perhaps now you can see, after over a century of this sort of nonsense, why the "whiteface" of *Dead Presidents* would be cathartic. Whoopi and Ted's prior, less original effort didn't go over so well. Some people got up and left, and some who left did not have nearly the same principles or talent as Whoopi; she shouldn't have allowed herself to be in a position where her lessers were in a position to look down on her. Ted's and Whoopi's lives were never the same after that. They were hounded by the press and by their consciences, written up in tabloids, and eventually they were torn asunder. Fortunately, movie stars are in the habit of changing mates on the fly. Eventually Whoopi married a man named Lyle who looked more than a little like Ted, and Ted married a woman named Mary who didn't look much like Whoopi. And as to whether they will all live happily ever after, we doubt it; movies aren't of the breadth, depth, complexity and substance of rivers, no matter how well dressed by marketing. People live ever after: Sometimes they live happily, sometimes they don't, depending on how the river is running that year.

# 8

## Sin and Juice

*. . . The men who murdered Virginia [City]'s original twenty-six cemetery occupants were never punished. Why? Because Alfred the Great, when he invented trial by jury, and knew that he had admirably framed it to secure justice in his age of the world, was not aware that in the nineteenth century the condition of things would be so entirely changed that unless he rose from the grave and altered the jury plan to meet the emergency, it would prove the most ingenious and infallible agency for defeating justice that human wisdom could contrive . . .*

—MARK TWAIN
*Roughing It*

**A**gainst my will and all better judgment, I was summoned to be a celebrant and profiteer in the O.J./double-murder/ marketing showcase/photo opportunity/tourism bonanza/ media fetish/racial feeding frenzy/"Trial of the Century."[1] (The "/" sign is called a slash. A comma usually does the job better; but as the link between the above listings of civilized

255

behaviors, the slash seems appropriate: This is not a story about the deterioration of society—this *is* the society.)

I was questioned by The Judge, in private chambers.

"I'm told you do not think you are fit to serve."

"No, sir," I said.

"Why not?"

"I know too much."

"What?"

"I know too much. I have no comment."

"No one who knows anything can have the nerve to say 'no comment' about this case. It is the people who know nothing worth telling who are the ones that won't shut up. You have heard of it, then."

"I'm alive, not deaf—I couldn't help it."

"Have you met the accused?"

"Yes, sir."

"Have you formed opinions about the case?"

"I see accounts of it in the newspapers and magazines daily. No way to go through them otherwise. I'm often heard sucking my teeth at joyful and interminable discussions of it on television and radio. The case has been obfuscated, then turned cattywompus by what must be the full memberships of both the American and National Bar Associations; the only fact they seem to know with certitude is their total hours billable. And I have been polled. Oh, Your Honor, have I! People have *demanded* my opinion, and on a daily basis—as if my opinion changed that often, as if it made any difference if it did, as if it reflects study."

"How did you answer the polls?"

"I told them what I thought they needed to hear at the time, Your Honor. You see, I do know right from wrong, and usually reality from fiction. So you do not want *me*."

But The Judge would not release me.

"You can put aside your opinion. You must serve," He said.

"Why? A jury trial will do no good."

"What do you mean?"

"A trial is no place to find justice in a case of a man, backed by rich men, who is accused of killing his wife—the key to that sentence being the possessive pronoun. Legally that is treated as a grey area. Besides, honest prospective jurors will be tossed out during the peremptory challenges. The lawyers will feel around along the bottom until they come up with liars who say they never heard of the case, or fools who actually *haven't* heard; never heard of a case on the very whiskers of the rats in the alleys and the beaks of birds on the wing. For such a humdrum crime as wife-killing—it is as commonplace a tragedy as anything on television—this case has drawn a bit more than its share of notoriety. You can kick up a divot of it anywhere; pick it up on the flatware, or the fillings in your teeth. The place to find jurors is the coma unit of the hospital—or maybe the morgue."

"Trial by jury is the best system you have."

"Then Heaven help us on this one, Your Honor."

"Serve, or be fined."

". . . I'll serve. Even though I already know the verdict."

"Oh?" said The Judge. "What will it be?"

"Which court?"

"What do you mean, which court?"

"There is the court of trial by jury, where money-immunity and general foolishness are the rule. Then there is the court of public opinion, which means to be equable and is—in all matters of ignorance. Then there is the court of blind justice."

"Give me a verdict for all three."

"In a court of trial by jury, he is *not* found Guilty. Which is not quite the same as being found innocent."

"And in the court of public opinion?"

"Another mishap—one to be profited from by some."

"And in the court of blind Justice?"

"Of that I have small doubt. But I'd rather not say."

"Why not?"

"I'd rather enjoy the first blush of 'presumption of inno-cence' involving a 'black' man in America. Usually it's been the other way around in the American system of justice. Given all the presumption of guilt toward 'black' men in U.S. history—and the cases are so many that a dime for each would quickly retire the national debt—from the Scottsboro Boys to Mike Tyson—that the 'presumption of innocence' would be first conferred upon *this* 'black' man is not only cautionary, it is the pinnacle of irony."

"How so?"

". . . I'd just as well not say if you don't mind."

"Oh, but you *will* say. If your testimony is relevant you shall not be a juror. You will be a *witness*, and I will send out a bailiff to find you an agent and a celebrity look-alike."

". . . Perhaps then jury duty *would* be best, Your Honor. If you will allow me to tell you my story in private, you can judge my character and prejudices. I think I am characterless and just prejudiced enough to be an alternate. I leave it up to you."

"Would you find him innocent because he is 'black'?"

"I find no one involved who is 'innocent.' "

". . . I like it so far. I'll hear the rest of your story."

"But it is such a *long* story, Your Honor."

"Out with it," he thundered, "or be jailed for contempt."

"Must I?"

"Bailiff!"

"I must, Your Honor. I see it now. It's coming back . . ."

**A**t the pleasure of the Court:

It all started with football. I confess I had admiration for Juice before I met him. He won the Heisman Trophy, symbolic of the man writers, broadcasters and other practicing invalids still consider the best college football player in America—off what little bit they know about it. The Juice got the Heisman while running for the University of Whatchamadoogee, back in 1968, when I was sixteen, feeling the heat rise down in the sticks. I came up down there playing football, because that was what men did, or so us boys were told. I went to the 'Rose High. We wore faded maroon-and-gold unis just like Whatchamadoogee's only they were in as bad a state of repair as our books. We ran our offense out of the "I" formation just like Whatchamadoogee U. I came up with Monte and Paulie. Monte played at the 'Rose with me. We played out and DB—sorry, wide receiver and defensive back. Monte should've played quarterback, but our version of The Juice was installed there. We had nicknamed him Speedy, or, The Perker. Nicknames like that are a dead give-away to future disenchantments: An aging man is not going to remain so speedy, and there will be times when he won't want the reputation for it. Speedy the Perker played quarter-back. He *should've* been in the tail—sorry, tailback—of the "I," like Juice at 'Doogee U. We did all right, though. We'd won nine games by the time we played Catholic Brothers in the Big Game of '69, at the grandest stadium in town.

Juice had taken 'Doogee U. to the New Year's Day Rose Bowl game in January of that year after unraveling a sixty-four-yard touchdown run against the Crosstown Rival—and it was nationally televised, that run, the hackle-raising pride, envy or fascination of all boys, including me, Monte, Paulie and you too if you saw it. Paulie was a running back for Catholic Brothers. He played with another running back named Mike in a split backfield set. These were some fast boys, Your Honor; sub-ten-second sprinters at a hundred yards.

Catholic Brothers and the Golden Wildcats of the 'Rose

were both undefeated when we met. The Brothers wore gold-colored helmets, like Notre Dame, but there was nothing very Christian about how they played ball. We also played like heathens, so it was a hard-fought game. I might add this to magnify your intrigue, as it surely will: The Wildcats were all "black." The Catholic Brothers, Paulie included, were all "white," except two "black" players they had who were fair to middling and not very much needed as I recall.

It was a talked-about game, a well-attended game; it was contested in a rough, uncompromising way—tooth and claw; it was a lovely war to be part of, remembered best and most warmly from the safe distance of memory and time. We struggled fiercely in a bloody, scoreless and spirited battle that was dominated by the forgotten defensive bodily sacrifices and heroics of boys who have now become middle-aged men whom you would not recognize as in any way athletic; old men with paunches now, trying to live out decent lives with what little future they have left; heroic sacrifices made by players who are now dead. And for what? For one evanescent moment, in an irretrievable past, we were all alike in our simple hopes, and very much alive in our simple flesh, our lives exalted above what they actually were. Any mortality of ours went virtually unnoticed.

Catholic Brothers bottled up our version of Juice, Speedy the Perker. We'd given them the edge—we always snapped the ball on the first sound after "Set!":

"Set! Fire!"

Always, Your Honor.

That's how arrogant, uncaring or unknowing our coaches were that year. We didn't care who knew we were coming. That was what the coaches said and that was what we believed. Instead of having us endure the discipline of a varied snap count, we put it out of mind, lined up and went on the first sound. We could outquick or outmuscle everybody in our way. Let the Catholic Brothers coaches notice it on film. Wildcats didn't care. We'd take what we wanted. As long as we won, everything else in life would take care of itself.

And it pretty much had, up until we met the Catholic Brothers and Paulie and Mike. The Brothers were good at football carpentry; they sawed down, cut off and put a hole in everything we tried. Our salvation was that when they had the ball, we were sort of on time with the tools ourselves— Monte, me (rarely me, only when unavoidable), mostly the rest, young men you never read or heard about or saw televised, like our middle linebacker Chris Jones, who could knock you stiff as a casual act and a common one too unless you learned the art of the evasive move and the quick strike.

Being able to deliver a "kill shot"—that's just part of the game, Your Honor. Monte and me, we didn't have time to notice any fetching quality in Paulie's ice-blue eyes: too busy trying to put a tattoo on his—sorry, tackle him. Slowly the game wound down. Emotions channeled through a stadium packed with a rainbow of people whose colors did not bleed well in groups; cheering, arguing, waving pennants, rocking to drumbeats, tingling all over while girls in tight sweaters with narrow waists and muscular legs bounded into the air between them and us, their beloved warriors.

Deep in the fourth quarter, one possession would tell the tale. Catholic Brothers had the ball, third and three, their side of the field. Stop them and they'd punt, we'd get the ball back—and a tie, probably, because we didn't have Monte at quarterback throwing to me or Snatcher, whichever didn't get double coverage. We had Speedy out of position and a ground game the Brothers brought eight rowdy young men to the line to stop. So the deep ball was definitely there. We had to stop them first. They gave it to Paulie off tackle and fired off right. We fired with them. We were sort of around there. We buried Paulie for no gain inside a roiling maroon cloud, streaked by bolts of gold, our hard plastic gear crackling like thunder. Now, I'd like to tell you about their punt and our winning touchdown, and of my heroic block—but I cannot, Your Honor, considering it is you, and seeing as how I'm sworn. We buried Paulie for no gain, all right. Only, he didn't have the ball. He sold us a fake: the handoff went to Mike, who ran for a touchdown. We lost, six–zero. Weeks later we played our last game, the aptly named Blues Bowl. At least we won that, fifty-two to fourteen.

I've helped win or lose many a game since; all kinds of games, not always involving a football. Years have passed. Yet I recall that game with regret, not so much that we won or lost, but we had more to show, should've done better— though Paulie may not vouch for it.

The Juice came into the National Football League that same fall, 1969, and after a shaky start, ran his way into the Pro Football Hall of Fame. This is like to fighting your way into Arlington Cemetery. A bronze bust in a hallowed and usually empty hall might inspire future generations afield, but being there doesn't do *you* much good. Getting there is all the fun of being in a Hall of Fame. Juice rushed for two thousand yards in one season—nobody had ever done it before—for the Buffalo Bills in 1973. Monte and Paulie were preparing to be drafted into the League; they had prepared by playing football for their respective colleges. I was mounting a transient life among the invalids who wrote about football and the like, who sit and decide who will get trophies and who will be inducted into the infamous halls of fame.

Considering what fame, middle age, permanent infirmity and obsolescence do to an athlete, it's hard to imagine the big rush. But there is a rush—not much different from a gold rush. Monte and Paulie got caught up in it, and they are no different from you or me.

My end of this industry was fairly manageable; I would work my way up to the enviable position of "covering" League games. And along that way I saw the Juice run his way into legend, running with an arrogant élan that makes a runner "great" and causes his name to ring in bars, hunt clubs, barbershops, golf clubhouses and other habitats. Juice was fast—world-class speed—and elusive; quick, explosive and deceptive, punishing when necessary; possessor of a *magic*. That was how he was described all his life by those like me. It was a correct description, but a complimentary one only for a few fleeting moments, and soon the chance for any more such moments had passed for good.

Back when he played, the Juice said nobody on the field could whip him in a fight. I later heard the same said of Marcus Allen, another great runner who broke many of the Juice's collegiate records, shattered his professional marks and made off with one or two personal ones, apparently. The best football players—I should say the most effective ones—think in such a lofty manner, or close to it.

Monte and Paulie played in the League nearly two lifetimes, each—three and a half calendar years being equivalent to a League lifetime. Paulie and Monte, along with Juice, played out the string in San Francisco, in 1980. By then all three wobbled about on misshapen knees that often cramped their ability to get out of bed, let alone run, though they were very good barometers, infallible at forecasting rain. When Paulie, Monte and Juice were playing out the string together, I was in the trade the hard way, reporting on the surface aspects of sporting life for *The Oakland Tribune*.

While I was in Oakland, that portion of *The Tribune*'s staff consisting of tyros briefly included a "white" kid from Buffalo named Mark, an ambitious, congenial fellow with dishwater blond hair and big square teeth like Chiclets. Upon word that Juice was coming to San Francisco, Mark said, "Hey, I saw him one night at a club. He came up and told a girl, 'Hey, baby, suck my cock.' "

I could not have been more astounded and offended if Mark had said I had done it; I didn't ask myself why I would take offense when Mark was not talking about me. By reflex I said, "We don't talk like that." Well, I shouldn't ought to have said it, Your Honor; just because I knew me didn't mean I knew Juice.

Later, Monte told me that he had been on one of two team buses after the San Francisco team had been downtown for some civic duty. Juice had just arrived. They were riding back to the team's headquarters when Juice commandeered the bus. Monte was sitting with a fellow nonentity who was playing out the string. He coaches over in Philly now. Funny how things go. The hardened and studious nonentities prosper in the face of adversity, for they know it all too well. The famous and the favored fall apart when the wheel stops going their way. Juice took over the bus, had the driver turn, grabbed the microphone and spoke over the loudspeaker. Juice showed the guys the sights of his hometown. Coit Tower? Golden Gate Park? Lombard Street? The wharf? The cable car? The Golden Gate Bridge? The TransAmerica pyramid? Hardly. "Look at that white girl right there. Look at those two—those are the kind of white girls I like," Juice said brazenly over the microphone, grinning and daring anybody to disagree.

That's one credit you have to give Juice. He always was aware of his role in society. Monte said he and his friend almost melted through their seats in confused embarrassment. Monte said none of the coaches or players said a mumbling word to Juice. The head coach, Mr. Bill Walsh, wasn't on that bus. Monte asked me, "What do you think of that?" I said,

"Not much; men will talk about 'pussy' like it is the key to life." And for all I know it is, Your Honor. But to announce a skin preference about charming qualities that go bone-deep seemed stupid, cavalier—or worse. And if history has taught us anything, it is this: That women whose mysteries move you—you never know what kind of a wrapper she will come in. Once certain conditions of comeliness are met—or go unmet—the wrapper becomes the least important part.

"Yeah, well, that's what Juice said, though," said Monte.

Later, Paulie came by and spoke to me. He was hemming and hawing and that's not like Paulie—we'd been there, at the point of impact, so the normal "black-white" lies were not available. So I said, "What're you hemming and hawing around for, Paulie?"

"... I was sittin' in the ho-tel, me and Juice and ——- from the Rams and —— from Seattle. We're all sitting there talkin' 'bout runnin' backs, and their place in his'try, and I'm pretty satisfied, 'n honored in a way, 'cause these fellas are the best at what we do, y'know, 'n I'm just ol' Paulie."

"Paulie, don't even try it," I said. "You can play." I added this unnecessarily, for Paulie knew he could play. He was in the League. He wasn't speaking of playing; he was speaking of magic.

"Anyhow, Juice up and says, 'I prefer white girls, don't you, guys? White girls will do whatever you want. Black girls, all they ever want is to get married. Never have to worry about the white girls wanting to take you home. Heh-heh ...' "

"He was talking to you?" I asked.

"Worse. Like I wasn't there."

"... Just forget it. It'll mess up your focus. Gotta rehab that knee of yours. Gotta concentrate on that."

I don't know if Paulie ever forgot, but I did. I pressed on, and wrote up football like it was going out of style, which it wasn't. I wrote up all kinds: college ball, Stanford, Cal, the Pacific Athletic Conference; I wrote up Oklahoma, and Georgia with Herschel Walker. I wrote up the Oakland team winning the Super Bowl in 1981 and the San Francisco team winning it in 1982. After the Oakland team won the Super Bowl in 1981 the big Oakland offensive tackle, Mr. Art Shell, grinned at me while standing in full battle dress on one of the wooden podiums they constructed for the conquering players. He smiled and said, "Eight-and-eight, eh?" He referred to my preseason prediction of the team's record. They'd done slightly better. I smiled back, because I had won the big press pool for predicting the score of this Super Bowl game. We batted our laughter back and forth and no doubt people thought something was wrong with us. Mr. Shell was an unusual example of a dominating player, because he could use his head as more than a bullet. When I would take a time-out from writing up football and sports to write about something else, Mr. Shell would stop me on the Oakland practice field and say, for instance, "I saw what you wrote on the editorial page and I think . . ." Then he would make a brief, cogent point that informed me of aspects of the piece I had not seen myself, and I was the one who had composed it. As to the incongruity of this bristling behemoth lecturing me so professorially—I leave that one to you, Your Honor.

I wrote up my history with Paulie and Monte when I got the chance so nobody could say they left the League without getting their nods. I wrote up players, coaches, games, assorted whatnots. I was praised, mostly for what I wrote about Paulie and that game a long time ago; praised for it by the Oakland owner, Mr. Davis, by the San Francisco coach, Mr. Walsh, and by many others, up to a point where it got ridiculous and I was offered work in the tiresome trade at *Sports Illustrated* in New York. I went there reluctantly from my beloved Bay and proceeded to write up Mr. Davis's team moving down to Los Angeles at the same time. While Davis was caught up in the aggravations of moving, he had the wool pulled over his eyes by a rich man named Trump, who didn't know beans about football, but "owned" a team in a rival league and offered one of Davis's quarterbacks a princely sum to switch leagues. Davis, feverish not to be out-riched, matched or bettered the silly offer, when he should have just waved goodbye. Then he was forced to watch his overpaid and mediocre jockey hold back his thoroughbred players like Marcus Allen from returning to the Super Bowl for the next five years or so. I sort of hinted around at this in *Sports Illustrated*, and Mr. Davis fell out of the mood to praise me anymore. I write what I see—what can I tell you, it comes with being a hack. I wrote up the San Francisco team coached by Mr. Walsh, moving up in the world to the high point of winning a fifth Super Bowl by 1995, behind Jerry Rice, the best to ever trot out there for my money. Paulie moved on into work at a couple of television stations. Monte moved into international sales, Juice moved on, ever so briefly, to the booth at Monday Night Football broadcasts for a network where he was both revered and patronized. Everyone had seemingly made peace with their lot, except maybe Mr. Davis.

In time, at the end of the 1980s, I happened to meet a television producer, whom I shall call Mr. O'Brien, a man of propriety, manners and visual sense, if not much of the more common variety. That is to say, he was naive to the fact that most other men do not combine any of these virtues well. He was "between networks," in the way some career wives are between husbands, I suppose, and working up a cable television show that I helped launch into its current decaying orbit. Any work is good work if it doesn't seem like work and you can get it. O'Brien was then hired by the NBS (close enough) network, and talked me into coming to work on the football broadcasts for a year. He had also decided to hire the Juice. Now, I didn't know any more about football than the average person who's spent twenty years playing or writing about it, but I decided not to tell O'Brien I was less than oracular on the subject and left him to his own evaluations, figuring to get a year's worth of work out of it and enough salary to be able to take the next year and write a book with the freed-up time.

Those O'Brien had hired and inherited were gathered together in a network meeting room and introduced to the support team. Juice was brought forward with great fanfare. It was said his "Q" rating was nearly as high as a religious prophet's—second only to yours, Your Honor. O'Brien had been a student at Notre Dame when Juice was at 'Doogee U., running rings around the Irish and earning a deathless place in the Hall of Fame in O'Brien's heart.

Later, we went out to Oakland and met up at a preseason network party held at a downtown hotel. I arrived and, to my surprise, saw Paulie. He said he was "freelancing" for the local affiliate, and I didn't press it. He had been assigned to help Juice, one of two or three helpers Juice had on network payroll or some other, and that was outside of the couple of handlers Juice had on his own, including his lifelong friend Al Cowlings, who went to high school with Juice in San Francisco, introduced him to his first wife (A.C. had wanted her for his own girlfriend, and once Juice found that out, he had to have her first), went to Whatchamadoogee with Juice, and played with him, Juice's call, at every stop in pro football that Juice had made. Now, you can call people like Paulie and Cowlings sycophants if you want, but I'm sure they had other duties. Paulie said he was the assistant to the assistant field producer. I asked him if he considered that work. We shook arms and laughed wildly at each other. Paulie's good people. He asked me about Monte and Speedy, and I said I hadn't heard from Speedy in years, but Monte was working in sales.

Just then another one of Juice's designated helpers walked up. "Hi, my name's Saar, good to have you aboard," he said. "Juice told me to come over here and tell you to get him some water." Then he smiled perniciously and waited expectantly—for what, remains a mystery even today.

I looked over at Paulie, who reddened and looked wicked daggers at Saar. "Hey, I know this guy. He ain't nobody's waterb—" I stopped Paulie right there, and then I told Saar, "Tell Juice I have no water. Matter of fact, I'll tell him myself."

So we walked over to talk to Juice, but as we approached, a young "white" man rushed up from the other side. His fiancée was the concierge on the floor of the hotel where Juice's room was. Or so he now said. Apparently, Juice had spoken to the young woman in private. Her fiancé was now flushed hot. "O.J., that woman you were talking to, the concierge, she's my fiancée!"

"That's good, that's nice," said Juice dismissively.

"No, you don't understand! She's my fiancée!"

"Sweet girl," said Juice, his eyes rattling back and forth like the peas inside of a couple of blown whistles.

"Juice," said the man breathlessly, "you can *have* her!"

We never got back around to the water.

Well, the season went on and so did I. Juice never had too much to say to me on the rare occasions when we were alone. Once or twice he did try to help me out. He told me to never stay at anything other than a Ritz-Carlton Hotel. Juice said he knew the owner of the chain, that the owner was his friend, and a great guy, and would not like it if Juice ever stayed anywhere but at the Ritz-Carlton. I told Juice the only way I could afford to stay at the Ritz-Carlton was if the owner liked my presence enough to pay for it. He laughed.

He also told me he had never been sick a day in his life, and the secret was to gargle with Listerine every morning. I tried it, but it didn't work so well for me. He didn't have much conversation for me otherwise. One of his assistants was usually there flitting about, or one of the Big Bosses.

The really Big Boss, head of this whole mess, had said he was a "liberal" when I first met him. I didn't know whether to say "That's nice; what hoops must I jump through in order for you to prove it?" or to offer my condolences and wishes for his quick recovery. I soon saw what he meant. One Sunday, just before we were to go on the air, Juice was standing with the Big Boss as I walked up. Later on, after the double-homicide, the people who had been Juice's sycophants talked about how when Juice had interviewed players, they always got around to talking about "pussy" during the breaks between takes, if not before. But nobody said that precisely the same thing happened with powerful men like the Big Bosses of NBS.

"C'mon, tell us about the time you did, how many was it at one time, in one night, Juice?" said the Big Boss, and as the Juice grinned and began to say, the Big Boss's eyes softened toward him. Big Boss turned to me and said, "Juice is a legend."

I was struck speechless, Your Honor, and that is a hard thing to do to me. I said I had work to do—they were paying me to come up with information about the League, not to regale them with stories about my narrow band of sexual conquests, especially since I had normally been the conquered one in these engagements. I reeled away, mumbling about needing to make some calls before that show started so I could earn my keep. The Boss looked at me and frowned and said to one of the producers (not O'Brien, who was a decent man), "What's wrong with him?" And for a while there I wondered if something *was* wrong with me, before deciding that whatever was wrong with me was not as well displayed as what was wrong with this situation. I thought this was a game the Juice was playing, and a dangerous game; I have made enough comments on roles "black" men are given in the society. I was taken aback because I'd never before seen the lineaments of the game displayed thusly in the Halls of Power.

Late in the year, the whole crew went to Denver for a big game. The night before, the crew decided to go out on the town together for the sake of relaxation and camaraderie. Since by then I had developed a tendency to be away from the group, I decided I should make an exception and tag along with the technicians and crew members and Juice and his sycophants. I did not want them to think something was wrong with me so I took the invitation and about eight of us went out, including Juice and Paulie and Saar. I did not know we were going to a bar with a western motif where naked women were displayed, gyrating and enticing men who were drinking and howling and waving small banknotes around. As I walked in, I saw Saar studying me as if about to enjoy an impending predicament. Paulie looked at me and swallowed hard, then shrugged and chugged on a beer. I didn't stop to think about it then, but I think Juice and I, and maybe one of the tech guys, were the only "black" people in the joint. Although you can't count Juice as "black"— nobody in the body bar did, at any rate. He was welcomed as the Second Coming, the "white" people parted before him and slapped his back and put him up front so he could take a better look at the naked women and tell all the other men which of them was acceptable, and even perhaps choose one, if she and her husband were very fortunate. One man, whom I took to be a proprietor of the place, walked up to Juice with a woman who wore nothing but a bow tie, her naked breasts hard and stiff and pointing out unnaturally, made so rigid by the surgical implantation of perhaps the same mysterious polymer that goes into the shells of football helmets.

The man said, "Jewyce, wont you to meet mah wahfe."

The naked woman giggled and extended her tiny hand. Juice took it and shook it, appraising her up and down as though she were an Angus heifer he might soon bid on. The man stood there and beamed the whole while. I thought of Roxanne Pulitzer, wife of the newspaper heir and a purveyor of bimboism; she had written in a tell-all book that sometimes, during the lulls in the ménage à trois and bestiality and whatever else it was she and her famous husband did to stave off boredom in the bedroom, in order to steel his resolve, she would mention that she would like to be, let us say, managed, by O.J. Simpson, while her husband watched.

This was the surreal world O.J. gladly walked. In time, he knew no other, nor, apparently, did he care to. I told Paulie I had to get out of there. I left, and noticed Saar watching me with a smirk on his face. He knew what was going on. Later Paulie told me that on the plane on the way back from Denver, a businessman had come up to Juice and Saar—Saar was never far afield from his meal ticket—and started talking about how much his mother loved Juice, loved him as she loved no other, except the former baseball slugger Willie Stargell (the businessman's family was from Pittsburgh), and that she would be fit to be tied to get the chance to meet Juice. Juice asked if the man's mother would be meeting him at the airport. The man replied that his mother was on board. So Juice told the man to bring his mother up to first class. He'd love to meet her.

"She's on the plane, Juice," the businessman said, "but she's down below. We're taking her body back to be buried . . .

"But Juice, if you would come to the funeral, it would make her the happiest woman on earth! Will you come, Juice?"

Juice said he doubted if he could make it; but the man was welcome to take his best wishes back to coach.

Paulie said Saar and Juice were bemusedly quiet for a while, until Saar said, "Wow, I've seen a lot of amazing reactions to you, Juice, but never any like that!"

Paulie said Juice agreed, that had been something else.

Then Paulie said Saar asked Juice if all this adulation and idolizing ever went to his head. Paulie said Juice looked at Saar and said that at times he'd felt like the son of God. Paulie looked at me, as if waiting for some reaction. But in spite of everything, there was something about Juice, something forgivable, so I said, "Well, Paulie, we're all the children of God." Paulie shook his head and grew sober. "Naw, man. He said *the* son of God."

The NBS football crew took a late New Year's Eve flight to Miami to cover the Orange Bowl that year. Because only mad dogs and TV people fly on New Year's Eve, the plane was nearly empty, save for the production crew, producers and the "talent," the misnomer applied to those who appear on camera. Paulie was on the plane, and Saar, and the show's host, and even O'Brien, I think. As we boarded, I saw one of the stewardesses look up and simply say, "O.J. Simpson!" We were heading for South Florida—home of the Pulitzers, though by now I had discovered it didn't matter where we went in America, reaction to the Juice was the same.

Shortly after takeoff, the stewardess whispered to Juice and batted her eyelashes and went into a first-class lavatory. Then Juice gave the high sign and went into the lavatory behind her. A voice said, "Watch this!" I don't know if it was the host, or one of the producers or crew, and it probably doesn't matter, because it seemed to me everyone fixed on the lavatory door. Soon Juice emerged from the lavatory, beaming. He did not smoke, that much could be said for him at least; but he produced a cigarette. He flipped it into his mouth and pantomimed a deep inhalation and then a relaxed exhalation. And everybody who saw this got it and cracked up, turning red with laughter that was not the kind that forces you to join up. Maniacal laughter, I think it's called. I admit, even I shook my head and smiled, if ruefully. The host was giggling like a schoolboy playing hooky. He turned to me and said, "Did you see that? Hunh? Hunh?" I said, "Afraid so." This most recent public sortie of the Juice's was of amusement and comfort to the host.

Years later, long after Paulie and I had left NBS, that same host was plying his trade toward professional basketball. A young pro basketball player named O'Neal had become the subject of national interest—making commercials, music videos and being fantasized about. NBS happened upon a videotape of O'Neal, made while he was doing a radio show with a fellow who had been his roommate at LSU—a guy sort of like Paulie, I suppose, except not as good an athlete. O'Neal was obviously comfortable with this fellow, who no doubt gained a radio show in part because of his acquaintance with the new stud of the day. A video of the radio show was aired during halftime of an NBA playoff game. The host set up a "clip" wherein O'Neal's ex-roommate asks him to describe his version of the final moment of a championship game. Then the clip was shown. A relaxed O'Neal took the mike and in a near-perfect parody of a television play-by-play commentator, said something like this:

"Five seconds left in the NBA championship game, four, there's O'Nealouthighwhatishedoinghe'swayoutofhisrange! He's launching a three-pointerwhatishedoingit'supit's GOOOOD!Idon'tbelieveitAHdon'tbelieveit!!O'Nealhashitan impossiblethree-pointeratthebuzzerandtheOrLANdo MagicarethcNBAchampionshahaIcan'tbelieveitdidyouseehim

wayoutofhisrangelikethatdidyouseewhatthekiddidthey're
goingcrazyhereinOrlandoO'Nealisrunningaroundthecourt
ohmyGodIcan'tbelieveitIcannotbelieveitdidyouseewhatthe
kiddidinallthehistoryofsports . . ."

And on like that for a while before ending by vibrating his
head like a tuning fork, his lips making a yo-yoing sound out
of Merrie Melodies cartoons, and then laying his head over
to the side, as though he had passed out from sheer emo-
tional exertion. It was a superb satiric commentary on the
art of sportscasting. The camera came back into the network
studio and the host sat there flummoxed. To his credit, at
least he admitted it, and after several attempts to explain
what was coming up while still trying to process what had
just transpired, he announced that O'Neal had flabbergasted
him, and "threw" the action elsewhere. A man that big and
that "black" had that facile a brain? It would take some time
to figure out something to rationalize that one away.

So anyway, me and Juice worked the sidelines of the Orange Bowl game. He worked one sideline and I worked the
other, and O'Brien said it was a pretty good job we did. Four
years later, on New Year's Day 1994, we were back on the
Orange Bowl sideline again. Juice was still working for NBS
and by then I was long and happily gone. As we watched the
game, I noticed a particularly effective player, the fullback
from Florida State. His name was Floyd, though he liked to
be called "Bar None." One of his injured teammates stood
on the sideline near us and after one of Floyd's earth-
churning efforts, he turned and said with high admiration,
"That boy gon' kill somebody." All in all it was an accurate
way to describe a football player who could have an impact
in the League. One other thing, Your Honor. The quarterback for Floyd's team in that game was named Ward. He
won the Heisman Trophy too. And his coach pulled him out
of the game on second-and-goal with less than a minute left

in the game after Ward had driven his team all the way down the field, with his team down by a point. The coach of his team sent in the field goal unit. This drive was for the national championship, and this particular team had lost the national championship on failed field goals twice in the preceding four years. Now the coach took out Ward, the Heisman Trophy winner, put the "black" quarterback above all, and he sent in the field goal kicker. The kicker made the kick, saving the coach's reputation, perhaps in just about all eyes but mine, but now the Florida State team had only a two-point lead, and there was still over half a minute left. The opposition closed to within range and lined up for a forty-seven-yard field goal. As they lined up to try it, Juice was pretty mad, and so was I, so I said, "You know that kicker's going to make this, that would be the truth of ball." But the kicker missed, and Ward and Floyd's team won the game almost in spite of their coach's unspoken opinion of one of them.

It may be of interest to learn how I came to leave NBS. It was by mutual assent, though I have the feeling I still would have been dismissed even if I hadn't wanted to be. Back in that 1990 season with the Juice, the crew had gone out to Los Angeles to do some work on Mr. Davis's team. Marcus Allen played for them then, but was falling out of favor with Mr. Davis. Of greater interest to me at the time, Mr. Art Shell had just been named as the head coach. I thought this was fitting and proper and couldn't wait to tell him so. Juice and me and a few crew members descended upon Mr. Davis's team's training facility. I still knew quite a few of the boys, and pleasantries were exchanged all around, although they knew or would soon get the word that I was a hack and would write what I saw. Since in television there isn't much call for writing, they were safe, with me being at NBS and all. And they were particularly safe with Juice. Some of the old heads still marveled when they saw him, although the younger players would merely nod, as though he was someone they had heard of, but he'd never raised a hackle anywhere on their much younger bodies.

Just then, one of Mr. Davis's hirelings waddled out and announced that yours truly was not welcome at Mr. Davis's team's practice facility, and that if I wanted to come to the game I could buy a ticket like everybody else. I wanted to say that judging from the half-empty stadium, there were plenty of seats available, and there might not be if Mr. Davis had let go that lame quarterback and kept Marcus Allen happy. But I couldn't say that because I had just shaken hands with Art Shell so this put us both in a compromised position. You see, as a writer, you welcome this kind of threat, because their throwing you out is going to give you something good to write about. But TV requires a certain degree of cooperation from the subjects and it doesn't play well not to be there at all, so TV people take pains to be ingratiating, while I have been trained not to take any such pains, not if I don't care to. At the same time Mr. Shell had just been hired as the first "black" head coach in the League in generations. Mr. Shell and I retired to a small room. I said, "Art, you're an organization man. Now, normally this would be interesting, but I won't compromise your position. I'm out."

Mr. Shell, for his part, sighed and said, "Thanks, man."

I thought that was the end of it, but I was mistaken. The next Sunday we were in the makeup room at the NBS studio getting ready for the show. At first there were just the makeup person and me; then Juice came in, saying nothing, not even so much as a bah humbug. Then the rest of the "talent" came in—the host, my partner, Mr. Beathard, in our little segment of crime during the show, a couple producers and O'Brien as well. As soon as Juice saw the room was populated well enough for a minstrel show, he began. "Boy, you should'a seen [Wiley] running away from that practice field last week. They said they didn't want him there and he took off!" Juice assumed a limping gait that was all elbows and feet that appeared to be hurting. Old Stepin Fetchit would've turned green with envy. "Yah, this is what he looked like. He was moving!" The occupants of the room were convulsed with laughter. However, I was not. And it's not that I do not deserve to be ridiculed; it's that I deserve to be ridiculed by those who owe me some ridicule. One could very easily see how I had made Juice's life so miserable by trying to do something with mine. So without any consideration of the ramifications, I merely said,

"Fuck you, Juice. Okay? Fuck you."

Understand that I know the dangers inherent in speaking to the Juice this way better than most of you, having attended many prizefights and football games and other war footage. Juice could have crushed my head like a grape, probably. But that had nothing to do with what I said to him. And eloquence and art and tact had nothing to do with what I said, although that much is obvious. Any latent fears about my personal safety were less than fear of undue besmirchment of my smidgen of character. It had nothing to do with not being afraid of him. Courage is just a nice word for fear management. So I said it, and at the time I said it I meant it. Everybody in the room, host, producers, makeup people, O'Brien—they all froze solid. The banter stilled and died a quick and beautiful death. And I knew at that moment I was gone from NBS as soon as the Big Bosses could manage it and there was nothing anybody, including O'Brien, could do about it. And I was *glad*, Your Honor. Because I had broken the script of Juice's surreal life, which nobody else ever did. *Glad* that I had broken the script, glad that I had broken it in this particular way. On our otherwise silent way onto the set, I said to Juice, "Look, man, I don't mean no harm, but where we come from"—I meant the neighborhood of football—"an ass-whupping ain't shit, you know?" And a look passed over the Juice's face that I cannot fully describe, because the word that best describes it is *malevolent*, Your Honor. He could have killed me then, or tried to, if he could have been sure that the "white" men would stand there and watch him (which they would have) and then testify on his behalf if he had been tried for it later (which they would have) and claimed ignorance. But the script had been flipped, and he was not so sure, and in that hesitation the moment was gone, and we moved on as if nothing had ever happened, but of course it had.

I saw all this, Your Honor, and if I had not seen it I might not have believed it. I saw how his behavior was encouraged, by "white" as well as "black"—more so, even. He was the epitome of acceptable "black" manhood—a premier athlete who had hauled wood for acceptable institutions and was docile before them and accepted perks from the executives and remembered the names of their children, though, as it turns out, he couldn't have composed a declarative sentence to describe them—not that he would've been asked. It was an unneeded skill and it might be dangerous. All he had to do was be the warrior, the athlete, with all its attendant roles, *and nothing more.*

Jim Brown, Juice's forerunner, came by the set later that year, before I finally took my leave. I did finish out the year, and was surprised when everybody was so nice to me, in a stilted sort of way, including Juice, through the final gun of the last game NBS covered that year. O'Brien called me shortly after that and tried to apologize, but I told him none was necessary because, as I saw it, we had both done our jobs. I had caught Jim Brown watching me back then, watching for breaks in my manner, for my flaw, for something that would explain how I came to be at NBS. His face said he didn't believe I could be there unless there was something wrong with me, and you know what, Your Honor, I'd begun to agree with that look; without a certain obsequiousness, how could I be there in the first place? Only by the naive grace of the man named O'Brien, who was merely looking for competence and merit, foolish man. He is one of the rare ones. Usually that's not what they are looking for at all. Like Jim Brown, I was not surprised when I learned of the murders. The difference between me and Jim was, I would not have said so on national TV.

"Fascinating, if long-winded," said The Judge. "Do you think any of it has any actual bearing on the case?"

"Your Honor, at the pleasure of the Court, my words have a bearing only on my own feelings and opinions, and not on the O.J. Simpson Trial of the Century. My feelings and opinions are these: It seems to me that it is not 'black' people who constructed the hoopla and the commerce and the underlying conundrums of racism and sexism surrounding this trial. It was not 'black' people who put up a two-hundred-thousand-dollar reward for anyone who could unearth evidence to prove the Juice's innocence. The owner of Gimbel's department store did that. It was not 'black' producers who decided this trial was fit TV programming for the entire calendar year of 1995. And it was not the best 'black' defense lawyers in America who catapulted onto the Juice's bandwagon: The best 'white' defense lawyers did that, and surely not for the money, for the wealthiest sultan of Araby would be tap city after six months' worth of billable from this all-star cast of barristers and attendant snoops, assistants and technical experts. So why did those 'white' lawyers join up, except—perhaps instructively—for the late William Kunstler? That brilliant 'black' lawyer, Mr. Johnnie Cochran, was *summoned* to the case. He didn't volunteer. Neither did the lisping, well-intentioned and desperately mediocre 'white' wet-dream version of affirmative-action 'black' prosecutor, Mr. Christopher Darden. Neither of *them* volunteered, although as far as images of 'black' people are concerned, Mr. Cochran has so far been the saving grace of this grim farce; he also brought in Mr. Carl Douglas, so at least two 'black' men involved in the fiasco of the century come off as functional.

"But it wasn't 'black' people who took the handcuffs off Juice after he was initially taken into custody following the murders. It was privileged 'white' men who did that. It wasn't 'black' people who retained attorney Robert Shapiro on the Juice's behalf. It was the 'white' chief executive officer of the ultra-rich King World video distribution company who did that. It wasn't 'black' people who negotiated with Shapiro's lawyer on his fees for setting up the legal Dream Team. It was Juice's 'white' business manager, Skip Taft, who did that. And it wasn't any 'black' people who then told Juice he could turn himself in anytime he wanted to: 'Next Wednesday, Juice? By noon? Okay, fine with us. We'll be here. See you then.' 'Black' people live in an alternate universe from that. It was privileged 'white' men who gave Juice leeway. It wasn't 'black' people who provided a slow-moving escort to the Juice when his Ford Bronco was on the leisurely lam. It wasn't 'black' people in those police cars following at a respectful distance. Guess who. It wasn't 'black' people who determined the prosecution's case should hinge on the testimony of detective Mark Fuhrman, or on that utterly ridiculous 'it-has-to-be-one-man' scenario. One man couldn't have done what Juice was accused of doing *and* gotten rid of bloody clothes and a knife at the same time. Not without help. But it wasn't 'black' people who ordered the police to stop looking for perpetrators and/or accomplices. Again, this line of prosecution 'attack' was another brilliant accomplishment of the privileged 'white' men. So even if Juice were found guilty, why am I being told, by privileged 'white' media pundits, that it would be 'black' people who would riot? Nobody *I* know would riot, and I get around. It would seem to me that privileged 'white' men would have the most reason to riot. But, of course, there are some 'black' people who, when you go out of the way to tell them they should riot, will take you up on it.

"And, Your Honor, none of that has anything to do with who cut Nicole Simpson's throat and stabbed Ronald Goldman to death. Neither does the matter of whether or not detective Mark Fuhrman, who 'found' the controversial (and superfluous) bloody glove on the Juice's estate after the murders, is a racist. I'm sure he is a racist, and a flaming one, why wouldn't he be, he was a cop in L.A., wasn't he? He seems prototypical of the big-city policemen almost everywhere—unintelligent and undiscerning, vain, venal, utterly unreflective, drunk with power, eminently bribable, all in all a by-the-numbers cop profile. So why wouldn't he be a racist? After his interviews with a screenwriter were published in court and witnesses testified and his rank bigotry was exposed, I was asked for some words on what it must be like to live in a world where such policemen existed. I offered up this: In this world, there were not just policemen like Fuhrman; there were bank mortgage underwriters like Fuhrman; college professors like Fuhrman; high school principals like Fuhrman; journalists and editors like Fuhrman; doctors like Fuhrman; lawyers like Fuhrman; senators like Fuhrman; real estate agents like Fuhrman; car salesmen like Fuhrman . . . you get the drift. What do you mean, 'How do you live in a world with Mark Fuhrmans?' You don't. You die in it.

"When it comes to loading his problems up on 'niggers,'

Mark Fuhrman beats the hell out of Mark Twain's Pap Finn, and that is no mean feat. In fact, if Mark Twain were still alive, the O.J. Simpson murder trial would probably kill him. Or he'd kill it. Long before Juice's murder case, Fuhrman had said, and on tape, 'First thing, anything out of a nigger's mouth for the first five or six sentences is a fucking lie.' So who is Fuhrman telling on here, 'niggers,' or himself?

"Remember the lesson from *Huckleberry Finn*, that the spoken word always reflects first on the *speaker*, and not the subject. For what was it Fuhrman was doing when he was taped, or when he testified under oath at the Juice's trial, for that matter? Was he telling the truth every five or six sentences? According to sworn witnesses, he said, 'The only good nigger is a dead nigger,' and referring to himself as a cop, 'You're God.' Then he said, and on tape, 'We've got females and dumb niggers and Mexicans who can't even write the name of the car they drive.' But apparently the prosecution isn't much on cars either. The prosecution didn't put up the Juice's attempt to take it on the lam in a Ford Bronco as evidence in the trial, or his passport, or the ten grand in cash he was carrying, or even his interesting suicide note; instead, they put on the impeccable Mark Fuhrman. This is the wellspring of inspired human genius!

"Isn't it?

"What of the superior mentality of Fuhrman himself? Maybe he salted and cooked the crime scene with evidence, and maybe he didn't, but the crime scene definitely didn't *need* any salting and cooking, on that we may be in agreement, so Fuhrman skulking about like some twisted version of the Scarlet Pimpernel became the undoing of the very justice he claims to champion and want so badly. Fuhrman is so smart compared to the 'niggers' he despises that he might now go on and discover the antidote for penicillin. But, as a bigot, Fuhrman is an easy target and I could make a pincushion out of him all day but that has nothing to do with who cut that woman's throat.

"That the Los Angeles police were overbearing or conspiratorial (they usually are, aren't they?) has nothing to do with who cut that woman's throat. That the prosecutors were vain, vexed, slow on the uptake and more than just bordering on incompetence themselves for even bringing up Fuhrman has nothing to do with who cut that woman's throat. That the veritable army of a defense team was skillfully and appropriately obtuse has nothing to do with who cut that woman's throat. That Nicole's family sold her down the river and even her father turned his back on her when she showed him pictures of her battered face has nothing to do with who cut that woman's throat. That Nicole Brown Simpson had done questionable things at the Juice's behest, then on her own, and became what's called a 'ho' or a 'bitch' by all those men, both 'black' and 'white,' who say she 'played' Juice has nothing to do with who cut her throat. That you, begging your pardon, Your Honor, have allowed people like me with our half-baked opinions and prejudices to be so long-winded has nothing to do with who cut her throat. None of it does. It is simple, Your Honor. Just ask the Juice: 'Do you know who killed the bitch?' "

"Watch the language."

"I plan to, Your Honor."

"Say 'the B-word' instead."

"All right, I will. But what about The Question?"

"He said he was absolutely one hundred percent not guilty."

"Not only said it, Your Honor, said it with nostrils flared and with a dip of his head, like a proud, kept thoroughbred stallion. But, no, ask him again. This time ask him if he *knows* who killed her. Just ask him. Yes or no. If he says, 'No,' then he *is* a nigger—one not unlike Mark Fuhrman. If he says, 'Yes,' then he's just a man. He hasn't left himself much choice, Your Honor. And I'm afraid the rest of us are left with even less."

"So are you saying you think he did it?"

"Your Honor. Please. I'm saying that what you have here is three hundred thousand dollars' worth of trembling prosecutors with a half-baked case going up against ten million dollars' worth of nothing-to-lose defense attorneys who know a half-baked case when they see one. I'm saying the state's dozen prosecutors were so worried about whether they were being made to look like, well, three hundred thousand dollars' worth of prosecutor, they forgot to do their jobs. Their jobs looked easy enough from over here."

"Objection!" says one of the prosecutors.

"Second that," I said.

"Overruled, both of you!" said The Judge to the prosecutors. Then to me: "Easy enough? How so?"

"Well, just a couple of instances, Your Honor. That Kato Kaelin alibi. In the first place, he was Nicole's friend, but he's staying at Juice's manse, because Juice doesn't think it would look good for him to stay at Nicole's? What was Juice doing in their business? Weren't they divorced? Kato is the alibi? They went to McDonald's in a Bentley? And not one prosecutor asked if they'd ever gone to McDonald's together for any reason before—let alone in a Bentley. Not one prosecutor asked if this was a first.

"Then there was the airport hotel where Juice stayed for a few hours once he flew to Chicago. Not once was he asked if he had ever stayed at that hotel before—or if he had ever stayed at *any* hotel in Chicago before that was not the Ritz-Carlton.

"And ask about Al Cowlings's frequent availability, and Robert Kardashian's impassive face. Why I bet, even when Juice is found not innocent, but not guilty either, Kardashian will look like the cat that not only ate the canary but also owns his own pet shop. The freeway 'chase,' the suicide note, and ten thousand dollars he had on him, and, well, just little things like that, Your Honor."

"But all of that is not proof of anything," said The Judge. "You cannot convict a man for murder on that."

"I'd convict Juice for accessory to murder only if everyone else is indicted as accessories before and after the fact. This is some class-action guilt right here. If I may, Your Honor."

"Proceed."

"**P**retend you are blind. Like Justice. Take The Case apart layer by layer. An ex-wife and one of her consorts are murdered. The ex-husband was in close proximity and there was evidence of blood in his car, at the scene, in his home, and a long history of physical abuse. He is your prime suspect before you even get to any of this evidence because of one word rumbling around in your mind. Precedent. Two kinds prevail here. The second is the unspoken precedent of believing a 'black' man guilty until he is proven innocent.

"But the first is a man's ability and proclivity to end any disagreement with his wife the real hard way. I decided to keep newspaper clippings of similar murders reported after the Simpson-Goldman murders of June 12, 1994. I gave up that enterprise after six weeks because I was running out of storage space. I found this kind of crime happens *every single day*—or so close to every day even You would not feel the difference, Your Honor. Precedent says the incidence of murder of wives by husbands or ex-husbands is rivaled only by shoplifting or incest. One man in Maryland, a 'white' truck driver, came home and caught his wife in bed with another man; he sat up with her for a while contemplating her offense then blew her brains out with a 30.06 rifle from point-blank range. The judge gave him eighteen months, and said he only did that for appearance' sake. He happened to be a 'white' man. In another case occurring around Washington, D.C., the husband who did the murdering was 'black'; that he was from Alaska was the only novel part of it. He killed his former wife and her lover even though they were in separate places—the lover working at a swank hotel in Bethesda, Maryland, the ex-wife at a hospital in Virginia. The man commuted to pull it off, then drove to the Lincoln Memorial and shot himself in the head. Why would he take such pains? I believe he thought if he exhibited this behavior, then perhaps what the privileged said about him was true—he was a murderous savage at bottom and such conduct was inevitable. But it was not his lineage that drove him, Your Honor. It was his feeling of power and control over the life of his former wife—his feeling of ownership over her. Some people call it jealousy, but this gives jealousy too bad a name.

"Now, I've heard it said that The Juice, owing to his choices in women and habitat, wanted to be 'white.' Your Honor, you will forgive me, but a bigger crock of shit I never heard. Juice didn't want to be 'white'; the pathetic role he participated in all his adult life, a role he played as the illiterate Mandingo sexual athlete hail-fellow-well-met who never had anything but a smile for the privileged and nothing but the back of his hand for the unprivileged, his acceptance in this role, his comity within it, his experience—his world—was *based* on being 'black'—but a certain kind of 'black' was required. He spun a tangled web of stereotypes and for it he was dearly loved and paid a handsome wage. California estate, blond, blue-eyed wife, millions in assets, access to executive chambers and jets, endorsements, broadcasting salary, all of this for a washed-up jock who played in the days before million-dollar salaries and couldn't spell? If Juice were 'white,' he could not have had any of that presumed abundance for those attributes. Juice couldn't write a legible letter, much less a notification of bankruptcy. Off the field, he'd *required* help, by all definition. And he got it. He got loads of it. And he didn't get it from 'black' people. Juice made 'whites' feel comfortable with his kind of 'blackness.' He didn't want to be 'white.' He wanted to be *privileged*. And he was."

"Objection," said a defense lawyer while checking his watch. "Witness is speculating."

"Your Honor, I agree. I object to it myself."

"Overruled," said The Judge. "Continue."

"Begging the court's forgiveness, Your Honor. Power has never convicted itself of anything. And it is Privileged Man's unwritten law that he can kill his wife, or any of his ex-wives, no matter how they are currently situated. In this case, the man was 'black,' in the most acceptably grinning, athletic, illiterate, doggish, benighted, irredeemably and warmly-acceptable-to-the-white-folks-in-charge sense. This is the Nigger Ralph Ellison loathed. This is not Twain's Jim. Juice did not possess such dignity. This is not even Uncle Tom. Juice was the 'black' man that 'white' men wished him to be. Your Honor, I should explain, before the tabloids take that and run with it, the way you must read that is, He was the Unprivileged man all Privileged men wish Unprivileged men could aspire to be. And what makes the trial of utility in this society driven by mass media is that the victims were 'white' and Juice was 'black.' This made it fascinating and this is the kind of fascination that keeps audiences glued to the set so that they may be sold a certain brand of beer and soap. It had to be this that made it so profitable an exercise, because this sort of crime is carried out every single day; and if Juice had murdered a 'black' wife, we would not be enduring any of this, Your Honor. Look out a window and you may see an example of the crime, even as we speak. A crime like this standing alone is passé. It was explained that Juice was a famous public figure, and that was why it was given such saturating attention. Well, yes, Juice was famous by the time the bodies landed, but before that he was famous? To whom? The young? They didn't know beans about Juice. The middle-aged power-brokering 'white' man? Yes.

"The assumption of fame is a building block of pathology. Fame is one DNA strand of insanity. At the time of the murders Juice was a sportscaster and an actor manqué who possessed not range of expression but only duality of it; he was either smiling or bewildered in every role he ever played. This was the act he carried off in order to get the big shots to give him roles in the first place. As an actor—well, I had thought there were lawn jockeys that were more expressive and had better acting range than Juice, but then he was carrying out one act already. He made a living off a recurring role as a car dummy in the forgettable *Naked Gun* series of movies; sometimes a real car dummy was his stand-in. Your Honor, I'd seen him brag about this embarrassing and recurring role to young blond women in Miami Beach bars and waited with him for them to be impressed—and await it yet. Juice was the cultural equivalent of a Frisbee prior to June 13, 1994. Young people had no clue. A 911 dispatcher, whom Nicole called in panic after one prior beating, asked, 'Is he the sportscaster or whatever?' in response to Nicole's saying, 'He's O.J. Simpson! I think you know his record!' Which record? A 1989 nolo contendere case of spousal battery, or his exploits on the football field and in rental car commercials? I cannot be sure what she meant, but, Your Honor, I am allowed to guess, aren't I, and I do fear it was the latter. For Nicole bought in to the bargain.

"And theirs, Juice's and Nicole's, was a sick love, based on mutual obsession, carried out in public. She was becoming a husk of the girl-woman Juice had bought and paid for, and all she had developed was what she had gotten him with—an allure that must ultimately fade. And her family went along with it. For she showed her own father photos of her bruised face. He went on to work at the business Juice's contacts had provided him. She confided in her sister, and her sister borrowed thousands of dollars from Juice in protest, and then told Juice he took Nicole for granted, and was surprised when Juice wanted to throw her out of the house for saying it.

"And Juice did anything with and to just about any woman he wanted, and he made Nicole like it too, and join in, if it occurred to him. And they believed this to be a lifestyle of the rich and famous, and it probably is, Your Honor, it probably is. Even A.C. was hooked into it. Even he got mad at 911. When he and Juice took that ride on the freeway—A.C. had a white Ford Bronco, just like Juice's, Your Honor, and A.C. is a little too available in this scenario; in the Shakespearean tongue, 'A.C.' comes out 'Iago'—A.C. called 911 to say he had Juice, and, presumably, he was important now. He told 911, 'This is A.C.' When the operator understandably said, 'Who?' A.C. was incensed and insisted, 'You know who I am!'

"Oh really?

"In fact, Your Honor, Juice, not to mention his entourage of miscreants, was a nonentity to most young people—and had become one to Nicole and his then-current girlfriend, Paula Barbieri, who was cooling her heels in Michael Bolton's Las Vegas suite when Juice called her six times on the day of the murders. But young people and nubile women and 'blacks' do not run the TV networks, newspapers, magazines, hotel chains and department stores, and they do not conduct very many polls. Yet polls were conducted about the guilt or innocence of Juice, and the results of the polls were always—always, Your Honor—reported in the media by

race. Now, I had never heard of any sort of similar polls being conducted concerning any question of whether criminality has a 'black' face. These grim pollsters (it has been my
good fortune not to have run into or known anybody who
has run into any of these pollsters, concerning this or any
other subject; perhaps the same three hundred are polled
over and over again) said, 'Seventy percent of white people
think he is guilty, and seventy percent of black people think
he is innocent.' What these polls didn't once note was on
what basis people were answering them:

> In our late canvass, half of the nation passionately believed
> that in silver lay salvation, the other half as passionately be-
> lieved that that way lay destruction. Do you believe that a
> tenth part of the people, on either side, had any rational ex-
> cuse for having an opinion about the matter at all? . . . Does
> this mean examination, or only feeling? The latter, I think . . .
>
> [—YOU KNOW WHO]

"Yet these results were reported by the media with the chas-
tising looks they give you while they are manipulating you,
encouraging your moral outrage. Ordinarily, guilt of a
'black' (unprivileged) man is assumed. That is as much Privileged Man's Unwritten Law as the ability to snuff one's wife.
The polls were the first I ever heard of that asked, Do you
think a 'black' man is guilty? Never heard of much call for
such a poll before. The privileged ran with this poll further
than Juice ever ran with the rock. But there is nothing in the
precedent of the American legal system that would make a
'black' person answer a poll about the guilt of a presumed
'black' man any other way. Where is the big surprise? All
those of questionable guilt, guilt by heredity more than of
any crime, and *now* here you come taking polls? The one
time when precedent of presumption of 'black' guilt is solid,
superseded only by the presumption of 'white' privilege?

Well, hell no then, he's not guilty, said the unprivileged who were polled, meaning *they* were not guilty—that their uncles, brothers, husbands and fathers who had been victimized by the many historic peers of Mark Fuhrman were not guilty; Juice, whoever he was, looked 'black' from over in the Bronx where they were. The manipulation implied in *taking* such a poll is considerable. If I didn't know better I'd call it rabble-rousing. Incitement to riot.

"There is another crock, Your Honor. One of the aging lawyers who have staged a comeback through this trial via the media and television said that if Juice was convicted, 'black' people in Los Angeles would riot. He lives in Utah and apparently feels he would know such things. Oh? Which 'black' people would these be? They are not the 'black' people in my barbershop. Young and old, they curl their lips and say to me, 'What did he ever do for anybody like me?' I've heard them say it, Your Honor, and could tell they meant it. If and when Juice is convicted, there will not be any riot, or even much angst, other than in boardrooms and country clubs, and that will be a brief period of angst at best. At the same time, when the Juice is not found guilty, a great many 'black' people will be happily relieved of the monotony of working under a separate scale of justice. When they cheer— and they surely will—they will be cheering *Johnnie Cochran*, for winning the intellectual exercise. *Cochran* will be the hero to 'black' people, not Juice. It will not matter to them that the scale of justice they have just joined is one tilted only toward the privileged. They won't care about that. They will be figuring that if Claus Von Bulow got off even though he sedated Sunny Von Bulow, then Juice should get off. They'll figure if William Kennedy Smith's lawyers outlawyered the state's lawyers and got him off, Juice should be awarded the same dubious privilege. That's what they will feel. I understand those feelings, and those feelings will be blamed for the verdict, when really the verdict is about a half-baked prose-cution case (why, Your Honor, was the prosecution case so half-baked) and rich male privilege. A great many 'black' people will be happy about what the verdict symbolizes.

"So you can pretty much have it, Your Honor, I'm through with it, although I must add this. If it had been me instead of Ron Goldman delivering a pair of glasses back to Nicole Simpson, this would be a different case. Because whoever killed me between 9:30 and 10:30 P.M. would not have had the time or the energy to catch a midnight plane from the L.A. airport to Chicago. He would have had to use the San Francisco airport. First of all, little pieces of me would have been found all along the Pacific Coast Highway, all the way from Brentwood to San Francisco. The police report would have read thusly: 'We had a trail of blood from Brentwood, through Malibu, Santa Barbara, San Simeon, San Luis Obis-po, Big Sur, Carmel, Monterey, Castroville, Half Moon Bay, Pacifica, into San Francisco. We found the body on Geary Street. He died of loss of blood suffered through countless slash wounds in his buttocks area. His thigh muscles and calf muscles were all torn loose. At first we thought it was knife wounds, but they were torn from the bone from pure exer-tion, it looks like, and the soles of his feet were skinned, not from knife wounds, but bald like an old tire.' No, Your Honor, it would have taken some running down to kill me on that night. In fact, I might have run to Chicago myself."

"That's not funny," said The Judge.

"Well, if not, it's not because I didn't try.

"The motive does bother me, Your Honor, because Juice had seen Nicole do just about everything. He had asked her to do just about everything, probably. So jealousy looks a lit-tle bit tame for this one. He knew she'd been with Marcus Allen, he may have even seen it, because he'd seen her with this Keith guy who owned the restaurant. He'd watched her with him—where you and I might have turned away if it had been our ex-wives with somebody else, he watched. So maybe jealousy is not the full motive.

"He called Paula Barbieri six times after being rebuffed by Nicole on that fateful day, and Paula wasn't there, she was hanging out with Michael Bolton in Vegas, and so poor Juice, in his late forties, was finally rejected by women and all alone. Did he sigh? Did he read a book? Did he determine to meet someone new? No. He called his boys, A.C. and some of those other fellows who revere him so. Why, Your Honor? Well, these are questions for the court to ponder and not me; not for long, though. Motives are for detective novels. You don't need Easy Rawlins or Sherlock Holmes for this one. Those were detectives with honesty and integrity to them, so they would not fit into this scenario at all. They would not even submit a bill on this one. Imagine asking one of those detectives to get to the bottom of this case. They'd look at you, and then tell you that the bottom of the case is right there on top:

" 'Do you *know* who killed the bitch?'

"Your Honor, be honest, we don't all *know* who did it, but we all have a feeling that we know who *knows* who did it. If we want to pretend we don't, that's up to us. Just ask him. Simple as that. Until he says, he's being used, like many other symbols these days, as some kind of public example. But of what? That is the only mystery here, one I'd like to get to the bottom of."

"One more question," said The Judge. "Whatever happened to Monte, Paulie, Speedy, Davis, Shell—all those men you knew?"

"Well, lemme see; Mr. Davis finally moved his ball team back to Oakland, where it belonged, although he still doesn't have a quarterback to write home about. Art Shell had a winning record coaching the team, in spite of his lack of a great quarterback, or any kind of running back once Marcus Allen left and went to Kansas City. Mr. Davis fired him anyway, so Art Shell went on to be an assistant coach at Kansas City, and he never suffered a moment's loss of dignity that I could see, and he'll be head coach of another team one day, if I ever own one. Paulie, he went on back down to the sticks; he's coaching ball down there I hear, and also knowing when it's going to rain ahead of time. I talked to Monte, and he'd run into Speedy, who wasn't looking too well. Monte said Speedy was angry with him, saying it should've been him who played in the League, and not Monte—it should've been him making out well in international sales, not Monte. Monte put up with that garbage for a while, then he told Speedy goodbye, and left him there trembling, looking like he was about to try and kill somebody if he got the edge on them; then Monte went on back to Jamaica, or London, or South Africa, or Nigeria, or one of the other places he lives and does business in these days.

"When I told Monte about the trial and Juice, he didn't seem surprised. Monte said it's a total freak show once you get up into that rare air of power and professional athletics mixed together, especially in L.A., where ain't nobody straight. Monte said he could see it in Nicole's face—freak show. Monte says football players don't always leave that violence on the field, and that they like their women available at all times; he said it was a life of everything goes, anytime, and whatever feels good, do it, and ain't nobody straight in L.A., and that everybody had talked about Juice and A.C., and that when it's a total freak show like that, sometimes you grab whatever you find close at hand, and that maybe Nicole was going to blow the whistle on it all, the whole damnable thing. That helps motive along. The motive wasn't jealousy. The motive was *fear*. The fear of being a human being and not the son of God. The fear of having to stand in line just like everybody else. The fear of being left alone. But *whose* fear? If Juice did this sin, there's no getting away from it. To put it in your kind of language, Your Honor, the sins of the father are visited upon the sons. O.J. Simpson is going straight to Hell. The only question being, is everybody else going to follow him? So far, the answer is—yes.

"But don't let me sway the court any, Your Honor. This court is swayed enough under its own head of steam. So it comes down to your judgment, Your Honor. Not lawyers' judgment, not a jury's judgment, not public judgment, not media judgment. The Judge's judgment, Your Honor. You know best. I'm just trying to get by."

". . . You may step down, sir."

". . . Thank you, Your Honor. And don't mention it."

# 9

## Why Niggers Steal, Are Violent and Stay on Welfare

> *... they gave a blackjack to a man who was in jail too, and told him to beat me ... he beat me until he was exalted ...*
>
> —FANNIE LOU HAMER

**W**illiam and Ardelia had been married eleven years. They lived in a place not unlike yours and they had been blessed with two adorable, inquisitive children. The boy looked like Ardelia. The girl looked like William. Were they happily married? Ah. Hmm. Well. The first three years were unadulterated bliss. They could hardly stand to leave each other's sight. Then the children came. After eleven years and two children, it is better not to ask if they were happy. Wait eleven more years and then ask; if you can remain their friends that long, you'll have earned the right to ask. After eleven years it was apparent that they were together. Happy? Making it. And happy to be making it, yes. But together through thick and thin, often the former. Marriage has less to do with happiness than with diplomatic compromise; it also has to do with biting your tongue, aging gracefully and caring boundlessly for the children. Were they committed to each other? Why, yes, now that you mention it—not that *they* did—but after eleven years together you are committed whether you mention it or not.

At the beginning of the twelfth year of their long union, William began to act strangely. Once he was complimentary of her to his friends and even the general public. Now he began to mock her. When he was younger he had bragged to his friends about her loveliness, and about the inspirational dimensions of her bodily endowments. His friends smiled, raised their eyebrows, dug deep and repeatedly into each other's rib cages with their elbows, and laughed in sinister manners indicating they knew such women themselves—then behind William's back they asked Ardelia if she was considering giving out free samples. Ardelia had always known how to handle them, and she never let on to William that his good friends all tried to beat his time behind his back. Now he became derisive about her appearance, to a new set of friends. Finally, he accused Ardelia of infidelities. Then he began following her around, checking her odometer, glaring at the gardener who came to trim the hedges, even though that trusty soul was sixty-five and the unhappy proprietor of a painful hiatal hernia. William began picking up the extension, listening, pretending he didn't know Ardelia was on the phone in the first place—as if she wouldn't know better:

"William, is that you?"

"Sorry. Didn't know you were on. Who you talking to?"

Once upon a time when they were younger, they had gone out together and could work any kind of party separately but as one. They would enter arm in arm with beaming smiles and crack out of the sides of their mouths, "Look at this wild pack of patronizing nitwits, will you, please?" Then they would captivate the crowd and be swept off on their separate ways, only to reunite at the other end of the room, wink and feel they'd put one over. They were envied. Now, on the rare occasion they went out, William offered a malignant scowl as they entered a party, directed at Ardelia. "Who you looking at?" he gritted. Then he clung to her like a creeping vine yet spoke not another word or even showed a tooth until they left the premises. They were no longer envied.

William's conduct caused Ardelia no end of misery. Life was hard enough without mysterious accusations coming from out of the blue. At first she was flattered, in a vague and uncomfortable way. Then she ignored him, hoping the behavior would go away. The behavior intensified. Finally, in order to placate him, for the sake of the children, and mostly because she was at her wit's dead end—she began to change. Where once she walked proudly, her head held high, her stride elegantly long and thrust forward, as sure as the finest model's on the best runway, she now began to walk with head hung low, her back bent, her magnificent bosom held concave. Where once she had been friendly, willing to meet and enchant all comers, now she would not speak or smile. She began to wear loose, ill-fitting clothes—the better to hide in. She gained weight. Her friends asked if William didn't mind. She did not answer. William had encouraged it. It was the only action she had taken lately that seemed to satisfy him. She pulled her hair back severely and kept it that way. She spoke in monotones. She even went against a law her parents taught her and allowed her personal hygiene to slip. She wore less makeup—then no makeup. She did all this not to please herself, but because she had begun to doubt her own worth and competence, and felt a desperate need to assuage William's expressed doubts and chronic fears about her faithfulness.

It was not nearly enough. William berated her in front of

the children and hawked her every move. "I know you're messing around on me, Ardelia," he said. "I know you are."

At one point Ardelia became frustrated enough by William's continued suspicions to actually have a conversation with him about it: "William, what are you talking about? Between getting you out of here with a fresh shirt, clean underwear and breakfast in the morning, getting those children out of here in the same shape, keeping the house clean, doing laundry, cooking, managing repairs, running the greeting card business out of the basement, doing the shopping and on top of that occasionally helping you fulfill your evening manifest destiny, honey, believe me, I'm too *tarred* to mess around." Then she smiled, tentatively.

Her attempt at disarmament enraged him.

"I don't care what you say," he gnashed. "I know you're messing around on me. It's written all over your face. I *know* you. But that's all right. That's okay. You be careful now, Ardelia, because you never know when or where I might show up."

Ardelia bit her tongue and became more unlike herself.

One Wednesday, Ardelia went grocery shopping. She always went on Wednesdays. While she was loading the bags into her car, along came her friend Tracey. Ardelia had not seen her in months.

"Ardelia, is that you, girl?"

"Tracey! I've missed you."

"I could hardly tell it *was* you! What is this you got on? What is all this muu-muu? Girrrl, if God had gave me a body like that one you got—or had . . . Uh, how's the kids and William?"

Tracey saw Ardelia was made nervous by the mere calling of her husband's name. So she repeated it. "William. How's he?"

"He's . . . foine. Everybody is . . . I gotta get home."

"What's the matter, girl?"

". . . It's William, Tracey. I don't know what to make of him anymore. He's been acting like a complete stranger."

"Stranger? How?"

Ardelia's loyalty to the sanctity of her marriage was far greater than her loyalty to gossip with her friends. So she did not get heavily into it. They talked for only an hour or so. She explained that William suspected her of "messing around," and was jealous. Beyond jealous. Obsessed. Tracey sighed and said she wished she had a man who cared enough about her to be obsessed. And that made Ardelia pause. She told Tracey that William didn't have anything to be jealous about. Tracey mentioned Hank. Hank was a co-worker and friend of William's, or he had been a friend until William caught him sizing up Ardelia one day—at least it looked that way, to William. William ended that friendship under a fast pretext, though they continued to work at the same office. When Hank would ask innocuously, "So, how's Ardelia?" William would speak ill of her, hoping for Hank's dispassion, and though Hank seemed unintrigued, William was unconvinced. His thoughts in this area were misspent; Ardelia had never had any desire for Hank. Hank was an attractive man, anybody could see that; but she was William's wife and that was the way she ordered it up. Ardelia told Tracey there was nothing to Hank and her. That had been William's imagination. Ardelia said she hoped it wasn't Hank that William was worried about. Tracey told Ardelia it seemed like she was the one worried and she shouldn't because men were men and women had to know how to handle them. Then they hugged goodbye and Ardelia drove home feeling better. She decided she would "handle" William, not stopping to consider that William was not a horse. She took two bags from the car and went to the house. William flung the front door open. His brow was troubled.

"Where you been?"

"Where've I been? To the market, that's where. Don't you

see these groceries? There's eight more bags in the car. Help me? Or call William Jr. so he can help me."

"They're at your mother's. She said you were at the market too. Y'all must think I'm some kind of fool or something. You think I'm the kind of punk who'll stand by and let his woman mess around on him? You think you can make a fool out of me, Ardelia? Think I'm soft? You've been with him, haven't you? Haven't you?!"

"William, what are you talking about?! I just said I've been to the market. Now, will you help me get these bags?"

"Naw, you been with him! Whore! Slut! Bitch! I *know* you've been with him! I can *smell* him on you!"

And he struck her across her cheek with the back of his good hand, knocking the bags from her arms. Ardelia was stunned, hurt. She sank to the floor. Something in her was about to cry out and plead for the return of his better reason—but that was superseded by a feeling of . . . what was it she felt? Anger? Rage? And what did she think? *He hit me. I can't believe he hit me. After all I've done for this family, he hit me. Who kept this thing together, man? I kept this thing together, man! Who had the children and raised them right? Who cooked the meals? Who kept this house in order while you went golfing and stayed late at the office? Who washed and ironed the clothes? Who kept the children safe? Who helped them with their homework? Who tended to you when you were sick, disagreed with you when you were convinced a chest cold was tuberculosis? Who lent you the sympathetic ear when work got you down? Who held you when you cried? Who stood up for you to the neighbors?* A slow, vengeful smile now crept across her face. Ardelia was in few ways unintelligent. She knew she could not fight William— though she considered it. But he was stronger. She couldn't leave him. She had the greeting card business on the side, but she couldn't keep herself and two children going on that and also help her poor mother. So what did she do? She said to herself, "If that's how it is, if I'm going to be suspected, if I'm going to get beat for it—then maybe I will 'mess around.' "

And she did. She contacted Hank, inventing a fancy for him. In her new and vindictive state of mind, she didn't find it difficult to lie and to make herself believe in the invention. Hank, for his part, was glad to hear from her. They consummated the affair within two weeks, in blue flames of gaseous ardor. Hank was good for about six months' worth of blue flames before he cooled off. William's accusations and abuses continued unabated; no more, and certainly no less. So Ardelia found herself another Hank. Then another. Ardelia soon went downhill. Her once-beautiful body rose in the wrong places, flattened in the wrong places; her taut skin sagged and became blemished; her children entered delinquency; she began to smoke, drink and swear most comically; the greeting card business folded more from no effort than no customers. Eventually William caught her in bed with Hank No. 3 and shot her in the forehead with a pistol he had bought for her, so that she could protect herself from society's villains.

Then he lay down next to her, begging her forgiveness. He will beg forgiveness from you today, if you visit him over at St. Elizabeth's Mental Hospital. For Ardelia and William, it was a case of the self-fulfilling prophecy. And it could have been avoided if Ardelia had realized the missing part of the puzzle, the piece that forever eluded her. What was this missing piece?

*William was "messing around." William was "cheating." And his subconscious guilt over that betrayal manifested itself in his suspicions about Ardelia and his mistreatment of her.*

Ardelia had been so busy worrying about what William

thought of her, trying to change herself so he would not think that way of her, until in her frustration she became what he claimed he most despised.

She was so busy answering questions that she failed to ask a key one: "I'm not doing nothing, what *you* doing?"

Ardelia's demise and William's place in a home for the criminally insane could have been avoided if Ardelia had thought it through and realized a cardinal rule of life: *Whatever someone is accusing you of doing, nine times out of ten that is (perhaps even precisely) what the accuser is guilty of thinking . . . and doing.* And once you have a firm grip on this cardinal rule, you will be happier. For when you face a charge like the one leveled on the cover of the July 1995 issue of the magazine *Civilization*—"Afrocentricity: Why Blacks Dream of a World without Whites"—you can understand what is really meant by that, realize it doesn't reflect on you, sit back and relax.

# 10

## A Profuse Apology

I hearby submit an official apology for the incompetence, criminality, shiftlessness and stupidity of the African-American, the sum of which has held America down mightily. I apologize for their failure to agree to my own proposal that they all throw themselves off the nearest rooftops to save us the trouble of thinking up less obvious methods of disposal. Orderly rooftop-diving would not only save on brain drain but could be televised for profit, since the production costs for such an operation would be reasonably low and each episode ends with grisly, riveting and well-deserved deaths. This one is sure to be a real winner, ratings-wise, and profitable, very, and the profits can be used to pay off what is obviously owed. Burial is optional, occurring at the discretion of Accounting, and only if a way can be found to expense it without counting against the net-net-net.

In spite of the burden of hopeless "black" people riding its strong back and big shoulders, over the scant 130 years since manumission, the United States has risen to become the richest, most successful, most artistic, most imitated, most envied, most talked-up, bragged on and memorable society in the long march of humankind, the A-Number 1 power in the world and the history of civilization; I apologize that the "black" citizens, despite a head start, had nothing to do with this construction except for causing delays; poor put-upon America, where the big problem for most of its fine citizens is which diet to break next, where the internal danger is imposed by people who are not starving or homeless, but who make too much money to stay sane.

Starting from far back in the world's pack in 1865, America is now the most culturally influential, innovative, powerful and feared place, home of the world's most comely inhabitants—after some pruning is done—and, generally speaking, the most properly and successfully run enterprise going. There is no corner of the globe that does not speak the unspoken American language: "How much?" And if it weren't for the "black" Americans, by now the United States would've spun off the Earth entirely, into a newly calibrated trajectory up above it all, where the sun would revolve around it, no doubt; where privileged Americans would spin off new fiber-optic and computer-friendly galaxies, rivaling the galaxies already there—a genetically engineered new universe where there would be no calories to burn, no typos to curse, no women out of their place, no misspelled words to look up, no God to circumvent and then pose as, no Jews to scapegoat, no niggers to blame and none to die so America might stay upright.

I am sorry I read Mark Twain so thoroughly.

I am sorry I wrote about him so abysmally.

I'm sorry to have made you sorry that you ever heard of him.

I'm the sorriest spectacle you ever saw, taking it all around.

I want to apologize ahead of time for writing anything else after this. No need for me to over-apologize about it, though, because a book or a script that doesn't get made into a movie just sort of lies around being quiet and doesn't bother anybody much. But I'm bound to write anyway and I apologize for that—for being able to write in the first place. I was told these writings of mine would do nothing but stir up trouble and I was told right.

On the other hand, perhaps apologies are unnecessary here and I should submit an invoice instead. What do you think?

## Chapter Two

1. ". . . My First Lie, and How I Got Out of It."

The eminent writer and sports biographer Robert W. Creamer sent me the following letter on the above-named essay.

Tuckahoe
June 20, 1995

Dear Ralph

You may recall that when we were speaking on the phone (just a few minutes ago) I dug out from my bookshelf my ancient Mark Twain book titled in full *The Complete Short Stories and Famous Essays of Mark Twain*, a one-volume edition published by P. F. Collier & Son and purchased by me around 1934 or so. After we ended our conversation I picked up the Twain book, opened it at random and began reading "My First Lie, and How I Got Out of It." It began with typical Twain humor and hyperbole—doesn't remember his first lie but does remember the second, which occurred when he was nine days old. Says he had noticed that when a pin was sticking in him "and I advertised it in the usual fashion," he would be petted and coddled. Says he liked that, so he lied about the pin, "advertising one when there wasn't any." Twain says anybody would have done it; George Washington did it. And on and on.

Very funny stuff, and I found myself chuckling as I read. Or, I should say, as Twain deftly reeled me in. I didn't notice myself being reeled in as he went on to say that almost all lies are acts, and that people begin to lie that way as soon as they wake up, and go on all day. Twain calls this "the lie of silent assertion" and says we tell it without saying a word. That's where he netted me and then, after his lighthearted beginning, he gutted me and gutted all his readers by sliding into this at the start of the fourth paragraph:

"For instance: It would not be possible for a humane and intelligent person to invent a rational excuse for slavery; yet you will remember that in the early days of the emancipation agitation in the North, the agitators got but small help or countenance from any one. Argue and plead and pray as they might, they could not break the universal stillness that reigned, from pulpit and press all the way down to the bottom of society—the clammy stillness created and maintained by the lie of silent assertion—the silent assertion that there wasn't anything going on in which humane and intelligent people were interested."

Maybe that's hack writing. Maybe it's improvising. And maybe it's sheer genius.

Bob

2. Chapter 12, "Jim Standing Siege," from *Tom Sawyer Abroad*, Mark Twain.

The next few meals was pretty sandy, but that don't make no difference when you are hungry; and when you ain't it ain't no satisfaction to eat, anyway, and so a little grit in the meat ain't no particular drawback, as far as I can see.

Then we struck the east end of the desert at last, sailing on a northeast course. Away off on the edge of the sand, in a soft pinky light, we see three little sharp roofs like tents, and Tom says:

"It's the pyramids of Egypt."

It made my heart fairly jump. You see, I had seen a many and a many a picture of them, and heard tell about them a hundred times, and yet to come on them all of a sudden, that way, and find they was *real*, 'stead of imaginations, 'most knocked the breath out of me with surprise. It's a curious thing, that the more you hear about a grand and big and bully thing or person, the more it kind of dreamies out, as you may say, and gets to be a big dim wavery figger made out of moonshine and nothing solid to it. It's just so with George Washington, and the same with them pyramids.

And moreover, besides the thing they always said about them seemed to me to be stretchers. There was a feller come to the Sunday-school once, and had a picture of them, and made a speech, and said the biggest pyramid covered thirteen acres, and was most five hundred foot high, just a steep mountain, all built out of hunks of stone as big as a bureau, and laid up in perfectly regular layers, like stair-steps. Thirteen acres, you see, for just one building; it's a farm. If it hadn't been in Sunday-school, I would 'a' judged it was a lie; and outside I was certain of it. And he said there was a hole in the pyramid, and you could go in there with candles, and go ever so far up a long slanting tunnel, and come to a large room in the stomach of that stone mountain, and there you would find a big stone chest with a king in it, four thousand years old. I said to myself, then, if that ain't a lie I will eat that king if they will fetch him, for even Methusalem warn't that old, and no-body claims it.

As we come a little nearer we see the yaller sand come to an end in a long straight edge like a blanket, and onto it was joined, edge to edge, a wide country of bright green, with a snaky stripe crook-ing through it, and Tom said it was the Nile. It made my heart jump again, for the Nile was another thing that wasn't real to me. Now I can tell you one thing which is dead certain: if you will fool along over three thousand miles of yaller sand, all glimmering with heat so that it makes your eyes water to look at it, and you've been a considerable part of a week doing it, the green country will look so like home and heaven to you that it will make your eyes water *again.*

It was just so with me, and the same with Jim.

And when Jim got so he could believe it *was* the land of Egypt he was looking at, he wouldn't enter it standing up, but got down on his knees and took off his hat, because he said it wasn't fitten' for a humble poor nigger to come any other way where such men had been as Moses, and Joseph and Pharaoh and the other proph-ets. He was a Presbyterian, and had a most deep respect for Moses, which was a Presbyterian, too, he said. He was all stirred up, and says:

"Hit's de lan' of Egypt, de lan' of Egypt, en I's 'lowed to look at it wid my own eyes! En dah's de river dat was turn' to blood, en I's looking at de very same groun' whah de plagues was, en de lice, en de frogs, en de locus', en de hail, en whah dey marked de door-pos', en de angel o' de Lord come by in de darkness 'o de night en slew de fust-born in all de lan' o' Egypt. Ole Jim ain't worthy to see dis day!"

And then he just broke down and cried, he was so thankful. So between him and Tom there was talk enough, Jim being excited because the land was so full of history—Joseph and his brethren, Moses in the bulrushes, Jacob coming down into Egypt to buy corn, the silver cup in the sack, and all them interesting things; and Tom just as excited too, because the land was so full of history that was in *his* line, about Noureddin, and Bedreddin, and such like monstrous giants, that made Jim's wool rise, and a raft of other *Arabian Nights* folks, which the half of them never done the things they let on they done, I don't believe.

Then we struck a disappointment, for one of them early morning fogs started up, and it warn't no use to sail over the top of it, because we would go by Egypt, sure, so we judged it was best to set her by compass straight for the place where the pyramids was gitting blurred and blotted out, and then drop low and skin along pretty close to the ground and keep a sharp lookout. Tom took the hellum, I stood by to let go the anchor, and Jim he straddled the bow to dig through the fog with his eyes and watch out for danger ahead. We went along a steady gait, but not very fast, and the fog got solider and solider, so solid that Jim looked dim and ragged and smoky through it. It was awful still, and we talked low and was anxious. Now and then Jim would say:

"Highst her a p'int, Mars Tom, highst her!" and up she would skip, a foot or two, and we would slide right over a flat-roofed mud cabin, with people that had been asleep on it just beginning to turn out and gap and stretch; and once when a feller was clear up on his hind legs so he could gap and stretch better, we took him a blip in the back and knocked him off. By and by, after about an hour, and everything dead still and we a-straining our ears for sounds and holding our breath, the fog thinned a little, very sudden, and Jim sung out in an awful scare:

"Oh, for de lan's sake, set her back, Mars Tom, here's de biggest giant outen de *'Rabian Nights* a-comin' for us!" and he went over backwards in the boat.

Tom slammed on the back-action, and as we slowed to a standstill a man's face as big as our house at home looked in over the gunnel, same as a house looks out of its windows, and I laid down and died. I must 'a' been clear dead and gone for as much as a minute or more; then I come to, and Tom had hitched a boat-hook onto the lower lip of the giant and was holding the balloon steady with it whilst he canted his head back and got a good long look up at that awful face.

Jim was on his knees with his hands clasped, gazing up at the thing in a begging way, and working his lips, but not getting anything out. I took only just a glimpse, and was fading out again, but Tom says:

"He ain't alive, you fools; it's the Sphinx!"

I never see Tom look so little and like a fly; but that was because the giant's head was so big and awful. Awful, yes, so it was, but not dreadful any more, because you could see it was a noble face, and kind of sad, and not thinking about you, but about other things and larger. It was stone, reddish stone, and its nose and ears battered, and that gave it an abused look, and you felt sorrier for it for that.

We stood off a piece, and sailed around it and over it, and it was just grand. It was a man's head, or maybe a woman's, on a tiger's body a hundred and twenty-five foot long, and there was a dear little temple between its front paws. All but the head used to be under the sand, for hundreds of years, maybe thousands, but they had just lately dug the sand away and found that little temple. It took a power of sand to bury that cretur; most as much as it would to bury a steamboat, I reckon.

We landed Jim on top of the head, with an American flag to protect him, it being a foreign land; then we sailed off to this and that and t'other distance, to git what Tom called effects and perspectives and proportions, and Jim he done the best he could, striking all the different kinds of attitudes and positions he could study up, but standing on his head and working his legs the way a frog does was the best. The further we got away, the littler Jim got, and the grander the Sphinx got, till at last it was only a clothes-pin on a dome, as you might say. That's the way perspective brings out the correct proportions, Tom said; he said Julus Cesar's niggers didn't know how big he was, they was too close to him.

Then we sailed off further and further, till we couldn't see Jim at all any more, and then that great figger was at its noblest, a-gazing out over the Nile Valley so still and solemn and lonesome, and all the little shabby huts and things that was scattered about it clean disappeared and gone, and nothing around it now but a soft wide spread of yaller velvet, which was the sand.

That was the right place to stop, and we done it. We set there a-looking and a-thinking for a half an hour, nobody a-saying anything, for it made us feel quiet and kind of solemn to remember it had been looking over that valley just that same way, and thinking its awful thoughts all to itself for thousands of years, and nobody can't find out what they are to this day.

At last I took up the glass and see some little black things a-capering around on that velvet carpet, and some more a-climbing up the cretur's back, and then I see two or three wee puffs of smoke, and told Tom to look. He done it, and says:

"They're bugs. No—hold on; they—why, I believe they're men. Yes, it's men—men and horses both. They're hauling a long ladder up onto the Sphinx's back—now ain't that odd? And now they're trying to lean it up a—there's some more puffs of smoke—it's guns! Huck, they're after Jim."

We clapped on the power, and went for them a-biling. We was there in no time, and come a-whizzing down amongst them, and they broke and scattered every which way, and some that was climbing the ladder after Jim let go all holts and fell. We soared up and found him laying on top of the head panting and most tuckered out, partly from howling for help and partly from scare. He had been standing siege a long time—a week, *he* said, but it warn't so, it only just seemed so to him because they was crowding him so. They had shot at him, and rained the bullets all around him, but he warn't hit, and when they found he wouldn't stand up and the bullets couldn't git at him when he was laying down, they went for the ladder, and then he knowed it was all up with him if we didn't come pretty quick. Tom was very indignant, and asked him why he didn't show the flag and command them to *git*, in the name of the United States. Jim said he done it, but they never paid no attention. Tom said he would have this thing looked into at Washington . . .

3. . . . *ten* such books.

Here is a preferred list of Twain's ten best books.

1.  *The Adventures of Huckleberry Finn*
2.  *The Tragedy of Pudd'nhead Wilson*
3.  *Life on the Mississippi*
4.  *Roughing It*
5.  *The Innocents Abroad*
6.  *The $30,000 Bequest and Other Stories*
7.  *The American Claimant*
8.  *The Adventures of Tom Sawyer*
9.  *Tom Sawyer Abroad, Tom Sawyer Detective and Other Stories*
10. *A Connecticut Yankee in King Arthur's Court*

If you do not prefer those, here are another ten.

1.  *The Man That Corrupted Hadleyburg and Other Stories*
2.  *Sketches New and Old*
3.  *The Prince and the Pauper*
4.  *The Mysterious Stranger and Other Stories*
5.  *Mark Twain's Notebook*
6.  *Mark Twain's Autobiography*
7.  *How to Tell a Story and Other Essays*

8. *What Is Man? And Other Essays*
9. *Europe and Elsewhere*
10. *Joan of Arc*

If you do not prefer any of these, there are others, but by now you should have a good idea if you follow the train of thought or not. If you don't, you have not wasted time, for by now you have amassed an impressive pile of kindling for your fireplace.

4. Critical essays on *The Adventures of Huckleberry Finn.*

The most divergent criticisms under one cover are found in a 1970 W. W. Norton edition of *The Adventures of Huckleberry Finn.*

James E. Cox's critical and biographical profile from the 1968 *Encyclopedia Americana* is worthwhile. It is reprinted as the introduction to the Grolier edition of *Huckleberry Finn*, as part of that publisher's World's Greatest Classics series.

## Chapter Three

1. On Garrick's last trip in, he and Cole and I played a mental game while on our way to one of the fieldhouses. We called the game "NBA General Manager—Everybody Plays the Fool Sometimes." We chose, or drafted, our own personal all-time basketball teams. Once a player was drafted, you couldn't get him, which made it harder. Since Garrick was from out of town, as well as the best player, we allowed him the first draft pick. He knew what to do with it. Then Cole picked. Then I picked twice. Then Cole picked, then Garrick picked twice, then Cole picked, and so on, until we had a team of eight players—five starters and three subs. At the time Garrick was sixteen, Cole was thirteen and I was forty-three. I was surprised when I ended up with old-school guys and a couple of decent ringers from today. At first glance, it seems Garrick got the best of us—and well he might have, with the first pick, who was Michael Jordan. But at second glance, I think the old

man's team would scrap. Upon a third look, it may just be that Cole would win in the end.

| Garrick's Squad | Cole's Squad | The Old Man's Team |
|---|---|---|
| Michael Jordan | Penny Hardaway | Hakeem Olajuwon |
| Magic Johnson | Kareem Abdul-Jabbar | Wilt Chamberlain |
| Larry Bird | Bill Russell | Julius Erving |
| Chris Webber | George Gervin | Jerry West |
| Bill Walton | Charles Barkley | Oscar Robertson |
| Dennis Rodman | James Worthy | Isiah Thomas |
| Shaquille O'Neal | Tiny Archibald | John Havlicek |
| Joe Dumars | David Robinson | Scottie Pippen |

## Chapter Four

1. . . . bombing of the Alfred P. Murrah Building in Oklahoma City

April 20, 1995, *The Washington Post*, A1, "Bomb Kills Dozens in Oklahoma Federal Building."

April 21, 1995, *USA Today*, 1A, "Bomb Forces Question: How Safe Are We?"

April 21, 1995, *The Washington Post*, A1, "2 Sought in Bombing, $2 Million Reward Offered: As Hours Pass, Hope Becomes Victim Too."

April 24, 1995, *USA Today*, 1A, "McVeigh's Life One of Anger, Turbulence."

April 25, 1995, *The Washington Post*, D1, "The Book of Hate."

April 25, 1995, *The Washington Post*, A1, "Clinton Assails Spread of Hate through Media: Probe Focuses on Bombmaking."

April 28, 1995, *The Washington Post*, D1, "In an Instant of Unspeakable Horror, a Roomful of Toddlers Becomes America's Kids."

May 1, 1995, *Time*, "When the Terror Comes from Within."

May 6, 1995, *The Washington Post*, A1, "Clinton Rejects 'Patriot' Claim of Armed Groups: Quiet Descends as Recovery Efforts Cease."

May 8, 1995, *Newsweek*, "After Oklahoma City; Remembering the Dead; Cracking the Conspiracy."

May 8, 1995, *Time*, "Enemies of the State; On Trial—the Militias."

May 20, 1995, *Washington New Observer*, 6, "Oklahoma and the Spectre of Political Terrorism."

July 10, 1995, *The New York Times*, B10, "Oklahoma Witness Sees a 'Witch Hunt.' "

2. . . . the Smith case.

Nov. 3, 1994, *Atlanta Journal-Constitution*, A3, "Mother Targeted in Hunt for Boys?"

Nov. 6, 1994, *The Washington Post*, A15, "Black Residents Angered by Reaction to False Story; Anguished Town Says Goodbye to Young Victims"; A3, "Before Boys Died, Woman Saw Her Life Falling Apart."

Nov. 7, 1994, *USA Today*, 3A, "Town Feels 'Pain, Betrayal,' Outrage: Focus on Boyfriend's Letter."

Nov. 12, 1994, *Washington Afro-American*, A1, "35 Black Men Quizzed in Union, S.C."

Nov. 14, 1994, *Time*, cover, "How Could She Do It?"

Nov. 14, 1994, *Newsweek*, cover, "Sins of the Mother"; "Susan Smith's Chilling Confessions plus Why Parents Kill Their Kids."

Nov. 23–29, 1994, *The Brooklyn City Sun*, 28, "The Enemy Within—The Susan Smith Case."

## Chapter Five

1. ". . . Zero hour, hip-hop nation time, in a Doggy Dogg world of entropy where the enemy is us."

When I made up this line in the fall of '94, I was told how deeply resonant it was by editors at *Esquire* magazine. Especially the "enemy is us" part. That was downright lyrical, I was told. I was then asked by *Esquire* to confirm that the "us" meant "black" people. I said no, the "us" was only intended to *imply* "black" people in the negative; as was the rest of the paragraph; as were nearly all of the published paragraphs and other media and well-publicized artistic displays during this period of history. I was trying to be more subtle—the "us" that is the enemy was not *only* "black" people, but *all* people. So the "us" in the line meant the *one*, the collective one, and each individual one, the enemy that lies within all of us, including Wynton Marsalis—but lying most obviously within editors, perhaps. This was what the rest of the story would hopefully imply, leaving editors out of it. *Esquire* was less enthusiastic about the word's impact after I told them what I meant by it—that they too were included in the "us." It is not good to have to explain your words to people after they have read them. It is not necessarily bad either. The word "us" had not changed—only *Esquire*'s perception of it. Under one light it was heard as music, as only a good word and the right word can be heard. Under another light, it was horrible, dissonant, the wrong word. Luckily for "us" all, divining the truth within this word was a dilemma the readers of *Esquire* were ultimately spared.

—R.W.

## Chapter Eight

1. . . . "Trial of the Century."

June 15, 1994, *The Washington Post*, A10, "Handcuffs Don't Fit Image."

June 17, 1994, *USA Today*, 3A, "Simpson Mystery Keeps Building."

June 18, 1994, *The Washington Post*, A1, "O.J. Simpson Surrenders after Freeway Drama: A Golden Image and a Charmed Life Shatter."

June 19, 1994, *The New York Times*, A1, "Simpson Under a Suicide Watch, Is Jailed after Bizarre Chase: Behind Easy Smile, O.J. Simpson Was Hard to Read."

June 30, 1994, *USA Today*, D1, "Squeezing the O.J. Story; Media

Frenzy Feeds Hungry Audiences; There's No Escaping O.J. Drama."

July 3, 1994, *The Washington Post*, C9, "Why We Really Root for O.J.; The Superstar Suspect Embodies the Illusion of a Colorblind America."

July 10, 1994, *Los Angeles Times*, A1, "Focus on Simpson Troubling for Blacks"; "Death Penalty Unlikely for Simpson, Experts Say."

August 29, 1994, *Newsweek*, cover, "The Double Life of O.J. Simpson."

January 22, 1995, *The New York Times*, A13, "The Murder Case of a Lifetime Gets a Murder Prosecutor of Distinction."

May 4, 1995, *USA Today*, 15A, "O.J. Jurors: Try 'No Comment.'"

# INDEX

## About the Author

RALPH WILEY is the author of *Why Black People Tend to Shout* and *What Black People Should Do Now*. A former senior writer at *Sports Illustrated*, he now writes screenplays and is currently working on his first novel, *Flier*. He lives in Washington, D.C.